Over the Edge

Over the Edge

A Regular Guy's Odyssey in Extreme Sports

Michael Bane

VICTOR GOLLANCZ
LONDON

First published in Great Britain 1997
by Victor Gollancz
An imprint of the Cassell Group
Wellington House, 125 Strand, London WC2R 0BB

A catalogue record for this book is
available from the British Library.

ISBN 0 575 06450 1

Typeset by Anneset
Weston-super-Mare, Somerset
Printed in Great Britain
by St Edmundsbury Press Ltd
Bury St Edmunds

97 98 99   5 4 3 2 1

To my beloved parents:

Bob Bane, who never once suggested there might be anything
I couldn't do, and

Barbara Bane (1930–1995), who couldn't wait to read this book.

I hope you like it, Mom.

Acknowledgments

There are times when this book has seemed a Herculean effort. But it has been the enthusiasm of so many people that kept me plodding along. Below is a probably incomplete listing, but be assured that each and every one of you have a special place in my heart. Thank you for joining me along the way.

Guides: Steve and Deborah Ilg, Myrna Haig, Rachelle Roberts, Milt Bedingfield, Lisa Jaimison, Nancy Frederickson, Clark Man, Michael Powers, Mimi Borquin, Bill Lawrence, Steve Dunbar, Angela Hawse, Hal Watts, Wings and Ani Stock, Gary Gentile, John and Shelley Orlowski, Dick Eustis, Carolyn Reed, and Sonny the Bricklayer.

Fellow Travelers: John and Sandi Rodolf, Richard Lewis, Susan Smith, Dave and Deb Johnson, Alden Cockburn, Kelby 'I Can Scam It For You' Roberts, The Denali crew (Rich, Tom, Roger, Dr. Jim, and Tommy), David Feeney and the Scuba Network gang of lunatics, Michael Menduno, Mary Ellen Moore, Bob 'It Won't Hurt, Really' Potter, Natalie Bayol, the Dud Thames Bicycle Shop staff, Walter Brown, and so many others.

A special thanks to Roger Borthwick, for one hell of a Big Day: *I didn't win, Roger, but I finished.*

Finally, to my girlfriend, partner and cohort on so many of these adventures, Denise E. Jackson, whose selfless love and caring have opened up a world of new possibilities. Thank you.

Contents

1 To the Edge

You cannot learn to fly by flying. First you must learn to walk, and to run, and to climb and to dance.
– Nietzsche

It is ten degrees below zero outside my tent, and it has been snowing steadily for three days. I keep trying to think of new, inventive ways of keeping warm, but ultimately they all boil down to just one – stay in my purple sleeping bag as long as I can, trying to will my mind to blankness.

The wind roars, and the tent pops like a piece of rawhide on the end of Indiana Jones's bullwhip.

It is, I think, *Indiana Jones who has gotten me into this. At least, he's got to be partially responsible. He and his keyword, adventure.*

In a few minutes, I will have to snake out of my marginally warm sleeping bag, punch a hole up through the snow, crawl out, and start digging out my tent.

Welcome to Denali, Mt. McKinley, Alaska, Land of Adventure. I have come to this undefrosted refrigerator of a land to check an item off a list. No, make that, The List. Thirteen items, activities, events that have come to define the outer limits of my life – heck, the outer limits of any life.

It is an over-the-edge list, a collection of events that nightmares are made of:

Trapped in underwater caves . . .
Trapped on a frozen waterfall . . .
Trapped in Death Valley . . .
Trapped in Alcatraz . . .

And now, trapped on the highest mountain in North America, pinned in by a brutal blizzard and temperatures almost beyond comprehension.

Windchill? How about real damn cold?

I twist into as much of a ball as you can twist into in a mummy sleeping bag, avoiding the inevitable.

I am not supposed to be here . . .

I am in my forties, well past the derring-do years. I am a couch potato – well, maybe I *was* a couch potato. But I know emphatically I am not supposed to die in a blizzard on this mountain.

Or am I?

I remember the first time I saw the picture – Ansel Adams's flawless black-and-white Denali, standing over the remote and unforgiving Alaskan tundra like some Athabascan god. The great mountain seemed then, as now, as distant and as unreachable as the moon, a part of a world that exists only in myth. I remember looking at the picture, at its fine, seamless grain, and imagining the gravity of the great mountain pulling me north.

What is it like, I thought, looking at the tranquil picture of the mountain, *to fight your way to the top, through the snows and the killing winds and the endless, bottomless valleys of* ice?

What is it like to go to the very edge of the world and look over?

I remember shrugging. I would never know, would I?

2 The List

Disclaimer: Iditasport is difficult and hazardous under the best of conditions. You could be on your own in an area of Alaska where coastal storms meet the frigid cold of the Alaska Range and the Interior. No rescue can be anticipated. The appropriate knowledge of snow camping, frozen river travel, animal confrontations, illness, injury, gear failure or loss, self rescue, bad weather, hypothermia, frostbite, and the like must have been acquired before entering Iditasport. All too often, those not experienced in these conditions underestimate both the dangers and difficulties to be encountered.

This notarized release is designed to relieve everyone involved in Iditasport from any liability. This prevents you, or your next of kin, should the worst happen to you, including death, from blaming or suing Iditasport, its sponsors, or the land owners of the course, whether private, state, or federal. *Any decision you make is your own, and you are responsible for it.*
(Liability release for the Iditasport 155-mile bike race)

Sign Before You Climb! Rock climbing is inherently dangerous . . . You could die . . . Have a great day!
(Liability release for climbing, scrawled on a napkin)

But we're never gonna survive
Unless we get a little crazy . . .
(Seal)

Here is the exact moment when I realized that things had begun to spin out of control:

It is a west wind, a fifty-five-miles-per-hour freight train from the Midwest. Palm trees rock and snap; live oak branches the size of a kid's waist bounce off the highway, spinning into the boiling air. Miniature whirlwinds dance through the sand and gravel, pelting the car like a furious dry hailstorm.

Roger just grins.

'It's doable,' he says, watching a sailboat break loose from its storm anchors and head for the beach. A garbage can bounces by, just missing the car, only to flatten itself against a chain-link fence. 'Besides, what's the worst that can happen here?'

So we huddle alongside the rocking car, rigging two sailboards, slithering into our wetsuits like we have good sense. We haul the boards to the edge of the water, fighting the wind and the blowing sand, struggling to hold the tiny sails back in the face of the gale. A real sailor, in heavy-weather gear and carrying a rope, runs down to the water's edge, shouting to be heard over the wind.

'You're not serious!' he bellows in his best real sailor voice. 'You can't be serious, you crazy shits!'

'No!' I start to yell back, and then the wind, all fifty-five miles an hour of it, catches the sail. From the corner of my eye, for just a millisecond, I see Roger's board and sail explode out of his hands, blowing into the bay.

And then I am gone, a red-and-white rocket trying desperately to avoid skewering the rocking sailboats; the sailboard making a hissing sound like water slashing across a red-hot skillet as the board claws for the horizon.

The first drop on a roller coaster ... The first corner of a haunted house ... The first fumbled groping in the backseat of a borrowed car ... The pure, cold amber of crazy ...

12

Chain lightning and adrenaline, saltwater and the bitter taste of bile.

But that's not when I know things are unraveling. The exact moment comes an hour later, back on the beach, throwing up dirty saltwater and looking at the red, raw blisters across my palm. I am calm and happy, and it all makes perfectly good sense to me. I sit down behind the car, out of the wind, take a roll of silver-gray duct tape, and tape my hands, double layers over the blisters. My elbows feel disconnected; my back is a solid throb of pain. A muscle in my right knee twitches uncontrollably. Flexing my duct-taped hands, I reflect that I feel better than I have in ages.

The first drop on a roller coaster . . . The first corner of a haunted house . . . The first fumbled groping on the backseat of a borrowed car . . . The pure, cold amber of crazy . . .

Somewhere out there are the extremes, ringing the fringes of the sports world we're familiar with, a black hole for the imagination with the power to draw and hold even the most stalwart soul.

And the sports are booming.

Call them extreme sports, risk sports, adventure sports, whatever. The fact is that the extreme fringe of the sporting world is going through an unprecedented boom. Fueled by a virtual mania for *bungee jumping* – leaping off a platform with a rubber bungee cord attached to the ankles – such sports as rock and ice climbing, endurance ultramarathon running, snowboarding, downhill mountain-bike racing, skydiving and parasailing, radical in-line skating, and the more extreme versions of multisport events are all off the charts. The more bizarre the event, the more enthusiastic the participation.

The question is, of course, *why?*

Or maybe, *why not?*

My strength, I will later learn, is my ignorance. I sit in my car, the wind rocking my Windsurfer, now lashed to the roof rack, and begin making what my friends will eventually refer to as *The List*, a series of athletic events out on the pale. Later, The List will take on a life of its own, dominating not only my life, but my friends' lives as well. The List will change everything it touches, take me places I've only imagined. It will allow me to reach out and touch . . . something. Something desirable, something mythical. But as is true in all fairy stories, it will extract a price.

Of course, I don't really know this yet, as Roger and I pack it in and head for a pizza joint, Paranelli's, near the beach in Tampa. We get there, call some friends, order a pitcher of beer, and do what windsurfers do when they finish windsurfing – talk about windsurfing.

Friends arrive, and the conversation keeps swirling around the wind. Finally, I turn to Roger.

'I have an idea,' I say, a slight bit off kilter from the beer.

Roger nods.

'It was really . . . different . . . out there today,' I begin.

'Yeah,' says Roger. 'We didn't drown.'

'Yeah, yeah,' I agree. 'I liked it, you know?'

He nods.

'I liked the feeling.'

He nods. By now other people are paying attention.

'I bet you can get that feeling doing other stuff.'

Roger agrees.

'So my idea is to make a list of extreme sports . . .'

Roger is really brightening up now.

'The list . . .'

'Thirteen things,' Roger says. 'An extreme list ought to have thirteen things on it . . .'

'Then go do everything on the list.'

'Damn good idea!'

Everyone agrees.

So I get a cocktail napkin, borrow a pen from the waitress, and clear off enough space around me to write.

'Number one: Windsurf big air, like in Maui or the Gorge in Oregon . . .'

'That goes without saying, man,' Roger replies.

'Number two – what's that bicycle race where they go downhill at like sixty miles an hour, in California or somewhere?'

'The Mammoth Mountain Kamikaze Downhill,' someone chimes in.

'Okay,' I say, 'that's two.'

Three is a popular one, the Escape from Alcatraz Triathlon . . .

'. . . Where you gotta swim with all those sharks . . .'

'Take like a canoe off a waterfall,' someone says, and I dutifully write, 'Whitewater off a waterfall.'

'Rock climb!' Number five.

'Diving in underwater caves . . . That's some loony shit . . .' Number six.

'Climb frozen waterfalls.' Number seven.

'Jump outta airplanes!' Number eight. 'And do those parachute thingies, or kites, or whatever.'

'I read,' someone begins as we order another pitcher of beer, 'that there's some roller skate race that's been going on for ten years, through the hills outside Atlanta . . .'

Skates. Cool. Number nine.

'I need another scuba thing . . .' I start to say.

'Hell,' someone answers. 'Why not? You can't even swim, much less dive.'

'. . . Maybe really deep, like two hundred feet or something,' I say.

'Sounds good to me,' answers Roger, starting on the new pitcher. 'Is that ten or eleven?'

'That's ten,' I reply.

'Badwater,' a marathon runner says. 'It's an ultramarathon, like 150 miles or something, that starts in Death Valley and runs up Mt. Whitney.'

Number eleven.

'As long as we're talking crazy, how about the bike race in Alaska on the Iditarod sled dog trail in February . . .'

'Bicycling in Alaska in February?' asks Roger. 'That's seriously stupid.'

Number twelve.

'How about Big Number Thirteen?'

'I know what thirteen is,' I say quickly. 'Denali.'

'Denali?'

'Mt. McKinley,' I say. 'The highest point on the continent. In Alaska. An expedition to Denali is number thirteen.' *Thank you, Ansel Adams . . .*

'Sold,' says Roger.

The next morning, on the desk in my office, lies a cocktail napkin with thirteen items scrawled across it.

Suppose I really do the list? No, The List, uppercase. Suppose I really do it? How crazy is this stuff, anyway? Who are the people who think these things are fun?

I mean, it's easy to understand why a person might want to run three miles; harder to understand what drives a person to train to run almost 150 miles across one of the most godforsaken spots in the world, where the asphalt, I will learn, is hot enough to cause the air pockets in the runners' sneakers to explode and the final thirteen miles of climbing will bring them from scorching heat to cold approaching freezing.

It's easy to understand the urge to swim a couple of times a week for fitness at the local YMCA; harder to grasp the dark appeal of the Alcatraz swim, the bitter, cold waters sluicing in and out of San Francisco Bay, the fog and swirling currents, the real or imagined torpedo-like shapes patrolling the deep channels.

So I come to the risk sports looking, I think, for Indiana Jones. Or someone like him. Some part and parcel of our mythology, cowboy or samurai, riding the edge jaggies for all they're worth.

Instead, I will find a group of puzzled people with a tiger by the tail, interested not so much in mythology as in touching and holding an experience as ephemeral as spider silk, ghostly as morning mist over a Montana river, an experience made of equal parts muscle, adrenaline, and a mind that echoes a sneaker commercial . . . *just do it . . . do it . . . do it.* An experience I touched, however briefly, on a piece of fiberglass in a windy yacht basin.

'I think I know where you're going,' one of my many instructors will tell me as we hike along the frozen waterfalls of New Hampshire's Frankenstein Cliffs, named not for Mary Shelley's monster, but for an artist. The temperature will be below zero, and the winds from the valley below will scour the ice, tuning it as brittle and fragile as an old window pane. 'But how do you plan on getting back?'

But that is still a ways in the future; out of sight, out of reach.

I stare at my cocktail napkin.

Why not? How hard can it be?

I spend an afternoon at the library looking up events. There is precious little hard information. I can turn on the

17

television and see all manner of this stuff, but hard information is lacking. The more I search, the more extreme sports seem to be terra incognita, the place on the map where there's nothing but a hand-drawn dragon. *There are secrets here, I think, a world over the edge of the map. Secrets . . .*

Here is what I will learn, somewhere over the edge:

That extreme sports change the people who participate in them. While a bungee jumper might feel a certain rush of immortality, the other extreme sports offer something far less tangible – and far more rewarding.

University of Chicago psychology professor Mihaly Csikszentmihalyi writes of what he terms *flow*, a sense, to borrow an Eastern concept, of flowing with the universe. The flow state, he says, comes when we ask our body and mind to reach for the limits; it arrives when everything 'clicks,' and we are *doing* without *thinking* about doing. Our best moments, continues Dr. Csikszentmihalyi, occur when 'a person's body or mind is stretched to its limits in a voluntary effort to accomplish something difficult and worthwhile.'

Stretched to the limits . . .
Difficult and worthwhile . . .

I go back to my office and stare at my cocktail napkin:

1. *Windsurf Big Air*
2. *Kamikaze Downhill*
3. *Escape from Alcatraz*
4. *Whitewater off a Waterfall*
5. *Rock Climb*
6. *Cave Dive*
7. *Ice Climb*

8. *Skydive; whatever those parachute thingies are*
9. *Skate Marathon*
10. *Dive Really Deep*
11. *Badwater Death Valley Run*
12. *Iditarod Bike Race*
13. *Denali*

Outside, the wind still howls, and nothing seems impossible. I take a handful of aspirin, shower, and re-bandage my hands. Then I fish the morning paper out of the garbage and turn to the classifieds – *I'm going to need a mountain bike, I* . . .

3 Strength and Muscle and Jungle Work

Flush with the concept of The List, I start doodling around real plans – just how, exactly, do I plan to pull this stuff off?

I actually don't have a clue.

I need a plan. At first, the plan seems easy – I'll scrape up what money I have, go out to Death Valley, and tag onto that nightmarish run. Then I'll head on up north to do the Kamikaze Downhill. I'll learn to rock climb, then mountain climb, and get certified to scuba dive while I'm at it. I'll even learn to swim, something I've been avoiding.

In the cold light of day, and without the lubricating experience of pitchers of beer, The List looks pretty stupid sitting there on my desk.

There are a couple of problems that jump right out at me. Take the Alcatraz Triathlon, for example, item number three on The List. First and foremost is the fact that I can't swim. I am, in fact, slightly afraid of water. It's always been a joke among my windsurfing buddies. I can't afford to be thrown too far – beyond dog-paddling distance – from my board, since I swim like a concrete block.

Second is the fact that my bicycle, a fat-tired beach

cruiser with a little chrome bell and a carrier for a can of cola, has just been stolen. Assuming I use the pittance from the insurance company to buy another beach cruiser, I suspect that is not the type of bike used in triathlons.

Third, I haven't run a mile since high school, after which I had vowed to never run again unless I was being chased by something large and particularly nasty.

The Kamikaze? Item two.

I don't own a mountain bike; have never, in fact, even seen a mountain bike except for photos in *Mountain Bike Action* magazine. Aside from the bike, I have a critical shortage of one other element – mountains. As far as I know, one of the highest points in Florida is a few hundred feet high, and it's a garbage dump outside of Ft. Lauderdale.

Cave diving?

I'm not certified to scuba dive at all, and I'm not even sure how to go about getting certified.

Ice climbing?

Get real. The only ice I am really familiar with is in my freezer. The closest I've come to a frozen waterfall is on a Discovery Channel special.

Denali?

That stops me. What do I *really* know about Denali? That it's the highest mountain in North America, sure. That it's in Alaska. That Ansel Adams took pretty good pictures of it. That Inuits worshipped it. That, real or imagined, it calls to me. But climbing it? I've seen all the movies. I know that mountain climbing looks cold, unpleasant, and decidedly dangerous.

I thumbtack The List to the whitewashed wall of my office, next to the window looking out on the palm trees and neat lawns of my Florida neighborhood.

The List might have stayed there forever, except for one of those little quirks of fate that periodically comes spinning into peoples' lives, spreading chaos and unintended consequences. As it happens, my sometimes workout partner Susan Smith doesn't have a lick of rhythm and, about a week after I thumbtack The List to the wall, she proves it by stumbling in the middle of an aerobics class we are both taking. Within a day, she is hobbling around pitifully on a grossly swollen, black ankle.

Over coffee at the gym the next morning, she gives the medical update – basically a long list of things she can't do for a long time.

'What *can* you do?' I ask.

'Swim and bike, the doctor says.' Susan plays with her coffee spoon for a while before speaking again. 'You know your stupid list?'

'The one thumbtacked to the wall?' I ask.

'The one you talk about, yeah. Triathlon's on there somewhere, isn't it?'

I nod.

'Well, there,' she says, as if everything is now clear. '*That's* what we'll do. There's this short triathlon two months away. If we start training for it right now, we ought to be able to do it no problem. And that way, you'll get a start on The List . . .'

'Susan,' I say, interrupting. 'I can't swim. Your bicycle has a baby seat on it.'

'We can *get* bikes,' she says with the passion of a true exercise junkie looking at six weeks of rehab. 'We can *learn* to swim. I've checked into everything, and it'll work. It *will*.'

'Sure,' I say – not for the last time. 'We'll do a triathlon. In two months.'

Susan beams.

Our first trip to the bicycle shop is telling. We both show up the next Saturday morning, respective better halves in tow, at one of those shops that specializes in Lycra tops with a color resembling smashed bananas. Everyone in the shop is rail thin with legs the size of sumo wrestlers'. They have odd sunburns, from wearing those strange bike clothes. There is a subtle shuffling in the store; the serious bikers head for the back. The last guy left standing has to wait on us.

'We'd like to buy bicycles,' I say brightly.

'Ah,' says the clerk.

'For triathlons,' I add. The clerk looks us up and down.

'Really?' he says.

'Really,' I reply.

I start walking toward the brightly colored, sleek-looking machines hanging from the ceiling, but the clerk directs us to a different part of the store.

'Back here,' he says. 'I think you'll find more of a . . . price range . . . you'll be interested in.'

In the end, we buy bottom-of-the-line Cannondales, for $449.

'Excellent frames,' says the clerk, 'but the components are . . . well . . . compromised.'

'No problem,' I say, writing out the check. It is the first check I've written in support of The List. There should have been ominous organ music in the background – it isn't the *last* check I'll write.

With the Cannondale, I figure I'm halfway – well, one-third of the way – there. There is my small problem with the water. We respond to this by hiring, for the sum of $7.50 an hour, a swim coach who, by his own admission, specializes in three-year-olds. He's a little puzzled about why I want him in particular, but I tell him it will soon become clear.

We meet at a pool later in the week.

'Okay,' he says. 'What I want you to do, Michael, is swim a couple of lengths of the pool so I can get a feel for your stroke.'

'I can't swim,' I say.

'Everybody says that,' replies the kiddy coach. 'But go ahead and show me.'

I shrug and start dog-paddling. As soon as the water is over my head, I move smoothly to my second stroke: thrashing. The kiddy coach stands on the side of the pool scratching his chin.

'You can't swim,' he says.

'No kidding.'

He summons us back to the side of the pool. Susan, who can swim, strokes back. I climb out of the water and walk.

'What do we want to accomplish here?' the kiddy coach asks. 'Do you want to feel comfortable in the water? Feel safer with your kids,' he nods to mommy Susan, 'or just have fun?'

'I want to be able to swim half a mile in open water in six weeks,' I say, smiling happily. The kiddy coach actually starts to laugh before he glances over at Susan, who is nodding in agreement.

'You're serious?' he says, a phrase I will become very familiar with.

I nod.

'Why half a mile?'

'It's a triathlon; that's the swim distance.'

He nods.

'So you're not just talking about half a mile,' he says. 'You're talking about racing half a mile with other people kicking and thrashing and knocking your goggles off.'

'Right,' I say.

'I think we'd better get started,' he says.

We have successfully completed a one-mile run – although I did have to walk a little bit, maybe half. I realize that coaching myself isn't going to work. And not just for this triathlon. I am staggered by how much I don't know – and this is running, biking, and swimming. The implications for the rest of The List are sobering indeed. If I know so little about biking and running – forget swimming – how much *less* must I know about diving and rock climbing? I am unlikely to die in a local triathlon. I may wish I were dead, but really the risk is very low. I sit in my office and look at the thirteen items on The List thumbtacked to the wall. I can't say the same for all those items.

So Michael's Rule 1 emerges: 'Get instruction from people who know what they're doing.'

Accordingly, I attend a lecture on nutrition at the local YMCA given by Myrna Haig, who is reputed to be the best triathlon coach in the area. She has bulled her way through all the local races and even competed successfully in the legendary Hawaii Ironman. Instead of the Amazon I expect, I find her a petite, dark-haired woman with a blaring voice and a spectacular sense of humor.

After her talk, I hang around. 'I'd like to do a triathlon,' I say.

'Cool,' says Myrna. 'Next season, you'll be rarin' to go.'

'In six weeks.'

She stares at me, but amazingly doesn't blurt out what I expect.

'It's going to hurt,' she says.

'But is it possible?'

'Like I said, it's going to hurt.'

The problem, as it turns out, is one of start-up. It's not that I'm in bad shape; it's just that those particular words don't mean anything. There is no mythical 'in shape.'

Being in shape, says Myrna, depends totally on what one wants to do.

'For example, you're obviously in shape for windsurfing, because you windsurf just fine. All that extra weight doesn't bother you,' she says. Tact is perhaps not her strong point. 'But for running, any extra weight hurts. And triathlon is that much worse. The whole is much worse than the sum of the parts.'

She explains this while I sit on a stationary bicycle in a gym, seemingly hours before dawn, spinning like a hamster on amphetamines. I spin on the stationary bike for an hour. Then I stretch for fifteen minutes and head for the weights, which occupy my time until the sun grudgingly comes up. On alternate days, I either bike or run with my workout partner. Three days a week, at lunch, I get my swimming lessons. In the evenings, I swim – or occasionally run a short distance.

'Strength and muscle and jungle work,' I chant from an old Warren Zevon song. 'Strength and muscle and jungle work . . .'

On every Monday, my rest day, I will stay in my bed and hurt like a horse beaten by a savage owner. My shoulders will ache; my tendons will cry for mercy; the muscles of my legs will quiver like frightened birds, even when I am sitting down. I will get up only long enough to start the coffee and get a handful of aspirin.

'Well, it's your stupid list,' says Susan. 'You don't *have* to train this hard, you know.'

But I do, I think. The List is becoming a reality; I'm starting to sneak up on it. With each seemingly endless bike lap around Davis Islands, a residential development near my house, I seem to be a little closer to the jumping-off point. *Well, The List is not totally impossible.*

Slowly, but surely, I learn to swim, just like any happy three-year-old.

'I'm going to try this with you, Michael, and I don't want you to be insulted,' the kiddy coach says one day. 'The problem is you want to hold your breath when your face is underwater, which is causing you to run short of air, which is causing you to panic.'

'This is,' I admit, 'a problem.'

'So we'll try this. I tell my kids to actually say, "blow bubbles" when their face is underwater,' he says. 'So I want you to say, "Mikey blow bubbles," all the while blowing bubbles. See?'

Mikey blow bubbles?

I nod. I put on my goggles – the first pair I've ever owned – take a deep breath, and head toward the deep end of the pool.

Mikey blow bubbles . . . Mikey blow bubbles . . . Mikey blow bubbles . . .

To my complete surprise, it works.

At dinner with my friends later that night, one leans across the table and grins. 'Mikey blow bubbles,' he says.

Suppose, I think, *I do the entire List. How does it have to work?* In addition to training like a lunatic, I am poring through books on sports training. Unfortunately, what I'm finding is they're all very sports specific.

'Well of course they are,' says Myrna one morning after I point this insight out. 'The best way to train for running is to run; the best way to train for biking is to bike. That's the way the body works.'

'But what if,' I persist, 'you don't want to just run or bike or even just do triathlons? What if there's a broad range of activities you have planned? Don't you need to be able to shift gears?'

'What is it you plan to do?' she asks suspiciously.

So I tell her about The List, about windsurfing big air, about the Kamikaze, about Alcatraz and climbing Denali and skydiving and all the rest of it.

'Holy shit,' she says. 'I knew you were crazy from the start.'

'What's crazy about it?' I persist.

'About half of that stuff is fatal,' she says. 'The other half is real hard.'

'Okay,' I say. 'It's a training question. Can I train for a range of outdoor sports?'

'Yeah,' Myrna says, 'but it's going to hurt.'

This, I think, *is not news.*

The triathlon is two weeks away, and that knowledge has settled into the pit of my stomach. I have actually been able to swim eight lengths of the pool without grabbing onto the side. My excitement at this fact is slightly tempered by the fact that a half-mile is thirty-two lengths of the pool. And, in addition, I wonder who is going to paint a black line along the sand floor of the Gulf of Mexico so I'll know which direction to swim.

'No time for finesse, Michael,' says the kiddy coach. 'You're just going to have to stop and look.'

The biking and the running, though, are going just fine. Your body bitches and moans and whines about the load; then one morning you notice that it's no longer bitching and moaning and whining. It's as if your body is a totally separate entity from your mind. It wants to do what it wants to do, and it doesn't like your pesky mind telling it what to do. So it tries every trick in the book to make you stop doing what it doesn't like and start doing what it likes. Then one day, it decides it likes the workload.

'It's like there's a little guy inside you,' says Myrna, 'and you're always negotiating.'

Okay, I think to my body, *I'll deal. We have a long way to go, and we're going to be pushing very hard. I'm going to ask you to do stuff you're not going to like; but afterwards we can rest, hit the beer, whatever. I won't break you, won't do any permanent damage. You just gotta go with me when I need it. Unscientific as hell,* I think, *but it's all I got.* There is no response from my body, at least none that I can tell.

If I'd been sleeping the morning of the triathlon, the thunder would have woken me up. Lightning arcs across the sky as I load the bottom-of-the-line Cannondale on the back of Susan's car. Before we're halfway to the race site, before the sun has even considered coming up, it is pouring rain.

'Maybe they'll cancel,' I say.

'Naw,' says Susan. 'Our luck's not that good.'

We join a long line of cars, and while we're waiting to park, the rain stops.

Shit, I'm actually going to have to do this . . .

First you swim half a mile, then you bike fifteen miles, then you run three miles. In between the three events, you stumble around the transition area and pretend you know what you're doing. I lay out my running shoes and a towel next to the bike. Then I take my goggles and a swim cap and go stare at the water. It is about twenty minutes before dawn and the water is black and cold.

It's your stupid List . . .

We line up by age groups, and, upon sunrise, we get in the water. *It is,* I imagine, *much like being in a blender with five hundred of your closest friends.* Arms and legs are thrashing; the water is boiling; there's the occasional curse.

Eventually, I'm able to swallow my panic and start some semblance of swimming.

Mikey blow bubbles . . . Mikey blow bubbles . . . Mikey blow bubbles . . .

I raise my head and see that I am swimming at a ninety-degree angle to the rest of the swimmers.

Whoops . . .

But the swim passes much faster than I had expected (and luckily the water at the turnaround point is shallow enough to allow me to stand up for a minute while the crowd of swimmers pass). And the bike and run go slowly, but well. Neither Susan nor I finish last, which was our clever pre-race strategy.

'I knew you could do it,' says Myrna, toweling the dirty saltwater off her back.

'How?' I ask.

'Because you're crazy,' she says, not particularly joking.

And now The List is real to me. It's doable, as my friend Roger is fond of saying. Not easily doable, but not totally out of reach, either. And I am beginning to think the deal with my body is doable, as well. *You deliver when I need it, and I'll never abuse you.* On the way home, I start laying out another training program, just as hard, but without such a specific goal.

'That was the hardest thing I've ever done,' says Susan, and I agree. 'You're gonna do The List, aren't you?'

'I think so,' I say.

'Who's going to coach you?' she asks. 'I think you're out there by yourself on this one.'

'I'll find someone.'

'Good luck.'

4 Brain Aerobics

Suppose, I think, *I just treat The List as a long triathlon?*
I've already gotten past the first step, which is always alleged
to be the hardest. If I just train and train and train, I should be
okay.

Okay?

Maybe not so okay. The more I plow into the research for
extreme sports, the more I find an interesting vacuum. I
can find lots of older material under the loose heading of
'adventure.' These stories have titles like: 'Headhunters!
How I Crossed Borneo with a Camel Between My Lips and
a Babe on My Arm.' This is not what I'm looking for.
There's also the deluge of sport-specific books: How to
Train for . . . practically everything. But each one I read
seems rooted in the premise that the sport described is
going to become your primary avocation, your religion,
your entire life.

What is missing is that ephemeral feeling I had windsurfing big wind; that feeling of having the nonessentials
stripped away by the wind, until nothing remains but the
pure processing machine. Yes, that feeling is tied into the
physical; but it's tied into the mental as well. When I reori-
ent myself toward sports psychology, most of what I find
is along the lines of: Visualize Your Way to a Faster Six-

Mile Run. Specificity again, with a different spin.

The windsurfing experience haunts me. I spend some time trying to divide out what was physically hard – holding a sail in a sixty-mile-per-hour wind, bouncing the board over the fierce wind-driven chop – and what was mentally hard – controlling a level of fear that I was totally unfamiliar with, a fear so profound and so powerful that it threatened to reduce my brain to nonfunctioning, gray Jell-O. Yet the most frustrating thing to me is that this physical stress/mental terror produced the most sublime of experiences that had nothing to do with either stress or terror. Instead, the combination of the two seemed to kick me to a whole different level, a whole different experience. The question seems to be, what was that experience?

'Oh,' says a friend of mine who's been sharing my now-standard early morning runs, 'you mean The Fear.'

'The fear?'

'No, no,' she says. 'Not the fear, lowercase, but The Fear, uppercase.'

'What's the difference?' I ask.

'Let me give you an example,' she says. 'Each year, my family does some sort of camping trip together. Last year, we decided to learn to rock climb. So I'm out there on this ledge, maybe fifty feet above the ground. And I've got a rope on and everything, but I look down and I just seize up. It's like a system malfunction or something. I couldn't go forward; I couldn't go backward; I couldn't go up; I couldn't go down. When I closed my eyes, all I could see was this white light. That's The Fear.'

'What did you do?' I ask

'Nothing,' she says. 'There was nothing I could do. I stood on that ledge for an hour with all these people talking to me, telling me it was okay. Then I climbed down.'

'But it's more than The Fear,' I persist. 'It's like The Fear kicked in some kind of accelerator that maybe caused me to go out and recruit some additional brain cells that were just hanging around doing nothing.'

She shrugs.

'You had a good day,' she says.

But I am convinced it was more than a good day. The List, I know, is all tied up in that singular experience, that sense of everything *working*, of being caught up in an experience bigger than I am. Since The List began growing in importance in my mind, I've been regularly asking the same questions of friends and acquaintances: Why do some people feel obligated to go to extremes? What is the appeal of the edge?

The answers have a boring monotony about them:
Because some people are stone crazy. Or, because
some people are addicted to adrenaline.

That can't, I think, *be all there is to it.*

My friends shrug.

What I really need, I think, *is a guide to brain aerobics.* I start searching for that guide in the *dojo*, the gymnasium of the martial artist, where I have spent more than a few years training. What I remember is an interesting fact about sparring, fighting. The more you think about fighting while you're in the circle, the more you tend to get your chimes rung. This I learned through painful repetition. I found that I fight best when I am not 'there,' when the personality, the me, is strictly along for the ride. It took me years to figure out that when I got mad, I kept getting bopped on the head. But being 'absent' didn't mean I wasn't aware. On the contrary, I was never quite so aware as I was when I was stepping into the dojo's fighting circle.

'Awareness,' wrote Bruce Lee, the patron saint of all

martial artists, 'has no frontier; it is a giving of your whole being, without exclusion.'

I was coming to accept that, at least for me, awareness and fear are pretty chained together. After all, in the dojo, it was a fear of seeing stars and spending the next six weeks taping my ribs that seemed to move me to a different state; in windsurfing, it was the fear of sleeping with the fishes that tripped my experience.

It was also clear to me that time itself seemed chained to those elements of awareness and fear.

One of the first things I learn in my contemplation – which I had already learned intuitively – is that time is not what we think it is. When we think of time, we see a linear beast; it starts in the past, and it goes to the future. A minute is a minute. But somewhere out on the edges, a minute is no longer a minute. Time stops making linear sense and becomes something much more subjective.

In 1982, Larry Dossey, a Texas medical doctor and professor, wrote a book called *Space, Time & Medicine*, where he touched briefly on an interesting point. 'Many athletes have described experiences of time that resemble nonlinear, nonflowing spacetime,' he writes. The book has a number of anecdotes aimed at showing time not as the spinning hands of a clock, but some plastic pseudo-substance that changes, depending on our experience.

Dossey sums it up this way: 'In baseball, the bat and the ball are one; the batter can't miss. For the pitcher, the curve ball breaks perfectly, the fast ball is alive and hitters are retired in effortless sequence. For the basketball player the ball and the net form an arc of oneness from the moment of the ball's release. In all these moments there is an inexplicable and ineffable sense of perfection and flow.'

Hummm . . .

Much of the early research on risk concentrates on a phrase I am coming to hate, *thrill seeking*. I am not sure what this means, and it doesn't seem to me that the researchers are that far ahead.

'People,' Melvin Konner writes in *Why the Reckless Survive*, a book from 1990, 'don't think clearly about risk.' He then cites earlier research that lumps 'sensation seekers' into four dimensions: thrill and adventure seeking, experience seeking, disinhibition, and boredom susceptibility, sort of the collected pathology of high risk. People in that category, he notes, also seem to have an inordinate amount of sex, presumably, I think, with each other.

'And don't forget,' Myrna Haig reminds me, 'flee or fight.'

Ah, yes, flee or fight, that chemical leftover from our ancestors' days on the veldts of Africa. At its very basic, flee or fight is really very simple – when presented with a threat, our body gears up to either fight the threat or get us the hell out of the way.

There are a whole series of well-documented physical changes that occur as our body revs up. Adrenaline gets us ready to lift cars off babies; *endorphins*, pain blockers, prepare to insulate us from the consequences of lifting that car. More importantly, there is a body of new research suggesting that fear heightens our learning ability: something that scares the hell out of us is more likely to be lodged permanently in our memory cells.

'If you touch a scalding radiator when you are three years old,' says Michael Davis, who studies so-called fear learning at Yale, 'you never touch a radiator again.'

I'm getting somewhere, but it takes yet another psychologist to put it together for me. The link that Dr. Mihaly Csikszentmihalyi provides is that he gets beyond the negative connotations of fear learning to suggest that things that are hard, things that are scary, things that push us to our limits and beyond can create a unique mental occurrence.

He calls such occurrence *flow*, an optimal experience.

'When all a person's relevant skills are needed to cope with the challenges of the situation, that person's attention is completely absorbed by the activity. There is no excess psychic energy left over to process any information but what the activity offers,' he writes in *Flow: The Psychology of Optimal Experience*. 'As a result, one of the most universal and distinctive features of optimal experience takes place; people become so involved in what they are doing that the activity becomes spontaneous, almost automatic; they stop being aware of themselves as separate from the actions they are performing.'

The concept of flow – defined by Dr. Csikszentmihalyi as 'joy, creativity, the process of total involvement with life' – is hardly new. The great Japanese swordsman and Zen master Takuan wrote hundreds of years ago:

The mind must always be in a state of 'flowing,' for when it stops anywhere, that means the flow is interrupted and it is this interruption that is injurious to the well-being of the mind. In the case of the swordsman, it means death.

The Chinese sage Chuang-Tzu wrote, 'Flow with whatever may happen and let your mind be free. Stay centered by accepting whatever you are doing. This is the ultimate.'

Our top sports figures or artists or performers consistently talk about 'flowing with the universe,' 'going with the flow,' 'being totally involved.' Yet we continue to think of risk in terms of *rush*. As if the adrenaline is the entire experience.

And is such a cheap experience worth having?

Dr. Csikszentmihalyi's contribution to my thinking is that he doesn't look on risk-taking as a pathology, a disease.

I stumble on some of the last pieces of the puzzle in an odd place. Massad Ayoob isn't a psychologist or an athletic trainer, though he's actually a little of both. Rather, he is a cop, who teaches self-defense strategies, both armed and unarmed, to cops and civilians. When we first start talking, he quickly takes over the conversation. People in high-stress situations, such as cops, he says, have to learn how to function in those situations. That includes dealing with the huge chemical dump triggered by flee or fight.

'You know how time changes, usually slows down?' he asks.

I nod.

'You can use that,' he says. 'If time is slowing down, and you expect time to slow down, you have more subjective time to act. But you've got to be ready for it if you're going to be able to use it.'

Life-threatening stress, Ayoob adds, also triggers a whole series of *perceptual narrowings* – tunnel vision, acute hearing, loss of fine motor control of the muscles.

'Your body's giving you a different set of tools,' Ayoob says. 'Like any tools, they have their limitations. But if you learn to use them, you've got a hell of a better chance of coming out of this stuff alive.'

Our current culture of cynicism masks a deep-seated fear of change and the risks that drive the change. In our personal lives, we accept the government's (and the legal system's) position that life should be free of risks – hence the proliferation of liability laws. Our businesses have been hampered – even crippled – by steadfastly clinging to a status quo that clearly isn't working.

'Rather than encourage the type of cautious experimentation that defines good management,' says Daniel Kehrer, 'many American companies have so far spent their greatest resources trying to *avoid* risk.'

And yet there is always a hunger.

The urge for risks in sports, muses sports philosopher and martial artist George Leonard, runs counter to the tendency in modern industrial society to reduce or eliminate risks from every aspect of life. 'The arena of sports,' he writes, 'has provided a place for people to take calculated risks without breaking the law.'

My experience on the Windsurfer is even more complicated than I'd imagined: it warped the very limits of time and space. *But as people, aren't we more complicated than we'd imagined?*

As I think more and more about The List, there is one more quote that comes to mind. It is again from George Leonard, in his small book entitled *Mastery*. 'Whatever your age, your upbringing, or your education,' Leonard wrote, 'what you are made of is mostly unused potential. It is your evolutionary destiny to use what is unused, to learn and keep on learning for as long as you live . . . How to begin the journey? You need only take the first step. When? There's always now.'

There is still one last building block I need to discover. I come across a reference to an athletic trainer named Steve Ilg, of Santa Fe, New Mexico. Ilg teaches what he calls Wholistic Fitness, and his basic mindset is that people are whole units and need to approach training from that perspective.

'Specialization,' he writes, 'is for insects.'

I find a copy of his book, *The Outdoor Athlete*, and I am

struck by his beliefs about training, about mental training, and about the edge.

'For the most part,' Ilg writes, 'the mainstream regards multisport athletes as oddities, like we're some eccentric aberration of the gene pool. As close to the multisport wilderness that the orthodox sports media will venture is the triathlon. But here's where the problems begin. Triathlon is not a good example of a multisport. It's still a specific sport, all endurance oriented. Genuine multisport performance requires fitness at the extremes ... At the elite level, the true multisport athlete should be able to run or cycle at an ultra distance, back squat two and a half times bodyweight, climb at a 5.12 level and do it all with spiritual depth ...'

Okay, I'm not sure what he's talking about, but it's starting to make sense. I give him a call and, without preamble, launch into an explanation of The List. He listens, asks a few questions, and finally comes out with the best comment I've heard in a long time: 'Cool.'

I have found a guru for the edge.

5 Hanging Out in Death Valley

My first clash with reality comes when the rubber meets the road, or, more accurately, when my sneakers meet the dirt. I am methodically (and painfully) turning myself into the slowest runner in the world. Train though I might, in the end, I suspect running will have the upper hand. Still, it's a necessary step, I grudgingly admit, if I am ever going to get anywhere. I can see the edge, and it seems off at the edge of the horizon.

This necessity of running is triggered by the first contact between The List and the obstacles. I have decided, for reasons that are not totally clear to me, that the Death Valley run, item number eleven, will be a good starting point to get me out of training and into doing. It takes me a couple of weeks of phone calls to find out anything about that Death Valley race, which turns out to be the Hi-Tec Badwater 145-miler, sponsored by the Hi-Tec sneaker company.

I learn this from an ad, a fount of information, in an old magazine someone loans me. I learn, for example, that the race, 145 miles of living hell, across Death Valley, over two mountain ranges, and up the highest peak in the continental U.S., was created to promote a trail-running sneaker, which is no longer being manufactured. Upon seeing a picture of the sneaker, I understand why it is no longer being manufactured. In a world of sleek, high-fashion athletic shoes, the Badwater sneaker is butt ugly.

I call the toll-free number listed on the old ad and eventually end up talking to Dave Pompel, the genial Hi-Tec exec who handles the race.

'Can I,' I ask, 'just jump in and run the next race?' – which happens to be a few months away.

'No,' Pompel says.

'Why not?'

'Because,' he continues, 'this is one of the hardest running races in the world, and – correct me if I'm wrong – you don't strike me as being an elite ultramarathon runner.'

'Well,' I reply, 'there's something to that.'

'Also, the race requires a sag wagon carrying your water and medical support,' he says. 'I don't suppose you have a sag wagon lined up?'

'Well,' I say, 'not exactly.' I think about the situation for about a minute while Pompel patiently waits. I need to do something or The List is going to die before it even gets good and started.

'Can I come watch?' I hear myself asking.

'By all means,' says Pompel. 'And bring a bicycle.'

Perfect!

I have already purchased, in addition to my shiny road bike, a battered mountain bike from the classified ads, which I'm going to use in the Kamikaze Downhill. Death Valley, two mountain ranges, and the climb up Mt. Whitney ought to get the kinks worked out of the bike.

'I'll be there,' I say. 'Death Valley in July sounds wonderful.'

'Bring water,' Pompel adds. 'And lots and lots of sunscreen.'

The cheapest airfare is into Reno, which is, of course, nowhere near Death Valley. Nonetheless, my bicycle and I arrive in the ratty gambling town late at night, where we pick up a rental car and head through the relentless neon into the cool dark of the desert. I camp out in a cowboy motif motel near the desert town of Lone Pine and head into Death Valley the next morning.

Did I mention the heat?

By ten in the morning, it is skillet-hot. The whole world takes on the smell of red-hot iron, and the temperature of the rental car climbs perilously into the red. I look at the first rising hills, and I realize that the air conditioner, not perhaps an optimal piece of machinery, won't make the climb. I shut if off and roll down the windows.

I can find only one radio station as I creep into the blistering mountains, and the disc jockey is performing an on-air exorcism on one of Satan's minions, a sixteen-year-old fan of Dungeons and Dragons.

'I want,' the announcer shouts, 'to speak to the demon! Speak to me, demon!'

The boy makes a choking noise. 'I can't!' he screams, although it comes out something like, 'Ah caned! Ah caned!'

Suddenly, the boy's voice changes. 'Damn you!' he shouts in a new voice. 'Damn you and your Jesus!'

Amazingly, the announcer cuts to a commercial for Diet Coke. The car is moving about ten miles per hour up the steep grade. Every few miles there's an iron water tank for overheated radiators. The rising heat creates a twisted carnival mirror effect, and the distant mountains dance and twist. I wonder how far I am from the Charles Manson homestead.

'We now join live, on the air, a battle for a man's soul,' the radio announcer whispers breathlessly. 'There's some rough language, but, people, we are dealing with Satan himself, right now, live!'

I creep on.

'Was Satan, Beelzebub, the Beast Himself that made you kill those little animals, wasn't it! Wasn't it!'

'Damn you! Damn you! Damn You!'

I am beginning to wonder whether the race is such a great idea after all. When I top the last hill and I see the long roller coaster ride into Death Valley proper, it looks . . . hot.

I roll on through the desert, past ghost towns and moving sand dunes, until I come to a sign that reads, AHEAD – DATES!

After hours of steady exorcism, the idea of a date in Death Valley is a little frightening. But the sign refers to date palms, of course – an oasis in the middle of the desert. When I arrive at the hotel, it strikes me as hell's own Holiday Inn, a flashy stone building resort surrounded by date palms. There's even a pool, filled with German and Japanese tourists who appear to have all been dipped in the last existing batch of red dye #2. Welcome to Furnace Creek, and pass the sunscreen. This is race headquarters.

'Be gone, demon! Back to the pit! Be gone!'

When I shut off the ticking, clanking car, the demon is still hanging on, but I sense it's a close thing.

I check in, stow the bike in my room, and head for the mandatory pre-race meeting. There are fifteen entrants this year, and for the privilege of running across the desert and up assorted mountains, each entrant will receive a plastic water bottle and a T-shirt. Finishers will receive the coveted Badwater belt buckle.

The race is simplicity itself. At six tomorrow evening, the contestants will travel the few miles to Badwater, at 282 feet below sea level, the lowest point in the United States. It's called Badwater because there is, in fact, a pool of water there, so laced with alkalis of various sorts that it's a nasty, poisonous chemical stew. Badwater is south, deep into the valley, past the Devil's Golf Course, in the shadow of 11,000-foot Telescope Peak.

The air temperature at the race start will be around 125 degrees. Six feet above the blistering, shimmering asphalt – roughly at head level – the temperature will be closer to 160.

'Last year,' one of the racers chortles, 'some peoples' air pockets in their sneakers blew up!'

The runners will head north onto U.S. 190, the main two-lane blacktop that carves across this *Road Warrior* landscape. They will pass Furnace Creek, heading toward Stovepipe Wells, a wide spot in the road on the edge of the great migrating sand dunes.

With luck, the runners will hit the first of the mountain ranges, the Panamints, around dawn. They'll creep up the road I coasted down the day before in my car, headed toward 5,000-foot Towne Pass, where they'll have a relatively straight shot down into the brilliant salt flats of the Panamint Valley. The runners will have another climb into the tail-end of the Inyo Mountains before heading down onto the long, flat stretch into Lone Pine and the entrance to Mt. Whitney. The run from Lone Pine to the entrance to the Mt. Whitney park is thirteen miles, with almost a 9,000-foot elevation gain. At the portals the clock stops and the race formally ends, because the Park Service doesn't allow races to be run on public land. Most runners, though, Pompel confided earlier, will continue informally to the top of Mt. Whitney, elevation 14,494 feet.

The temperature at the portals will probably be in the forties, although it could easily dip below freezing. Snow is a possibility.

There will be no water on the course, no medical care available, no food and supplies for the run. There is also a sixty-hour time limit. The fastest runner will hit the portals in under thirty hours.

'Is this a great race or what?' says Pompel before the race.

I have decided I want to follow Marshall Ulrich, a thirty-something Colorado runner who has made the race his own. When I called his business before the race to let him know I'd be coming, his secretary told me he wasn't in.

'He's out running across the state,' she said without a trace of irony. 'He'll be back in a few days.'

When Marshall and I finally meet, he is what one would expect in a person who thinks running across a state – any state – is fun – thin, wiry, and intense. He takes me aside to tell me his finely honed strategy for the race.

'If I can run flat seven-minute miles for the first thirty-five miles, it'll get me through the hottest part of the run with a minimum amount of contact between my feet and the pavement,' he confides.

'Makes sense,' I say. I have run a seven-minute mile in my training – exactly *one* seven-minute mile, and then I had to lay down on the track. I am beginning to think very kindly of Dave Pompel's foresight.

I meet some of the other racers – a rodeo cowboy turned banker turned ultramarathoner, a phys ed teacher whose husband 'gave' her this race as a wedding present, a doctor who has just finished the Markleeville Death Race bicycle ride and whose support crew will carry a coffin filled with ice, a lawn chair and an inflatable palm tree, plus a square of AstroTurf as *de facto* lawn.

'Be gone, demon! Back to the pit! Be gone!'

Early the next morning, just as a cotton-candy pink dawn is touching the Funeral Mountains, I get up, slip on my shorts, T-shirt, and running shoes, fill a water bottle with warm, salty water from the tap, and head down the road, toward Badwater. The thermometer by the pool reads a paltry eighty-five degrees when I start running, but I know as soon as the sun clears the Funerals the temperature will click up faster than a New York City taxicab meter.

I run along the sandy shoulder of the road. The only sound in the desert is my sneakers, crunching sand. The heat is dry, brittle, like a long spell of fever or crumbling old parchment. I imagine the greedy atmosphere leeching the water from my pores, moisture vanishing before it even has a chance to become sweat.

The desert is still, digging itself in for the hellish day to come. The only plant I can identify with certainty is the Death Valley sage, unique to this corner of the earth, which I know by its dried arms. I follow the pavement until a turnoff onto a gravel road. I head down the gravel, deeper into the desert. The sun is beginning to make itself felt; half its blazing diameter is visible now above the Funerals. All across the gravel road are the twisted hieroglyphics left by sidewinder rattlesnakes in the gritty sand.

An hour passes, then another half hour. I finally stop, the sun blistering on my face. I've left the road and run up a jeep trail, which eventually dead-ends into a little box canyon. The snake tracks are thick across the floor of the little canyon, as if all the rattlers on the right-hand side decided to exchange places with all the rattlers on the left-hand side. I am sincerely glad I wasn't around when the word came to change sides. It is quiet and still, and all the people in the world are gone. I sit on an already warming rock and sip my tepid water, then run back the way I came, my treaded footprints overlaying the hieroglyphics. It is like running through a microwave oven.

Before the race starts, I walk down to the murky pool at Badwater. The edges of the pool are crusted with white mineral deposits, and beneath the surface of the hot, deadly water, creatures dart. Life is persistent. Above us, high on the rocks, someone has painted '282 feet below sea level,' to be sure we don't forget.

Strangely, the next time I'm more than 200 feet below sea level, I won't be breathing air. But that's to come.

My plan for observing the race is simple – I'll ride my bike along with the runners, run some when I can. Get as close to the race as possible. It's the least I can do for The List.

At six in the evening, when the runners head off, the temperature is around 120 degrees.

I ride the first twenty-six miles – the first marathon – on my mountain bike, keeping tabs on Marshall, who is running effortless seven-minute miles, then drifting to the back of the pack, to talk to the doctor with the coffin. At one point, I pull a water bottle off the bike's down tube and proceed to spray 160-degree water onto my face. Note to myself: *Carry water on person; 98.6 degrees is substantially less than 160 degrees.*

Watching a running race is a little like watching paint dry, so once the full chill of the desert evening sets in, I ride the two hours back to my car with about a billion stars to light the way.

Feeling vaguely guilty, I go back to my hotel room and sleep for four or five hours.

By dawn, Marshall is through the mountains. I drop back, and eventually pick up the rodeo cowboy turned banker, who's hiking his way up the steepest inclines.

'Want company?' I ask, and he nods. I'm able to drop my bike with the lone support vehicle, cruising up and down the lonely highway, and join him.

'You know what the strangest thing about races like this is?' he asks.

'Other than the very fact of their existence,' I reply, 'I don't have a clue.'

'It's the changes you go through,' he begins. Then we walk along comfortably for a bit.

'In something like this, where you're being pushed to the mental and physical limits,' he says. 'Strange things happen to your brain. It's like every emotion you've ever had – love, hate, fear, anger, all of them – at one time or another out here, they all come out.'

He talks on as we walk steadily uphill.

'The thing is,' he is saying, 'you can't pay attention to those emotions, either the good ones or the bad ones. They're like thunderstorms in the desert. There's big noise and flashes and the trees shake and the wind blows like stink, but it passes. It passes. And what you've got to do is stand there and let those storms blow past.'

We walk awhile in companionable silence. Then he tells me about the rodeo, about his family, about running, about the endless string of miles that have somehow come to define his life.

'I think about that a lot while I'm out here,' he says. 'But heck, I think about everything.'

Later, I spend hours riding up and down the increasingly spreadout line. I ride uphill, singing to myself, in the full heat of midday. My body is completely covered, except for my face, which is layered with sunscreen the consistency of tar. I pull up my shirt sleeve to scratch my arm, and it looks like I've been dusted with flour.

Salt, I think. *The moisture is leeched away, leaving the salt.*

48

I continue my singing and pedaling until my brain belatedly engages.

I shouldn't feel so good bicycling uphill in 120-degree heat. Ergo, I am on the verge of heatstroke.

I stop pedaling, lean the bike against a convenient boulder, and force myself to drink a full bottle of hot, metallic-tasting water. In no time at all, I am rewarded with a splitting headache. Since I no longer feel like singing, I get back on the bike and start riding again. The seat is hot enough to sear my butt through the layers, and the metal of the handlebars is too hot to touch.

In the evening, right about full dark, one of the sag wagons for a woman runner flags me down.

'Run with her,' one of her team says. 'She needs some company.'

So we load my bike into the sag wagon, and they drop me alongside the phys ed teacher, then leap-frog miles ahead to the next stop.

The first few miles are what I'd expect, comparing notes on homes and families and training regimens. She and her new husband have spent hours and hours on the road, sneakers joined together in holy matrimony, and this race is his gift to her. She is very happy. But the miles wear on, and the hour is late.

'You know my husband, right?' the phys ed teacher asks abruptly, and there's an edge to her voice. It's after midnight in Death Valley, and there are still ninety miles of running left. The temperature has finally dropped below a hundred degrees.

'I hate him,' she continues. 'No, I want him to die. That's worse than hating him, isn't it?' I tell her I think wanting someone to die is worse than hating them.

'Well, that's what I want. I want him fucking dead.'

She runs for a while in silence, and I can imagine her teeth grinding in the dark.

'I hate this,' she says, and she is crying.

Every emotion, the rodeo cowboy, now far ahead, told me. *Every one.*

Time passes; the sound of sneakers; occasionally, in the distance, the cry of a night hunter.

'I have to sleep,' she says.

'I know,' I say, 'soon.'

The miles and the night pass.

I run into her the next day, after she's grabbed a few hours sleep in a real bed in a place called Panamint Springs. She squints at me through eyes that have seen a little too much nuclear-blast sunlight.

'Did we run together last night?' she asks.

'For a while.'

'Anything I said that sounded stupid,' she says, 'was the desert talking.'

'Never thought otherwise.'

Later, I zoom ahead to walk alongside Marshall up Mt. Whitney. He has been running for more than twenty-four hours with a total of forty-five minutes sleep. He is haggard, destroyed – a *haint*, my granddaddy would say, the walking dead – methodically placing one foot in front of the other, up the mountain. At one point, his support crew is worried that he doesn't have enough fuel left to make it to the top. They decide M&Ms is the solution and tell him to eat. But Marshall, at least the thinking, rational, laughing Marshall, is no longer home. He continues plodding up the mountain.

One of the crew puts a handful of the brightly colored candy in his right hand and rolls it into a fist. But the fist loosens, and the M&Ms dribble onto the ground.

Finally, his main support person puts a half-dozen M&Ms in his hand.

'Marshall,' she says firmly. 'Put the candy in your mouth.'

He does so, without taking his eyes off the road ahead of him.

'Chew it,' she says.

His jaws begin to work.

'Now swallow it.'

He gulps.

It is the most agonizing performance I have ever seen.

Twenty-nine hours after leaving Badwater, he arrives at the portals, accepts the congratulations, and goes to sleep. A few hours later, he gets up and runs to the top of Mt. Whitney and back down, setting an unofficial record.

I won't cheat again, I think, the desert rolling beneath the rental's wheel. *I won't stand by and watch again. The only way to be fair to The List is to do, not watch. Whatever it takes.*

6 Betting Time

Up until now, I realize, I've been playing at The List.

It is easier to talk about extreme sports than to do them. A part of me likes the journalist's position, being able to stay one step away, as I did in Death Valley, from the real thing. The problem is that experience, that fleeting, mistlike sense of flow, will always be just out of reach for the nonparticipant.

'There is no easy way into another world,' wrote novelist James Slater, and I am faced with the truth of that statement.

Extreme sports are all over the media, from commercials for soft drinks and sneakers to *MTV Sports*, dedicated solely to extremes. NBC devotes a ninety-minute show to the Escape from Alcatraz triathlon, complete with its now legendary swim through one of the world's great shark breeding grounds. Nike builds the advertising for their new bike shoe around the Markleeville Death Ride, a grueling 150-mile bicycle race through seven mountain passes in Nevada and California ... 'You've got 35 miles to go,' the ad reads, 'but at least you're still ahead of the hearse.' ESPN covers the Mammoth Mountain Kamikaze Downhill mountain-bike race, which, based on the sheer number of injuries, may be the most dangerous athletic event in the country.

I am confronted with the wisdom of Yoda, from the Star Wars movies. When Luke Skywalker responds to a request from Yoda by saying that he has tried his best, the little alien Zen master snorts. 'Do or do not,' Yoda says. 'There is no *try*.'

What is holding me back is the niggling knowledge that I'll be moving into the realm of increased consequences. A part of me enjoys the bravado of those increased consequences. But another part of me is mindful of my age, of how much longer injuries seem to linger.

I· am not a natural athlete. I am not an athlete at all, by my own definition of athlete. At times, I think my body, which I occasionally negotiate with, is engaged in an active conspiracy just outside my hearing.

I spend a couple of months working with a running coach, herself an Olympic-level miler. Actually, she was the second person I'd approached for some pointers in my running. The first, after watching me run, explained that he was a serious running coach, for serious runners. I was, at best, a jogger, which, I gathered, was something akin to what might be scraped off the bottom of a serious runner's sneaker. He suggested I call coach number two, who, he assured me, had time on her hands.

To her credit, she dedicates herself to making me run faster. We have numerous meticulously monitored running sessions. I spend blistering, hot days on the University of Tampa asphalt track, methodically recording my heart rate as I run myself senseless. We keep charts and graphs, monitor my food input, tweak my shoes. I run until I am sure my brain has become unmoored from my skull and is bouncing around its cavity like a wet tennis ball.

At the end of two months, we evaluate my progress, which has been . . . minuscule.

'I've never had a student who tried as hard as you,' she says, 'and got less.'

I occasionally wonder what pieces are missing from my

genetic code, what little strand of DNA got slightly amended in translation.

Whatever. But I realize that what's in front of me is going to be harder than what's behind me; more physical, more mental commitment.

There's more risk, I think resolutely, *but there's also more reward. I hope.*

Risk is inherent in life, we say. Every choice we make involves some risk, so we all are, by definition, risk-takers. *Life* is risk.

Well, maybe.

'Trying to find a really good definition of risk is like hunting along a sandy beach for a one-carat diamond,' writes *Parade* magazine editor Walter Anderson. 'Every grain may have the look, but none has the substance.'

What we really want to talk about is better described by business writer Daniel Kehrer as *dynamic risk*: 'Dynamic risks are forceful risks; they create their own energy and motion . . . These are vigorous risks, willfully undertaken.'

Novelist Michael Korda continues along this line. 'Sports and physical fitness, which both usually involve some risk, are, for us, an escape from work, a recreation, a self-absorbed experience, often more a question of body vanity than anything else.'

The flow state, Dr. Csikszentmihalyi says, comes when we ask our body and mind to reach for the limits; our best moments occur when 'a person's body or mind is stretched to its limits in a voluntary effort to accomplish something difficult and worthwhile.'

It need not be through sports, but sports can be the shorthand, the teacher, that shows us what an optimal experience feels like.

I think the event that pushes me to the next level is the Marine Corps Marathon in Washington, D.C., which a friend runs in the autumn.

I am stationed at a beautiful tree-shaded spot about 20 miles into the 26.2-mile run, next to a series of steps. I am watching the runners go by when one of the last of the wheelchair athletes reaches my spot. He is older than most of the wheelchair racers – my age; Vietnam age – and he is obviously exhausted. Since the wheelchairs can't make the steps, there is a ten-foot ramp next to the stairs.

The racer starts up the ramp, and his arms fail. Five more times he tries the ramp, muscles bulging, his face bright red from the exertion, and five times he fails. Most of the crowd, myself included, has gotten quiet. Other runners and the young Marines lining the course still shout encouragement, but the man in the wheelchair is in his own world. On the seventh try, his face is blank, his eyes focused on a universe that is ten feet long. He doesn't see the Marine behind him, openly crying. He doesn't hear the other runners' shouts or feel the presence of the crowd. He just goes up the ramp, an agonizing inch at a time. And when he finally reaches the top, he just smiles, waves, and keeps going.

Vigorous risks, willfully undertaken.

I return home from the marathon ready to up the ante, increase the bet. It is time to take some risks.

7 Chips, Flakes, and the Last Hard Men

Here is the first emotion I experience as a climber:

Fear. Gut-numbing, mind-bending, limb-freezing, this-is-not-an-alert fear. My palms begin to pour sweat and my breathing shallows out, until I sound like an overheated puppy. I feel the first stirrings of vertigo, as if the butterflies in my stomach have suddenly taken flight and are flying in some strange formation. What's worse, I'm still on the ground.

'It gets easier,' says my instructor, Clark Man of Santa Fe, New Mexico.

Good, I think, trying – not succeeding – to look cool in my Lycra. *It will have to.*

I was afraid The List was going to go stale, that I was going to go stale. I was itching to get back to the field, which gave me pause. *Why* was I itching to get back to the field? What was the particular part of the extreme experience that was so compelling? I'd been thinking about that subject when a member of my pre-List aerobic class asked me out for coffee one morning.

Could I explain, she asked me, why her 'normally solid

and sane' husband not only went skydiving and managed to sprain something, but was insisting on doing it again.

'It's one of those guy things,' she said, her English accent making 'guy thing' into a pejorative. 'Testosterone.'

I didn't know her husband; maybe he *was* suffering from testosterone poisoning. He wouldn't have been the first person I'd met who was. But I figured I at least needed to give his defense a stab.

'Suppose,' I said, 'that one afternoon everything worked a little better. Your vision was a little clearer; your brain seemed to process a little faster; your body seemed to function a couple of years younger. How would you feel?'

'You'd feel great,' she said, skeptical.

'And would you want to repeat that feeling the next day?'

'You're cheating,' she said. 'There's no way he felt that way from just jumping out of an airplane.'

'Why not?'

'Because it's so *cheap*, you know,' she said. 'You give the people your money; you jump out of an airplane. So where's this mystical experience you're blathering on about?'

Where indeed?

But it makes more and more sense to me. I can get an easy confirmation with physical training – when we push our bodies, they adapt to the stress. We want to run faster, so the body recruits muscle tissue to help us. Tendons become stronger; muscles become more efficient. So what if we continue stressing both the body and the mind? Does the mind as well as the body go out and recruit other nerve tissues to help out? Do the muscles in the head become more efficient at problem-solving; stronger in their ability to think clearly while struggling through the chemical soup of flee or fight? If we accept that premise, then doesn't it also make sense that our bodies define this enhanced feeling as 'good'?

Whatever.

I get a cheap ticket to go to New Mexico to learn to climb. The choice of Santa Fe is twofold. I have read that the spectacular red rock cliffs around Santa Fe are perfect places to learn to rock climb. And, Steve Ilg is living in Santa Fe; it seems to me about time to sit down and talk to the master.

Rock climbing – scurrying up sheer cliff faces by the grace of muscles, balance, gymnast's chalk, and funny-looking shoes – is well on its way to becoming one of the glamour sports of the 1990s. Some definitions are in order here. When we think *climbing*, we often have visions of a group of hardy Sherpas slogging toward the top of Everest – or, at least, a younger Clint Eastwood in *The Eiger Sanction*, hanging onto the 'Death Wall' of Eiger by his fingernails. That's *alpine climbing*.

Sport climbing bears the same relationship to alpine climbing that racquetball does to tennis – it's a smaller, more frenetic version of the original. Instead of climbing mountains, which might entail some rock climbing, sport climbers look for relatively short, difficult sections of rock cliffs to climb. And they might spend days, months, even years figuring out how to boldly go, as one T-shirt slogan puts it, 'where only small lizards have gone before.'

Muscles alone won't get you up the rock, I have been told.

'You can't just do pull-ups,' says Denise Jackson, one of the three or four people in Tampa who actually climbs. She is also my girlfriend, and yet another person who will be drawn into the orbit of The List. 'Climbing requires finesse.'

More than finesse, climbing demands balance, even

grace, a dancer's sense of where your body is and how it moves. It's a mental game as well, as you pick your way along a vertical route, searching for hand- and footholds that are as often as not made up of faith as rock. Finally, there's the undeniable element of nerve – for a species that spent much of its formative evolutionary years in trees, falling is one of the ultimate nightmares. No matter how safely anchored you are, no matter that *intellectually* you know you're not going to hit the ground, that you can only swing a foot from the rock, a part of you wants to gnaw into that rock with your *teeth* rather than experience the slightest fall.

I have this one basic problem about climbing, which is that I am seriously afraid of heights. When I first mention to my parents that I'm going to New Mexico to learn to climb, the announcement is met with gales of laughter. My mother recounts, in painful detail, one of the family nuggets: How, as a high school student, I was unable to walk up the stairs to the top of a fire tower, because I was dizzy from the height. How I stopped, in fact, on the second floor, unable to look down.

'I won't look down,' I promise. Still, though, it's a question I'm afraid I'll have to address.

'Like a lot of things in life that are worth doing, climbing has a risk attached to it,' Dunham Gooding, head of the prestigious American Alpine Institute guide and instruction service, tells me before lesson one. At forty-five years old, Gooding has been climbing twenty-nine years. 'Unlike most sports, though, in climbing, the consequences of errors are severe.

'Think,' he says, 'instructor. It's not all that difficult to learn the fundamentals of climbing and protection systems. 'With good instruction, you can substantially reduce your risks and progress quickly. Without it, good luck.'

Finding that good instructor, though, isn't necessarily as easy as finding the Lycra tights.

My first encounter with a potential guide/instructor, plucked from the Santa Fe phone book, is daunting.

'So,' says my potential guide, 'what'll it be? Top-roping, figure 5.5 to maybe 5.8. Boring, huh? How about me leading, maybe four-pitch, average 5.6, couple of 5.9 moves that I'll help you over. You'll flash it no problem, then we'll rap off the back. Whatdaya say?'

What I say is, 'Excuse me?'

Like any sport, I discover, climbing has its own specialized vocabulary, and my first step is figuring out what the heck these people are talking about. Next on my list of potential guides is Clark Man, who proves to be my decoder ring.

In top-roping, he explains patiently, the instructor sets an anchor at the top of a cliff, then threads the climbing rope through the anchor and comes down. Back on the ground, the student climbs while the instructor or another student reels in the other end of the rope. If the climber falls, the other person on the rope, the *belayer*, catches the climber. In *lead climbing*, the instructor climbs first, setting *protection*, various kinds of anchors, in the rock as he or she climbs, and hooking the rope into those pieces. When the instructor gets to the top or to a convenient ledge, the student then climbs and removes the protection, with the instructor above providing the belay.

'For new climbers, I prefer top-roping,' says Clark, 'because I'm able to see the student climb, point out techniques, and talk them over the rough spots.'

A *multipitch climb* refers simply to a climb where the rope is only so long, so at some point on a long climb, you're going to have to stop and reset the anchors. Think of the cliché, 'coming to the end of your rope.' In climbing, that's a reality. A *four-pitch climb* means you're going to have to stop on four ledges, pull the ropes up, reset your anchors, and start again.

All those funny numbers (called the Yosemite Decimal System) are a shorthand way of rating the difficulty of a climb. The 5 means that the terrain is difficult (or dangerous) enough that you need a rope and some sort of protection. The number on the other side of the decimal point tells you how hard the climb is. Obviously, 5.1 climbs are pretty easy; right now, the hardest climb in the world is a 5.14. Anything above 5.9 is harder than I can imagine doing. A 5.14 is the domain of either superhumans or Spiderman.

Also, ratings are totally subjective; from my own painful experience I found that an Arkansas 5.9 is different from a Colorado 5.9.

'There are two things you need to learn,' says Gooding. 'Technical skills – safety, technique, where to place your hands and feet, and protective systems. The other thing is judgment, and that comes from experience.'

Placing your hands and feet is hard enough. My first day, standing in front of a granite wall, I can't understand for the life of me how anyone expects me to get off the ground. No one is more shocked than I when, following Clark's instructions, I find myself actually moving *up*.

'One of the exciting things about climbing,' adds Gooding, 'is that it looks spectacular. It's really easier than it looks, once you know the tricks of the trade.'

Part of what allows me to move up is Clark Man's steady, low-key coaxing, like a person talking to a frightened and potentially dangerous dog. In his early forties, Clark is, by his own definition, an old hippie. He makes silver climbing jewelry, instructs, and occasionally competes in climbing competitions. We are near the research town of Alamagordo, climbing on a series of cliffs that look vaguely familiar.

'They should,' says Clark. 'They've been featured in just about every cowboy movie ever made.'

The trick (okay, the *first* trick), Clark says, is to focus only on the move in front of you. You're not trying to climb to the top, you're trying to climb to that little ledge about six inches from your left knee.

'Look over to your right,' he says when I'm about four feet off the ground. 'See that little bump on the rock? Take your right foot, right about the instep, and put it on that little bump. Now stand up on your right foot.'

And I move up another two feet.

'Did I mention I was afraid of heights?' I say.

'Several times,' replies Clark.

Part of the boom in climbing, I discover, is a boom in climbing technology. I am, for instance, wearing 'sticky' rubber climbing shoes. The rubber isn't really sticky, but it does adhere better than it has any right to on the rock. The soles of the shoes are also very, very stiff, making them unpleasant to walk in, but able to hold their shape on the little tiny edges of rock Clark persists in pointing out as places to stand.

The rope is connected to a climbing harness around my waist and upper thighs made of climbing webbing that is strong enough to lift a car. The buckle of the harness is aircraft aluminum, which you thread the waist strap through once and then back to tie it off. No harness, Clark tells me, has ever failed in climbing.

The most fascinating thing to me, though, is the *protection*. The idea is that when you're lead climbing, you want to protect yourself as you climb. The way to do this is to hook your climbing rope, which is being fed slowly to you by your belayer below, into various pieces of protection as you climb. Then, if you do fall, you can only fall twice the distance between you and the last piece of protection. Makes sense, right?

Originally, climbers used metal stakes, called *pitons*, hammered into cracks in the rock itself. The problem with pitons was that they were destructive of the rock and became permanent, unsightly features on the landscape. In the 1980s, as rock climbing (as opposed to alpine climbing) kept growing, it was strongly influenced by increased environmental awareness. The idea became not just to climb, but to climb clean, to leave nothing behind on the rock. English climbers had pioneered the use of *nuts*, as in nuts and bolts, for protection. A piece of climbing cord was looped through a nut. To use it for protection, the nut was slipped in a crack in the rock and the climber's rope attached by a carabiner. Then, the second climber could easily remove the protection. Nuts got sophisticated. Now climbers carry multiple sets of wired nuts, steel wedges crimped and soldered to a heavy loop of wire. The nuts are all different sizes, and there are several varieties of shape, ready for any size crack.

I am particularly fascinated by an even more sophisticated piece of protection, a *friend*, which is a camming device that compresses when the trigger is pulled and expands when the trigger is released. The cams can bite into the sides of a perfectly parallel crack, where a nut could find no purchase. Like nuts, friends come in all different sizes, from tiny to outright huge.

'Of course, learning to climb has to do with a lot more than the gear,' says Clark. 'It's a Zen thing, you know.'

(Denise has a theory about instructors in high-risk fields. 'There's an "instructor" personality. They're very quiet – a good instructor never raises his or her voice,' Denise says. 'But when they talk, you had better listen.')

'Most of the climbers I know who are good teachers don't like sticking their necks out,' Clark adds. 'The last thing you want in an instructor is a daredevil.'

The Fear is still there as I continue climbing, but it's

heavily diluted by a fascination with going *up*. I think there is a lot of leftover kid in most people, and that kid wants to climb stuff just for the sheer love of it. Sometimes – especially for those of us with a baseline fear of heights – that's hard to explain, just like it was tough to make Mom understand why we had to climb that tree in the front yard in the first place.

But it's not something you really have to explain to someone, is it? If anyone has any questions, talk him or her into a day of instruction. The first time your questioner finds himself or herself sitting on top of a cliff, breathing like a steam engine, soaked with sweat, and covered with chalk, just taking in the view, that person will understand just fine.

Climbing is appealing precisely because it goes beyond the usual push and shove of weight lifting or the steady rhythms of running and cycling to blend strength and motion and – I'm still working on this one – grace into a vertical ballet. Climbing is the flip side of the hammerheaded world of triathlon, which functions under the time-honored theory that way more is always better. Climbing refuses to respond to the hit-it-again-harder school of exercise. You have to *think*, not just *push*. You have to follow a vertical route that, on first inspection, might seem either impossible or invisible. You have to string together a series of moves that might involve everything from the big muscle groups like the lats and quads all the way to the tiny tendons of the fingers. You have to be able to flex like a dancer.

Later on that first day, Clark says to me casually, 'Take your right heel, raise it over your head and hook it on that little outcropping of rock.'

Excuse me?

To climb at all, much less to climb well, also requires that elusive body sense found in dancers and martial artists – *where is my body in space; where is my center?* All those things take place while a certain rear portion of your mind, the part that remembers climbing down from the trees eons ago, is screaming: *You're going to f...a...l...l...l...l!*

I never before realized exactly how high fifty feet is. Fifty feet seems the base of the clouds, the top of Mt. Everest, within a few feet of where Daedalus's wings began to melt. The view from the top of a fifty-foot cliff, out across a *Young Guns* landscape, is more than amazing. It is an impossible landscape of sweat and fear and triumph.

It is as addictive as roasted peanuts on a hot afternoon.

I finally meet Ilg at an alternative bookstore in downtown Santa Fe, a parallel universe to the high-ticket galleries and jewelry shops on the square. He's too busy to talk, but we make arrangements to meet at his tiny office in the midday heat of the following day.

Ilg is like a cross between a gnome and Arnold Schwarzenegger, small, smiling enigmatically, but seriously *ripped*.

His office is a spare room, cluttered with books, gear, and a small computer. It is hot, but without humidity; the heat has no teeth. Ilg's blond hair is spiked up and he has a silver loop high on one ear.

'Welcome,' he says, beaming. 'We have a long way to go.'

The great thing about climbing, he says, is that it helps a person appreciate that extreme sports are more than strength and muscle and sweat. 'It's about dance,' he says.

'Dance?'

'Dance,' Ilg beams. Ilg beams a lot. 'Our problem is that we compartmentalize our sports, our activities, our training. But that's not how we are – we're whole beings, and our fitness needs to reflect that wholeness.'

It is Ilg, after all, who has said that, 'Specialization is for insects.'

'Part of that compartmentalization,' he continues, 'makes us see climbing as different from running, or snowshoeing as different from dancing. In reality, they're all part of the same process. The experience is the same, which, of course, you already know.'

Strangely enough, I do – sort of.

Here is my favorite climbing story, which takes place a year after I sit in Ilg's office:

My left index finger is bleeding through the athletic tape and a tiny chunk of my right thumb is missing, as if I'd inadvertently pulled it out and left it somewhere on this Colorado granite. Which is, of course, exactly what I did. We are in Penitente Canyon, about four hours from Sante Fe, New Mexico, and a good two hours from the closest Mexican restaurant, no small feat in Colorado.

Penitente Canyon is a premier sport climbing area. Sport climbing is pure rock climbing, usually practiced on relatively short cliffs, say fifty to a hundred feet... It is hard, fast, and as addictive as Raisinets at the Saturday matinee.

In sport climbing, you're supposed to fall. That's how you discover just how good you really are, and how you get better. Say what you want, it's still harrowing to me to feel that first peel away from the rock ... *Millions of years of evolution tells me I'm f...a...l...l...i...n...g.*

We evolved from arboreal species; fear of falling is our most fundamental fear.

I stand at the beginning of the next climb, looking at the grey granite. Its texture is rough, gritty sandpaper shot through with sharp quartz. The first move is a high step. I'll get off the ground by using my sticky-soled climbing shoes to hold onto the rock while I pull myself up with my fingertips in a tiny crack. I'm almost ready to start when I notice something odd. I'm not nervous, although just a second before I wasn't sure I could do the first move. Instead of a blank rock face, I see a kinetic pattern, a series of moves, step-step-step. All I have to do is move. Before I can start thinking, I start up the face. The high step comes naturally, as does each successive move. My feet are always in the right places; my hands just where they need to be. Thoughts bounce through my mind, but they don't seem to be connected to anything in particular. I am past the crux, the hardest move, and to the top before I really have time to realize it.

And just as quickly, the world refocuses itself around me. My finger is still bleeding. My thumb still throbs. I am, however, not the same person I was, some minutes ago . . .

8 Down

Down, a world of down.

Here is the view from the top of Mammoth Mountain:

We are above the treeline, 12,500 feet on a knob of bald granite. Behind me, a line of Lycra-clad bicyclists snakes back to the ski gondola, which is how we got up this granite face in the first place. Most of them look like gladiators, plastic pads on the knees and elbows, plastic chest protectors and helmets that leave only the slits of the eyes showing. They lean against two-wheeled devices that look like a cross between a traditional bicycle and a UFO.

They are calm, some laughing and ignoring the wind-whipped dust devils that howl up the side of the mountain. My head is pinging from the altitude, my mouth dry and caked from a combination of nerves, lingering altitude sickness, and last night's tequila, 'a sure-fire cure' for the altitude sickness that didn't even remotely work.

Ahead of me are five more Lycra-ed warriors and steps leading up to a red ski chute. On the other side of the ski chute are three and a half miles of down. The Kamikaze trail. I am wearing two T-shirts and garish biking shorts – the two T-shirts being clever protection against the sharp rocks and gravel I will be sailing over at about forty-five miles per hour in just a few minutes. I look at the other bikers' plastic chest protectors and want very badly to throw up. But I am too scared to throw up.

'So how many times did you get to practice the course?' the bike rider behind me asks. He is in blue Lycra with garish elbow and knee pads. Veins pop out of his forearms. Even his mountain bike looks mean.

'Didn't get here in time,' I say.

'Do a lot of downhill races?' he asks.

'First one.'

He looks nonplused. His bike even quits snarling at mine.

'Where do you live, anyway?' he asks, curious as to what kind of fool would make the Mammoth Mountain Kamikaze Downhill his first mountain bike race.

'Florida.'

'Oh, wow,' he says. 'Good luck. And you'll need it.'

I carry my silver Cannondale up the red stairs and position the bike in the chute. I am trying to think of something clever, something devil-may-care, to say, but I seem to have temporarily lost the facility for speech. Ahead of me, the chute drops ten feet to the Kamikaze trail proper, which in turn drops away for about a hundred feet to a drop steep enough to make walking it hard.

'Pedal like a mother,' the guy behind me cautions. 'You lose traction, you gonna be sliding down the mountain on your butt.'

Although I can't see it, I know that the drop feeds into a 180-degree switchback, which I will slam into at about eight hundred miles per hour, a watermelon seed spat out of the mountain.

'What happens,' I asked another rider earlier, 'if I'm going so fast I miss the switchback?'

'Well,' he said, 'you've got about eight seconds to learn how to fly.'

'You good to go?'

The starter shakes me out of my reverie. Ahead of me, I see mountains. The sky is bright, high-altitude blue. The clouds are perfect picture postcard clouds. I want to remember them just this way.

'You good to go, man?' he says again.

'Yeah,' I croak. 'Let's do it . . .'

The List, The List, The List. How much mountain biking could one expect to find in Florida? Not surprising that I got all my information (misinformation?) from magazines. And while mountain-bike racing is all the rage in the bike magazines, it is in fact hard, as it involves riding a bicycle up a mountain. But the downhills, I reason, have a much better ring to them. With the downhills, gravity will be shouldering part of the load, while I just push the occasional pedal and steer. And mountain biking was born on downhills, specifically the steep hills of the Marin Headlands in Marin County, California, across the Golden Gate Bridge from San Francisco.

Of all the downhills – Mt. Snow in Vermont, Deer Valley in Utah – the Kamikaze, beginning at the top of central California's Mammoth Mountain, is the most feared. The reason is simple – speeds on the 3.5-mile course can hit sixty miles per hour, with big rocks on one side and a cliff on the other.

Over beer in the pizza place, this seemed terminally cool. At those speeds, flying over the gravel and the ground-up pumice sand of the old volcano, control is more of a hopeful illusion than a reality. Common sense is no longer your friend, just as brakes, when applied, will no longer exactly stop you, and handlebars, when turned, will no longer make the bicycle go where you want it to go.

Before I head out west to face downhills, I watch a video of a previous Kamikaze. A racer comes out of a sweeping turn at some speed approaching warp-3, and suddenly his wheel begins to wobble. In slow motion on my television screen, he heads toward an imposing boulder, which he smacks with his front wheel. The rider is suddenly and gracelessly no longer a rider. Rather, he is a flyer, airborne, sailing over the handlebars – or what is left of the handlebars. The bike seems to be busily returning itself to its component parts – wheels going in contradictory directions, lengths of aluminum tubing leaving the frame. It looks like one of those industrial assembly films run backwards.

The voice-over is solemnly saying that, based on the sheer number of injuries, the Kamikaze may be the single most dangerous sporting event in America.

'Turn it off,' my friend, who's been watching with me, says. She has been one of the voices of reason as I've compiled The List, pointing out in perfectly moderate language that, for example, I live in Florida, where the highest local mountain is a seawall. Where, she asks repeatedly, do I plan to train?

'I've seen all I want to see,' she says now. 'Have a great time out there.' She stands up and leaves the room. I glance toward my Cannondale, propped against the wall across from the refrigerator, in clear view of the television set. I am sorry I didn't blindfold it before the video.

I bought the bike for a hundred dollars from a newspaper ad taken out by a guy who'd just hit the Florida lottery for big bucks. It is yellow, two frame sizes too small for me, and has been ridden on the race circuit for two seasons. In short, it looks as if it has found it's own boulder to hit and disassemble itself. It was love at first sight.

'I'll need to change a few things,' I tell my friends, who have a good laugh at my ability to find such a great deal. 'But basically, I think it's a good ride.'

Of course, I need to replace the wobbly wheels ($250); the shredded, battered gears ($150); the bent handlebars

($85); and the cracked, yellow frame ($275 for a trade-in). I keep the seat, the seat post, the chain, and many other small, irreplaceable parts. The result is the sleek, fat-tubed, silver Cannondale leaning against the wall in my kitchen. It is a state-of-the-art bike – at least state of the art as defined by someone who's learned everything there is to know about mountain biking from reading bicycle magazines. It rides great on the beach. I jump it off a seawall and it lands fine.

My first test run is in Colorado, down the fire roads that weave around Vail Mountain. I have dutifully ridden up Vail Mountain on a shaky rental bike, a measly ten thousand feet high, and I feel like someone has scoured my lungs with a wire brush attached to an electric drill. I convince my instructor, a smiling monster named Karen, to let me lie down for a few minutes before we start back down. She smiles a happy Colorado smile, one that you automatically give to an inferior species such as myself, and lets me collapse on a warm rock like some basking out-of-state lizard. Before I can achieve REM-sleep though it's back-to-the-bike time.

This time, I reason, *it's down. No problem at all, with gravity and all that.*

'Follow me,' she says, then disappears down a steep gravel road. I follow, and by the second switchback I can still see the dust kicked up by her knobbies. She is waiting for me at the fourth switchback.

'You are never,' she says, without preamble, barely bothering with the smile, 'going to get down this mountain if you don't let go of the brakes.'

I notice for the first time that my hands have locked into rigid claws, reflexively curved around the brake handles. I tentatively try to loosen a finger, but the muscles in my wrist seem to have seized up.

'See?' she says, pointing at my claws.

'What happens if I let go and can't stop?' I ask, that being a perfectly valid question in my book.

'Silly Michael,' says Karen. 'You go off the mountain, and you die.'

'Oh.'

The previous day: In order to avoid a complete novice designation, I rent a mountain bike at the Copper Mountain Ski Resort, which is open for biking all through the summer. I choose a Haro Extreme bike, because it looks cooler than the others and because I don't really have a clue what other factors to consider. Besides, the 'extreme' part sells me. I also buy a book of local trails, three PowerBars, and a semiwaterproof jacket, which I tape to the top tube of the bicycle. Then I head off into the Rockies, sublime in my ignorance.

Because by this time I'm a pretty good bicyclist on a road bike, I decide to skip the basic fire roads and go straight to *intermediate single track*, which I have read about extensively in *Mountain Bike Action* magazine. Single track is just that – a single track that threads up, down, and through the mountains. I begin on a wide trail that winds through a mountain meadow, wildflowers still blooming.

Cakewalk, I think.

A hundred yards later, the trail narrows and heads up. I ride as far as I can, wheezing for oxygen, which seems to be in short supply. Finally, I dismount and start pushing my Haro Extreme up the mountain.

The trail turns into a twelve-inch-wide groove cut into the side of the mountain. To my left is up, steeply climbing into the clouds. To my right is down, a long, tumbling drop I prefer not to think about. I remount the bike and try to ride, but my eyes keep glancing to the right. Perversely, the front wheel keeps trying to follow my eyes. Finally, I settle for using the Haro Extreme as a sort of scooter, pedaling a little, pushing with my feet a lot.

This isn't so bad, I think.

When I reach my first downhill, I'm in pretty good spirits for someone who's been scooting a bicycle along a trail for hours. I start pedaling like a crazy person down the gentle incline. It's everything I imagined, a roller coaster without rails, but with spectacular scenery – sky, mountains, rocks, trees, streams, all whipping by like an impressionist painting. At the bottom I plow through a shallow marsh, spraying icky black mud over the bike, my legs, and the surrounding flora. I am having a ball.

The next uphill isn't nearly as bad, and I hit the downhill pedaling, picking up speed, aiming for the next shallow marsh. I am whooping happily as I plow into the marsh at about twenty-five miles per hour.

The marsh is at least three feet deep.

The bike nose-dives into the muck and stops, dead. I continue on, over the handlebars, my arms extended like Superman escaping from a telephone booth. I land face-first in the muck, my screamed obscenity muffled as my mouth fills with rich, black mud. For a second I just lay there, then quickly sit up, coughing mud from my chipmunk-expanded cheeks and trying to clear enough gunk out of my eyes to see whether I'm permanently blinded or just encased in a yeechy cocoon. When I can finally see something, I look around for the Haro Extreme, which seems to have disappeared. I finally see a single pedal sticking out of the marsh.

I pull the bike, which now looks like some touring vehicle for South Pacific mudmen, out of the marsh. Then I plop down and just look at the thing. It's hard to tell through all the mud, but the front wheel seems to have developed a strange cant. I pick the bike up and haul it to a shallow mountain stream where I proceed to toss it in.

Probably can't hurt it any more, I reason, then join the bike in the freezing water. *Probably can't hurt me any more, either.* The bike is still mostly covered in mud when I haul us out of the water, but at least I can see that it is actually a bicycle. Next, I take off the front wheel and, using a handy rock, beat on it until it is back in some shape resembling round. Then I wisely (and slowly) pedal back to the bike shop.

'Jesus!' exclaims the guy when I return the Haro Extreme, the front wheel bent, the bike and me caked with mud. 'What in hell did you do to it? Never mind. Leave it. It looks like a local's been riding it.'

'It's all in the brakes,' Karen is saying. 'Don't use 'em.'

I nod intelligently. What I'm actually thinking is, *Riiiiight. Bag the brakes. Wait till I hit something solid, maybe a tree, to stop . . .*

'It's a question of trust,' she continues. 'You trust the bike. The tires are gonna grip. The bike's gonna track in a straight line. All you've got to do is sit on it without falling off. You're not going to need to manhandle the thing to make it do what you want.'

I think of an old Bruce Springsteen lyric about racing cars, *As you jockey your way through the cars . . . And sit out the light, as it changes to green . . . With your faith in your machine . . . Off you scream into the night . . .*

I'm on a rental Bianchi that's a sort of baby-food green. I don't like it, but it did get me up the mountain. We've been doing fire road downhills all morning, and I'm beginning to believe Karen is right. The bike knows what it's doing.

It's a feedback issue as well. A road bike travels on a smooth surface, and the message it transmits back to the rider reflects that I once cracked sixty miles per hour on a road bike downhill, and I remember straining all my senses to catch even the tiniest messages coming back from the smooth asphalt, making microcorrections to keep the thin strip of racing rubber in a straight, straight line. The messages from the mountain bike are blunter – big rocks, loose gravel, the fat tires chewing up the surfaces. And I recall Ralph Waldo Emerson's words about skating over thin ice: 'Our salvation is in our speed . . .'

When in doubt, go faster. Trust the machine to keep going over pretty much anything. Let go of the brakes and your fears at the same time.

'You ready?' Karen asks. I nod, and we again head down the mountain.

Faith in the machine . . . faith in the machine . . . We are picking up speed. The bikes fly through the curves. I'm hanging a few feet behind her rear wheel. I ride the biological waves sluicing through my body, adrenaline making time go all mushy and soft around the edges, so slow that I see a piece of gravel, caught by my tires, slowly arc and bounce away, over the edge.

'. . . And you're in love with all the wonder it brings . . .
And every muscle in your body sings . . . As the highway
ignites . . .'

We fly into a long, steep drop, and I rip past her, taking advantage of my weight and gravity. I follow a line chosen by the bike, a bump here, a shift of weight there. I am *here*, but not *here*, in the calm center of a data storm. Sight, sound, smell, the feel of the wind against my face, the terrain through the pedal against the sole of my shoes to my rapidly numbing hands. The same feel of the big wind against a small sail, the curious blending of physical and mental . . .

And we are down the mountain, on flatlands, the speed rush behind us. I reel the bike to a stop and lean against a tree, waiting for my instructor. She arrives a moment later.

'You graduate,' she says simply.

The whole West is mountain-bike crazy. For those of you who've been in a cave the last few years, mountain bikes are the bastard offspring of those old fat-tired paperboy bikes from the 1960s and 1990s motorcycles. In fact, the first mountain bikes were old cruisers, beefed up and raced down the steep but trendy hills of Marin County. When the first manufacturers started making mountain bikes, a strange thing happened – people bought them like crazy. Not, however, because of the mountains. Although there was definitely the allure of buying a hard-core, off-road machine, what really fueled the mountain bike fires was the simple fact that the things are easier to ride than high-strung, narrow-tired road bikes. I mean, you sit upright instead of in some weird European crunched-up position; you get to roll right over rocks and gravel that would have previously landed you on your face; you can jump off curbs and be cool and finally, and not insubstantially, you don't have to wear all that drastically colored Lycra that only looks good on about three or four people worldwide.

My Cannondale, largely because of my ignorance, is a surprisingly unsophisticated mountain machine. For a start, it is *unsuspended*. This means that it does not have motorcycle-style shock absorbers in the front and rear. I will learn about the utility of these devices later, as I ice my inflamed elbows and wonder when the feeling is going to trickle back into my fingers. The more serious downhill racers' bikes have a huge front *chainring*, or gear, to help achieve escape velocity on the way down. Their bikes also tend to be overbuilt, since a little extra weight on a down-hill is a plus, and the last thing you want to happen at sixty miles per hour is for some new trick component to break.

On my few, brief rides before the race, I discover that my bike doesn't like to shift *under load* – that is, when I'm pedaling hard. This is probably a function, says a local bike mechanic, of the bike being assembled out of spare parts by people who had only seen mountains in Jeep ads. I agree that could possibly have something to do with the problem. We try three different front *derailleurs*, the device that pushes or lifts the chain onto different gears, and each time the bike balks under load. Finally, the mechanic pulls out the stops.

'Be back in a minute,' he says.

He returns holding a Coors Light beer can, which he proceeds to cut into little strips. He then reassembles the derailleur with beer can shims in place. It works like a charm.

'I wouldn't bet on this for too long, man,' he says. 'What are you planning to do out here?'

'The Kamikaze,' I say.

'No shit?' he says. 'If I'd known that, I would have used better beer.'

'You good to go, man?' the starter says again.

'Yeah,' I croak. 'Let's do it . . .'

There's a push, and a drop as the Cannondale comes out of the chute and starts down. I am in my biggest chain wheel – the gear in the front – and the smallest gear in my rear sprocket. I want torque. If I'm accelerating, my tires are gripping. I head toward the first steep drop, pedaling for torque and shifting my weight to the rear to offset the steepness. Adrenaline hits like a hammer as my body shifts into overdrive. My vision narrows – *flee or fight*, I think absently, *focus on the threat* – my hearing is keener, my palms are sweating through the thick gloves. In seconds I am through the steep drop – steeper than I've ever been down – heading into the first switchback.

Faith in the machine . . . Faith in the machine . . .

Time no longer seems to mean anything. People on bikes fly past me, sixty miles an hour to my piddling forty-five . . . *forty-five miles an hour . . . I'm driving along at forty-five miles an hour, open the car door, and step out . . .* Is the ground hard? My arms are numb to my shoulders from the pounding coming up through the forks to the handlebars. I force my eyes to look far ahead, checking the terrain I'm sailing toward, resisting the temptation to look directly in front of me. If the rock is that close, I'm already over it. I've either fallen or I haven't. Bruce Springsteen and Ralph Emerson alternate in my head, a sound track running in some closed-off compartment in my mind. *Salvation in speed . . . Faith in the machine . . . Salvation in speed . . .* I realize I am pedaling as hard as I can, breathing like a bellows, welded to the bike as we hurtle through another switchback.

I turn onto a wider road, and I realize, absently, that I am almost down. I pick up my cadence, urging the bike onward. One more turn and I see the finish line ahead of me. *I have been riding forever – hours, days, months, and suddenly it's over.* Nine and a half minutes have passed since I was pushed out of the red chute at the top of the mountain.

My legs are wobbly as I steer the bike off the course. I stop by a grassy spot and lay the Cannondale down, then plop down next to it. I feel like a friction toy rolled off the end of a table, mental wheels frantically spinning, adrenaline sloshing around, winding down. My vision and hearing are returning to normal. My muscles quiver, and I realize my thumbs and most of my fingers are completely numb. I am barely able to take off my helmet and wipe the muddy mixture of sweat and dirt off my face. I am completely alone. I know no one in Mammoth. I lean back on the warm grass, my ears buzzing from the altitude and the impending adrenaline crash.

I've dodged a bullet, I think. *I screwed up, didn't take the sport as seriously as I should have.* When I close my eyes, I see the switchbacks sailing past, flashes of blue sky and a red gravel road. I jolt fully awake, as if I've fallen into a *f...a...l...l...i...n...g dream. Lucked out*, I think. Exhilaration tempered with fear. I think about the rest of The List, watching the white clouds swirl above the old volcano. *It won't happen again*, I vow. *I won't die for The List. I won't.*

It is an hour before I wearily stand and push the Cannondale to my rental car. I drive down the mountain, go to my room, and go to sleep.

The next morning I get up early, ride back up the mountain, and ride the Kamikaze course a half-dozen times, pushing harder, faster, each time down.

9 Between the Rock and a Hard Place

Let me tell you about a bad a day:

I am in San Francisco Bay, and I am swimming. Alone. The water is bitterly cold, the wind-whipped chop and swirling fog making it seem even worse. I have come to this freezing bay to train for the Alcatraz triathlon, with its infamous autumn mile-and-a-half, shark-infested swim from Alcatraz to the mainland. But on this particular day it's too choppy and foggy to even make out the outlines of the old prison from my sea-level vantage point.

I realize I shouldn't be out in San Francisco Bay alone, that I have moved beyond acceptable risk into just plain stupid. I am, however, slightly lost. I have only barely started The List, and it has begun twisting my life around. I've run in Death Valley, done the Kamikaze, learned to rock climb. The general consensus among my best friends is that, having completed my 'midlife crisis,' it is now time to get back to the real world.

'Look how far you've gone,' says one friend, over pizza at the very same place where The List was created. 'The joke's on everybody else. Not so long ago, there was a fat guy sitting in this room, and now there's not. You're strong; you're fast. What are you trying to prove?'

81

That refrain has suddenly become very common.

What are you trying to prove?

I think I would be doing better if I had the correct answer, which is, I think, something like: I am trying
to prove . . . my manhood . . . that I'm not as old as
the calendar says . . . that I'm cool . . . that I'm attractive to members of the opposite sex . . . that I'm a
baaaddd dddoooggg . . .

Instead, I say the truth, which is that I'm not trying to
prove anything. I want, I say, to find out where the edge
really is; see what it's like out there; taste it; feel it; smell
it; touch it. I want that . . . you know . . . feeling of . . .
well, that *feeling*. I want my brain to work better. I want
to be caught up in that data stream, feel the bits and bytes
flooding through my eyes and ears and mouth . . .

'You want the rush,' my friends say flatly.

'I'm not saying I don't want the rush,' I reply, 'but I am
saying the rush is only a tiny part of what's there, the
experience.'

Heads nod knowingly.

'I want you to meet a woman I'm dating,' a close friend
of mine says one night. 'She's a shrink, and she's fascinated
by people with death wishes.'

'I do not,' I say emphatically, 'have a death wish.'

'Have some more pizza,' he says.

Later, I am at a party at a friend's advertising agency. I
am cornered by a young woman in a basic black dress,
long blonde hair hanging down her back. She steers me
out of the flowing herd, into an eddy, sits me down in a
desk chair, and pulls up a bench across from me. She leans
forward on her elbows, and I notice her eyes are a muddy
blue. *I am*, I think, *trapped in a Calvin Klein commercial.*

'Tell me what it's like,' she says, stopping just short of
licking her red lips, 'when you think you're going to die.'

I can't help myself. I break out laughing.

'I wouldn't know,' I say.

She is clearly offended.

'Wouldn't know or won't say?'

I take her hands in mine. They are slightly sweaty.

'I am not crazy,' I say. 'And I intend to live forever.'

I stand up. She jots her number on a piece of paper.

'Call me when you're ready to talk,' she says, tossing her hair.

On the way out of the office, I toss the paper in the garbage.

A couple of days before I'm scheduled to leave for San Francisco, my beloved Chow Chow dies unexpectedly. I pack for Alcatraz in a bleak, gray mood, dumping my clothes in a bag. I spend a strained evening at the bike shop watching the mechanic go over my bike.

'You might want to pay attention here, Michael,' says Bear, the mechanic, who reassembles the Cannondale as I wear the parts out. 'I believe you're going to have to put this bike back together when you get to San Francisco.'

I watch him spin the wheels and listen to the clicking of the gears. The next morning, I get up early, go to the airport, and get on the plane. I doze off and dream of struggling in bottle-green, cold water, losing my breath, thrashing and sinking and – I wake up with a start. We are landing in San Francisco.

I check in at my hotel, make a stab at reassembling the bike, then grab my wetsuit and a couple of towels. I hike through the party time of Fisherman's Wharf, down to the Aquatic Basin – a small boat basin at the end of the Wharf – slip out of my jeans and sweatshirt, and wrestle my way into the wetsuit. I stuff my street clothes in my backpack, then cram the backpack up underneath an old boathouse.

Without so much as a stretch, I hit the freezing water in a low, flat dive.

The cold seeps through my wetsuit; my shoulders ache; my mind rattles, focus lost, caught up in the motion of the bottle green water.

There's something underneath me.

My stroke falters, my rhythm broken. I swallow dirty, bottle-green water. I splash like a child in a kiddie pool. *This is not a joke – they're under there, in that bottle-green water. The deep ocean killers, the tigers, the whites. Stupid, stupid.*

Nothing. Nothing there but my imagination.

I begin stroking again, trying to get my breath under control. *Mikey blow bubbles*, I think, somewhat desperately. *Mikey blow bubbles.* But my stroke is all over the place. Instead of pulling water, the flat edge of my hand slips though the cold, dirty water of the Bay. I falter again. The fog seems thicker. I can just make out the entrance to the Aquatic Basin. I look around me feeling the animal in my head throwing all its force into the bars of its cage. In my head, I see the bars bending and straining under the onslaught. I look around me for a boat, for another swimmer, for a log, for heaven's sake.

But I am alone in the cold bay, trapped between the Rock and the Hard Place of my mind. The animal screams in my head. I tack back into the yacht basin, breathing shallowly, sweat pouring off my forehead into the cold, green water. It is maybe a quarter mile to shore, but my strokes are sloppy and my kick has fallen apart. The shore gets no closer. My arms and shoulders are aching now; my legs and feet are numb. I thrash, and what seems like a hundred years later I stagger onto the sand. I am burning up. I peel off the top of my wetsuit, sucking in huge quantities of the foggy air. Finally, unable to stand any longer, I collapse onto the sand and hug my knees, shivering and sweating at the same time. I bite my lip, and still a tear rolls down my cheek.

The next time I look up, I am surrounded by about a dozen foreign tourists, their cameras clicking away. Some laugh and point and talk in a language I don't understand. I put my head back on my knees, and eventually they go away . . .

'Once you're on the Rock,' goes the old country song, 'there's no escape from Alcatraz . . .'

I don't remember the first time I heard of the Escape from Alcatraz triathlon, but there's no doubt how it ended up on The List: the swim. The legendary swim.

There are lots of harder triathlons. The Ironman in Hawaii, for instance, or the Earth Journey – three days of living hell – in Vermont. But only one features a swim that was – and is – widely thought of as, if not impossible, at least stone cold crazy. To me, that mile and a quarter of treacherous water between the old prison of Alcatraz and the Aquatic Basin in San Francisco is so lodged in the national consciousness that I can't pass it up.

'Think about it this way,' a race organizer tells me when I call for information. 'We tell everybody to stop halfway across and take a good look, 'cause you're in a place damn few people have been and survived to talk about it.'

Hyperbole, to be sure. But, hey, even Clint Eastwood had trouble escaping from Alcatraz.

When I push the race organizers about why anyone would come up with such a race, now in its ninth year, they are blunt: 'Because,' one of them tells me, 'it's hard as shit. It's scary out there in the bay. It works on your head. The currents can be vicious. We've seen whirlpools develop. We've seen powerful – Olympic – swimmers dragged off course. And say whatever you want about how unlikely a shark attack would be, but they're down there. You know it. I know it. Everybody swimming in the race knows it. Let me tell you, that fact will never be out of your head, until you're too hypothermic to think anymore.'

To enter the race, I've signed the most comprehensive liability release I've ever seen. First is a general release, then paragraph after paragraph of what can go wrong – drowning, struck by a boat or ship, animal attack, et cetera – which I must initial. When I get to San Francisco, before I can pick up my race packet with my official race number, I have to sign yet another liability release. Finally, at the mandatory pre-race meeting, I must recite a liability release into a microphone. You cannot, one of the race officials tells the crowd at the meeting, claim ignorance.

The swim, billed as 1.5 miles, is only one-third of the race. There's a 25-mile bike leg that weaves through the Presidio, past Seal Rock, and out the Great Highway along the beach, looping back, crossing the Golden Gate Bridge, and finishing at the military base in the Marin Headlands. From there, you get a 13.5-mile run along the trails and roads of the Headlands, considered one of the tougher trail runs in the country.

The way it works is, just before dawn we'll all get up and hike down to Fisherman's Wharf. Then, a bagpipe honor guard will lead all 250 of us plucky souls onto a ferry for the ride out to Alcatraz, where we'll all jump off the ferry into the freezing-cold bay (actually, I exaggerate, the water temperature will probably be fifty degrees, easy), swim to the mainland, jump on our bikes, et cetera.

There are two things I've learned getting ready for Alcatraz. The first I've come to think of as the second law of The List: escalation – which is, roughly, that the closer you get to an item on The List, the more it seems that you should have picked something harder. Instead of swimming from Alcatraz to the mainland, what you should be doing is swimming the English Channel or maybe the Bering Strait. The law of escalation makes sense. The List grew from ground zero, a nonathletic-type person peeking through the keyhole at a distant world. The further I get into it, however, the more my view becomes that of a participant, surrounded by other participants. Some of those other participants, a very few, have done things that I couldn't have imagined when I started The List.

I discover, however, that even among elite participants, Alcatraz has an almost mystical feel to it. My informal poll on why people are here is usually answered, 'Because this scares the hell out of me.'

Another thing I discover is that no one actually knows anything. Everyone has an opinion on Alcatraz, but no one I know has ever done the race. Even the race organizers have their own weird spin on training: 'Spend a lot of time in real cold water.' Finally, at a post-triathlon party in Florida, I get the lecture that everyone has been waiting to give me.

'You're doing Alcatraz?' says a local triathlon champion, someone better on his worst day than I can aspire to be on my best. I'm surprised he knows who I am, much less what I'm doing.

'Where do you think you are?' he starts winding up. 'You live in Florida. The water temperature here is the same as a hot shower. Where do you plan to train for a freezing cold swim? Your refrigerator?'

I try to turn the lecture into a joke, but he's having no part of it.

'Seriously, Michael, you can drown out there,' he says. 'Alcatraz can hurt you.'

I start to say that I know that, but he turns away and heads out the door.

'Have a good swim,' he says, disgusted.

Granted, my training regimen seems a bit strange. I swim regularly with a masters swim group for my technique. Since my first triathlon, I've actually gotten to be an acceptable swimmer – in the pool. I decide that I need two additional items of training – cold water and a long, open-water swim. The first is easy. I will spend large amounts of time standing in cold showers.

'You're kidding,' says my occasional training partner John Rodolf.

'Any better ideas?'

'Well, just don't expect me to stand in there with you,' he says.

Secondly, as I live in Tampa, I will swim across Tampa Bay, which amounts to about two and a quarter miles.

'Remember when we were out sailing in the bay,' says Karen Luzier, who owns a wonderful sailboat. 'Remember that big tarpon with the huge bite taken out of its middle? What do you suppose is out there that can snack on a hundred-pound tarpon, and do you really want to swim with it? Besides, that's not really water in Tampa Bay – it's number-three diesel fuel.'

I finally talk my friend Louie into joining me for the swim on the basis that 'I've never heard of a shark in Tampa Bay, and, besides, if there were sharks, the Bay is so polluted that they would be too mutated to bite.' John grudgingly agrees to paddle a surfboard alongside us, to keep the thundering cigarette boats from turning Louie and I into chowder.

The swim goes off without a hitch. The water does, in fact, taste like diesel and has the consistency of warm chicken noodle soup, and the last twenty-five yards to the pier are unfortunately through a school of jellyfish. We emerge unscathed, except for John's sunburn. As we're walking away, the owner of the little pier's bait shop runs out and stops us.

'Did you two just swim across the bay?' he asks. Louie and I beam like proud fathers. 'You morons. We've been chumming for sharks all summer off this pier. The place is alive with 'em.'

Louie looks stricken.

'But you said . . .' he starts.

'Louie,' I say brightly, 'were we eaten?'

'You're not just crazy,' he says darkly. 'You're nuts.'

Sleep's pretty much out of the question the night before the race. I try calling people on the phone, but all too soon people remind me of the time zone difference between the West and East coasts. Around four in the morning, I give up the premise of spending anymore time in bed, get up, and methodically check my gear.

My bike is already racked in an old warehouse, about a mile from the Aquatic Basin. After the swimming portion of the race, we will run a mile to our bikes, hoping to get the feeling back in our extremities before we ride. I wish my bike were still here, so I could go over it one more time.

At five in the morning, in the dark, I take my wetsuit, running shoes, a can of Exceed Sports Meal – a chocolate energy drink so buffered that it will barely come out of the can, much less the drinker – a towel that I swipe from the hotel bathroom, a giant, economy-sized container of Vaseline, and an enameled pin of a great white shark, which I will clip inside my wetsuit for luck and head out.

My head is clear. The thinking is over. The worrying is over. I am in the quiet place, where there is nothing left in the world but the task in front of me. Somewhere in the back of my head, a green light that reads, 'Waiting for Data Input', is blinking. The animal of doubt and fear and pain rests, quiet in its cage.

I walk down the quiet streets of Fisherman's Wharf, past the crab-sandwich shops, the photo-processing kiosks, espresso bars, nautical-themed souvenir shops. The Wharf smells of old food and the fog; from the direction of the water, a disturbed sea lion barks loudly. At the Aquatic Basin, there's the usual pre-race hubbub, but it's subdued, muted in the fog. The sharp, piercing lights of television cameras stab through the foggy dark, touching the real athletes, the people for whom Alcatraz is simply another race. For the rest of us, outside the circle of lights, the race is something more than that. A test, surely; a validation, maybe. We are scared – I am scared – but the fear has no strength; I feel my fear the way you might feel a breeze on your face walking to the office. The breeze might be cool or hot, comfortable or uncomfortable, but it doesn't change anything. You note its touch and keep on walking.

I look out across the dark water, toward where the old prison will materialize, solidify out of the fog.

'There's not a lot of point in talking about it,' a racer said to me the day before. 'We all know why we're here, don't we?'

I set up my gear on the beach, put on my wetsuit, and mill around until I hear the first strains of bagpipe music. Then the whole ragged bunch of us hikes down Fisherman's Wharf to a waiting ferry, for the ride out to Alcatraz. Before the boat ride, of course, we get a pep talk. 'Just keep in mind,' says an organizer over a loudspeaker, 'that swimmers in wetsuits look like seals, which are the primary food for sharks . . . Swimmers, like seals, swim in a pack . . . Remember, sharks pick off the stragglers . . . Have a nice swim.'

In no time at all, we are at the prison – Rocky Beach, which is usually underwater – beneath the crumbling guard towers of Alcatraz. I've covered most of my exposed skin with Vaseline. My wetsuit is cut away around my shoulders to give my arms full freedom; this also compromises its warmth. The Vaseline won't offer a lot of protection from the biting cold, but it will, I hope, buy me a few more minutes before hypothermia sets in.

And hypothermia will set in. Despite the wetsuit, the fifty-what-ever-degree water, which conducts heat far more efficiently than air does, will begin sucking the heat out of my body as soon as I hit the water. As the temperature of the core of my body begins dropping, the rest of my body will begin taking heroic efforts to preserve the organism – me. First, we'll shiver, as my body tries desperately to keep warm. The swimming motions of my arms and legs will help, but won't be enough. Somewhere out in the bay, when my core temperature will have dropped around 5 degrees from its usual 98.6, my body will begin shutting down 'nonessential' systems, among them the one that thinks. At various times in the swim, kayakers will approach me and ask me my name. If I can't answer, the plan is to pull me out of the water and get me to the medical boat, hovering on the edges of the swim.

Good plan!

'It's time, campers!' and the doors of the ferry open. It's about a ten-foot drop to the water, and I get in line as quickly as I can. *Don't think . . . Jump in the water . . .*

I do. When I hit the water, it's like having dived headfirst into a concrete block. The cold takes my breath away, and as I sink into the bottle-green water, all I see are stars. A few feet below the surface, the stars clear and I struggle back up, dog-paddling to Rocky Beach. About a hundred yards out is the *rabbit boat*, its bright orange flag practically glowing in the fog. I sink chin-deep in the water, letting the cold soak through me, letting my breathing drift down, down, down. Then I dip my face in the water and hold it there. The saltwater tastes briny, dirty. I raise my face and look up the sheer cliffs to the old prison, then start swimming toward the start.

When the gunshot comes, it's anticlimactic. I take one more sight of the orange flag, put my head in the water, stroke. *Mikey blow bubbles*, I think absently. This phrase, I realize, has been hardwired into my head. I have a simple plan – watch my stroke to make sure my hand is pulling water, and raise my head every six strokes to watch the orange flag. Somewhere out there I know is a huge orange buoy, set this morning based on the latest information on the current. The overall plan is to swim toward the buoy, which is in the wrong direction for the Aquatic Basin, and the current will pull us home. I will also think calming thoughts for whatever companions I have down below. *I am not a seal . . . I taste like an old tire . . . If you're hungry, eat the woman in the nice blue wetsuit next to me . . .*

After about twenty minutes, the tops of my feet feel as if they're tangled in seaweed, a strange effect of the cold I've noticed before. This lasts for about another ten minutes, by which time my feet, along with my hands, are numb. I would like to say I notice my mental facilities slowing down, but it's not something you notice. Instead, thoughts just slip away. In the middle of the shipping channel, there are steady, oceanic swells. The water tastes like Tampa Bay, and the fog has cleared enough for me to see the ghostly outline of San Francisco. *It's real deep here,* I think, *more or less.* I raise my head and see the orange buoy, where I'm supposed to turn, and the brightly colored kayaks moving in and out of the swimmers.

'Hi!' someone says, frightening me.

Talking sharks!

But it's a paddler in a kayak.
'What's your name?' he says.

Name?

'Michael,' I say slowly. 'Bane.'
'You okay?'
'Sure.' *Why wouldn't I be okay?*
'Good luck,' and the paddler is gone.
I round the buoy. *I don't have to round the buoy, but I want to round the buoy. I like rounding the buoy.* The current is at my back. I am going faster. I have to watch my hands, though. For some reason, I forget to watch my hands and I stop moving. I am lying there paddling, but I don't seem to be going anywhere. When I remember to look at my hands, I see they are flat under, their edges cutting smoothly through the water. *Flat hand*, I think, and I start moving again. I like moving again. When I raise my head to sight again, I see the entrance to the Aquatic Basin.

Hot damn!

I swim through the entrance, and ahead I see the beach.

The beach!
I like the beach.

I swim until my knees hit the bottom, the sand; then I struggle up. The timing clock says forty-three minutes. *I like the timing clock.*

My wetsuit practically pops off when I unzip it. I stomp out of the suit and see my running shoes, right where I have left them. I slip my feet into the sneakers – elastic laces – and they pull right on.

'Hurry!' people around me are saying. I am hurrying. I pick up my tank top, then come to a dead stop. *There are four holes in it – one for my head, one for my right arm, one for my left arm, one for my whole body. But which is which?* I look around me and see others struggling with this question. I try one hole, and it's too small – my head won't fit. I take the shirt off and stare at it. *I've done this before* . . . On the third try, my head slips right in, just like that. People around me applaud.

'Run!' someone is saying, and shows me the way. On the mile run to the bike, I can feel my brain coming back to life . . . swimming back to the surface from whatever storage bin it had been relegated to by the survival tyranny of the body.

I couldn't get my T-shirt on?

At the bike, I chug down some Exceed, as much to dilute the dirty water of the bay sloshing around in my stomach as anything. Then I am riding. I race under Alcatraz rules, which means that I have to come to a complete stop at every stop sign and stoplight. The road is wet with drizzle, and I am flying through the hills. The Cannondale rolls smoothly, comfortably, familiarly. I sweep down the steep drop, past Seal Rock, to the Great Highway. I envision my feet spinning in perfect circles, to the rhythm of old rock songs. To my right, in the ocean, a single surfer catches a small break and carves toward shore.

A 180-degree turn at the zoo and I'm on my way back. I pass the same places, climb the steep hill at Seal Rock and, huffing and puffing like a steam engine, head toward the Golden Gate Bridge. The bridge is slick and windy. I grab a drink of water, then miss the holder when replacing the bottle. I see the bottle bounce once on the steel-grated roadway, then fall the long, long way into the cold bay.

As I start out on the run, I see the 'real' athletes coming in. They are racing the clock, drawn completely now into their own quiet places. They are away from pain, away from fear, lost in the rhythm of their own shoes on the wet pavement. I salute them, then turn off the road, into the woods.

The fog settles in for the run through the pristine Headlands. The trail is damp and at times slick. Occasionally, a beam of sunlight finds its way through the fog and the ground steams. The trail is a nightmare of shifting terrain. We might feed from a dirt road to a narrow trail along a ridge line, then do a steep, rutted descent to a sandy beach on a secluded cove. There is a choice then of soft sand or water. I take the harder packed sand and the water. The trail follows an old road back up, the steepest climb of the race. I run when I can; walk when I have to. With each turn in the road, it climbs higher.

I hear huffing, and for a time a woman racer with an English accent jogs alongside me.

'Every hill has a top,' she says. 'Every one.'

I hope she is not the woman in the blue wetsuit, whom I offered up to the shark gods at the beginning of the race.

The race turns off the road at its peak and heads along another ridge line. This trail is the narrowest yet, and in the deepening fog it seems a grey tunnel. I can hear my cross-country shoes smacking the rocks, feel the pain in my knees and hips from the bike and the trail so far. I seem to be completely alone, following a course that seems destined to go nowhere. There is a sharp pain in the middle of my back and I realize, for the first time apparently, that my neck is bleeding, chaffed raw by the collar of my wet-suit. *I wonder how high these ridges are . . . I wonder what I could see if the fog would miraculously lift . . . I wonder if there's anybody else here except me . . .*

'The mind wanders,' the banker running 146 miles across Death Valley told me. 'It seeks its own place. Just let it go. It doesn't matter.'

Each step increases the toll on my body. The cross-country shoes, while they grip the damp ground, have no support, no cushioning. The ridge line is all rock, and each step seems to reverberate up my legs, through my aching knees, into my head. The cool and the damp take their toll as well. *I think I'm rusting* . . . The trail weaves and bobs, off the ridge line, back into the woods.

Later, the woman with the accent will ask me, 'When you were on the ridge line, did you think you were in Hell?'

Now let me tell you about a good day:

I've been running for a couple of hours along the twisting trails of the course.

I run absently, aware of the sound of my cross-country shoes on the trail and little else. I am aware that my right shoulder aches from the swim, that both my feet are blistered, that I've probably pulled a muscle in my thigh on one of the descents, but the thoughts are far away, untroubling. I run a steep, stair-step decline, and suddenly I step out of the woods, onto the last mile of pavement. Race volunteers hand me a cup of water and shake my hands, and I jog off for the final mile. I run smoothly, my stride straight and true, my arms pumping effortlessly; if only for this moment, the athlete I never was.

As if on cue, the fog lifts for the first time that day. I see Alcatraz and the bridge and sailboats on a bay that is bright Caribbean blue.

10 The Ethnic Platoon Skates Again

Perhaps I am not born to skate.

This thought occurs to me while I'm lying on my back. in the middle of a crumbling, broken-glass-covered parking lot, watching blood dribble from my arm onto my T-shirt. So far I have skated, give or take a few feet, just under two yards. My new skates, black-and-fluorescent-green Rollerblades, however, have gone on without me. The net result of this tricky piece of work is that my skate-shod feet fly into the air, my butt smacks down on the asphalt, and lots of unsanitary-looking grit embeds itself in my elbows.

Item 9: skate marathon

The skate marathon I choose is the annual Athens-to-Atlanta Road Skating Marathon, a decade-old, 85-mile jaunt from the college town of Athens, Georgia, into metropolitan Atlanta. The race precedes the trendy ascendancy of in-line skates by about nine years – thus, I have this vision of a hundred refugees from a roller rink rolling through the Georgia hills. *All skate! All skate! –* The

Lycra brigade will roll along the backroads, which will also be open to more conventional traffic. *Ought to be fun . . .*

There is a thirty-eight-mile leg that is all rolling hills and not in urban Atlanta. I decide that The List does not require me to skate in urban Atlanta traffic – I may be, as my friends now claim, crazy, but I am not a complete lunatic.

It takes about three days to be able to regularly remain upright on the new skates. I have to keep telling myself to lower my center, get my center of balance as close to the ground as possible. I have a long time, months, until the race, however, and I figure all I have to do is keep skating. I also practice complex (read: impossible) techniques, like braking. I do this by skating up to the top of a parking garage, then turning around and skating down. If I fail to brake properly, I leave my signature in bright red on the wall of the parking garage. This technique is taught to me by a woman skater named Barbara Lane, who, one particularly memorable afternoon, leaves a twelve-foot swath of red along the parking garage wall.

Denise and I have worked our way up to six-mile skates, signing up for all the short skate races we can find, when I realize that the race is only a couple of months away. *This won't do.* We go out one afternoon and grind our way through a boring, hot twenty miles.

'Well,' she says, 'if we can skate twenty miles, we ought to be able to skate forty miles.'

I rub my aching back and worry about her logic.

Denise and I get into Athens on a drizzling Saturday afternoon in October and check into the race-central Ramada Inn. All sorts of strange people are milling around the lobby, as if several odd groups are having conventions at the hotel. Our first challenge is to figure out just how we're going to get home from the Dacula – no *r*, no vampires in Georgia – Elementary School, where the thirty-eight-miler ends.

When I ask one of the race volunteers about transportation back to Athens, she says, 'Beats me.'

Denise and I decide to rent a second car, drive it to Dacula the night before the race, park it, and use it to get back to Athens, which is a perfectly good plan until we discover that apparently every place in Athens that rents cars has closed at noon. I finally decide to take a long shot and call the used-car dealers. Somewhere fairly far down the list, I find someone who says, 'Come on down!'

And we do, to a 1950s prefab building and a flickering neon sign that says BUY HERE! PAY HERE! Inside, there are a couple of Army surplus metal desks and cracked wall paneling faded the color of old spilt coffee.

'Howdy!' says a big man behind one of the desks. 'You folks is in luck.'

I have an overwhelming urge to buy a car, which I sublimate.

Eventually, after more cash than paperwork trades hands, we end up with an 1980 vintage, oil-burning, smoking Ford for the day.

'We closed tomorrow,' our benefactor says. 'When you bring it back, just throw the keys through that busted window.'

We decide not to overly tax the Ford by shutting it off when we pick up the other rental (which we had rented in Atlanta the day before) and head to Dacula. Upon driving in the area of the course we'll be skating the next morning, I notice that Georgians have a different definition of 'a few little hills.'

The highway roller-coasters up and down, long climbs alternating with, to my eyes, terrifying downhills. Even training in parking garages hasn't gotten me used to cannonballing down a steep hill. The difference between a bicycle and skates is that a bicycle has real brakes, while in-line skates only pretend to have brakes. For every hill I drive up and down, my mood gets a little sourer. And, in addition, thirty-eight miles on twisting backroads in rural Georgia is a long way. *If it is a long way in the car – albeit, the Ford – how long must it be on skates?*

When we finally get to the metropolis of Dacula (past Winder, through Carl and Auburn) and find the appropriate place to leave the rental, Denise hops in the Ford.

'I thought you said the hills weren't bad,' she says.

'They grew.'

Back in Athens, we arrive in time to pick up our race packets, sign yet another liability release ('I know that skating on open roads is a potentially hazardous activity . . .'), and attend the mandatory pre-race meeting.

The crowded meeting room of the hotel is filled with what looks like a collection of warring tribes. There are street skaters from New York City, looking like only extras in that great urban drama can look; lean and mean professional skate racers from somewhere out west, in matching jerseys and matching rail-thin bodies; a large collection of bearded, tie-dyed folks who look more like vendors at Grateful Dead concerts than skaters; a smattering of nattily dressed yuppies; some foreign entrants with (honest) their own photos on collectable trading cards; California Venice Beach blondes, male and female; and a scattering of people who just look lost – the category Denise and I are in. To me, the room looks exactly like those old movies about World War II, where every platoon has the exactly correct ethnic mix. I keep expecting Lee Marvin to step forward and explain how he's going to whip us all into shape.

Instead, Henry Zuver steps forward and tells us where

we can expect the big hostile dogs on the course.

With that information, Denise and I head back to our room, to replace our everyday street-skating wheels with rock-hard racing wheels. Every sport has its gadgets, and in-line skating is no exception. Denise and I will be skating in *recreational skates*, in-line skates that you can buy over the counter. Her skates have four wheels, mine five: The theory being that the more wheels you have, the faster you can go, your rolling resistance being spread over a greater surface. The somewhere-out-west people will be using slickly designed, dreadfully expensive, equally dreadfully uncomfortable racing skates. Those little monsters consist of a hard boot molded to fit your foot (or the other way around, to hear some of the racers talk), bolted to a frame made of some mysterious space-age material. The frame holds five wheels, which spin on precision German bearings. The racing skates are as light as feathers, with the rolling resistance of a marble on a polished glass floor. Our concession to the race is to change to a harder skate wheel. The softer the wheel is, the greater adhesion it has to the road. While adhesion can translate into more stability, it also means more rolling resistance, so you have to push harder to roll the same distance.

Our new wheels are as hard as stones, with about the same amount of adhesion. This will enable us to fly through the Georgia countryside like Wile E. Coyote and his Acme rocket backpack, we figure.

Unfortunately, I have yet to learn the military truism that the battle plan seldom survives the first encounter with the enemy.

At dawn Sunday morning, Denise and I wolf down a quick breakfast, don our skates with the rock-hard wheels, and join the rest of the ethnic platoon in front of the hotel. Not only is it dark, but it is drizzling rain. The highway is glazed with water and shimmery rainbows of oil.

'This,' announces Denise, 'is not going to be fun.'

The platoon skates uphill en masse to the formal starting line. One person falls on her butt on the slick street. We mill around for a few minutes at the start line, then, unceremoniously, someone says, 'Go!'

So we go. Actually, the people in front of me go. The somewhere-out-west racers lower their bodies into an impossibly low, bent-over racing crouch, and sprint for Atlanta, ignoring the fact that the road is like an ice skating rink. The rest of the platoon, 250 or so skaters, start spreading out. Denise and I have opted to start in the rear. I have visions of working my way forward. I am reminded of the old Southern comedian Dave Gardner, who always said that, 'A man's reach can sure as hell exceed his grasp.'

The slick highway is a major challenge. Unlike bicycles, skates don't have a lot of glide in them – you stop pushing, they stop rolling. To maximize the push and the glide, the skater assumes an unnatural position – bent-over at the waist, the back parallel to the road, knees flexed. The driving leg pushes out, not back, to make the skater roll forward. The longer that outward push is, the longer you glide and the faster you go. The longer you glide, the less energy you're going to use.

I am learning that the endurance side of extreme sports is all an energy/output equation. How long do you need to go, and how much energy are you going to spend to go that far? The more efficient you are, the farther you can go on less. Efficiency, though, is one of those trick questions on the test. It is a factor made up of technique, equipment, and, for lack of better words, *body sense,* the ability to do the same task using smaller muscle groups instead of those big haulers like the quadriceps in the legs. Like in rock climbing – where if you constantly pull yourself up with the big muscles of the arm – the big muscles will burn out sooner rather than later, even if you're Sylvester Stallone (well, maybe not Sly).

The problem with all the wet asphalt in front of us is it raises pure hell as far as efficiency. Instead of long, graceful strokes propelling me along, I'm taking short, clipped strokes to keep the stones I'm skating on from dumping my butt on the ground. The short strokes don't propel me as far or as fast as longer ones would, so I've got to take lots more of them. The short strokes also alter my body position – I can't bend as low to the ground, because I'm pulling my leg up short.

Yeech.

We skate through Athens, and after a few twists and turns, we're out on the highway proper. It's dark, and I concentrate on the flashing red lights of the skaters who were smart enough to remember to bring lights. Denise and I take the first hill in the dark, which, given my dislike of hills, is perfect. I half brake, half slalom down the hill and arrive at the bottom in one piece. I may yet survive.

The sun eventually makes a grudging appearance through the clouds, gray tinged with a pale orange, as I skate past a field with horses. The horses shake their manes and run to the fence with a stiff, prancing gait.

'I realize how stupid this looks,' I say to the horses.

They nod in total agreement.

I wish I could tell you about how scintillating, how stimulating the race is, but, in fact, thirty-eight miles on skates is . . . thirty-eight miles on skates. There is a sort of brain death that sets in. I settle into a stroke rhythm, ignore the fact that my lower back feels like it's been smacked with a stick, and try to get my brain to completely shut down. I stutter my way down hills, then catch the people who passed me on the way up the next hill. Real skaters, racers, will barrel down the hills at speeds

103

approaching sixty miles per hour. Rationally, I know this isn't a bit different from bicycling down the same hill at the same speed. If anything, skaters are closer to the ground, which will ease the impact a bit if they fall. I have, however, hit the ground too many times on skates to ever feel comfortable when the speed creeps above twenty-five miles per hour or so. Ground is hard, my climbing instructors have told me. Indeed it is.

The first fifteen miles are as uneventful as anything I've done. Stroke, glide; stroke, glide. Watch the fields roll past; wave to folks on the way to church.

The next fifteen miles are tougher, but mostly because the road is nasty, wet, and bumpy. My skates vibrate so badly I'm afraid fillings are going to fall out of my teeth, and pretty soon my ankles are numb. This doesn't make that much difference, because I'm able to lace the boots tight enough to allow me to ignore the fact that I can't feel my ankles. It's kind of like having them in casts. I'm using a pair of off-the-shelf Rollerblades with thick plastic boots, like ski boots. The drawback is that I lose flexibility in my legs, which costs me efficiency points.

There are a couple of steep climbs, steep enough that at a couple of points, I feel like no matter how hard I push, I'm rolling backward. One doomsday drop culminates in a two-inch concrete lip on a little bridge. More than one person hits this tiny lip at about forty miles per hour. It's a physics quiz: The lowest two inches of your body, in this case your skate wheels, go from forty miles per hour to zero miles per hour in less than a quarter of an inch. The remainder of your body continues on, gaining speed, the remaining distance to the asphalt. How far will you continue to slide, assuming concrete has the abrasive factor of, say, heavy grit sandpaper?

It's a quiz Denise and I thankfully fail to participate in. After a few hours, I am mostly feeling tired. I bend over as much as possible to stretch my abused back, stretch my shins whenever I stop. As the morning wears on and traffic increases, there is the indescribable experience of being passed by a fully loaded eighteen-wheeler doing seventy miles per hour. There is a huge s...u...c...k...i...n...g feeling as the truck pulls me into its draft, followed by a moment of nausea as I imagine myself smeared along the Georgia countryside. Also, strangely, the highway gets much scarier as church lets out. Carloads of Sunday-go-to-meeting dressed people whiz by, shaking their fists and often shouting curses. A couple of times, rearview mirrors fly by inches from my face. I look up once to see a small child in a dark suit shooting me the bird through the back window of a car.

'Do you suppose,' I ask Denise, 'that this Sunday's sermon was "Devil Worshipers on Wheels"?'

'I think I saw that movie,' she says.

Along about mile thirty-five, three and a half hours in, I'm counting strokes, then trying to calculate how much longer I'm going to be out here. Various places on my feet have, despite my best efforts, blistered and are now somewhere beyond pain. My lower back feels as if someone has been driving self-tapping metal screws into it, and I can no longer remember all the lyrics to Elvis Presley's first ten hits.

Somewhere in the middle of this reverie, I look up and realize that I'm at the top of a long, steep hill.

The hell with it, I think.

I knot myself into a little ball, like Robert Redford in *Downhill Racer*, my clenched fists in front of my face, and cannonball the hill. The skates pick up speed like crazy, like somehow I have inherited the Acme rocket backpack. I feel time go soft as adrenaline slams into my system. My vision narrows, my eyes locking on the bumpy highway.

With my increased perception, I realize that I don't have a snowball's chance in Georgia of making it to the bottom of the hill on my feet. I am vibrating like crazy, and the more rigid my body becomes, the harder it is for me to remain in control. I unflex my screaming legs ever so slightly, raising my center a few inches – and I am on the ground, my tailbone slamming into the asphalt at about thirty-five miles an hour.

I see a universe of stars and a flash of pure, blue-white pain that makes my consciousness flicker like a match in the wind. The match flickers, then glows again, and I remember to spread-eagle out on the highway, giving me as much sliding surface area as I can get. Old guys heal slow, and I'd prefer not to break something – or have the Georgia asphalt belt sand its way to the bone. After what seems like a couple of miles and a very, very long time, I slide to a stop, exactly straddling the double yellow line in the middle of the highway.

'Oh god! Oh god!' Denise says as she skates back uphill to me. 'Are you hurt?'

I, in fact, can't seem to move. I lie there like roadkill, waiting for the pain level to drop from the hellishly agonizing level, waves of searing heat rolling off my tailbone. I finally perform some sort of limp fish flop maneuver and roll onto my belly.

'We've got to get you out of the road,' Denise says. There is traffic, and if I don't move soon I will become literal as well as figurative roadkill. I begin crawling to the side of the highway, with help from Denise. A carload of people stops.

'Can we do something?' they ask Denise. She shakes her head.

Kill me, I think. *Make it quick.*

'Are you sure we can't do something?' they say.

I make the side of the road and actually manage to sit

up. The pain has gone from hellish to simply awful.

'I'm okay,' I say. 'Thank you very much for stopping.'

They drive on.

'Is anything broken?' says Denise. She seems so calm and efficient that I figure she must be scared to death.

'Just a lot of blood,' I say. 'Nothing feels broken.'

'Can you stand up?' she says.

'Not yet, but give me a minute.'

We clean off the blood, and I eventually creak to my feet. Everything is swaying slightly, but I appear to be relatively functional. In a lot of pain, but working.

'What do you want to do?' she asks.

'Finish,' I say.

So we skate on. I now skate like Pinocchio, rigidly upright, my legs barely moving. The remaining two miles take us a little over an hour to finish. I gingerly sit down on the curb next to the finish line, unlace and unbuckle my skates, and pull them off. My socks are stained blood red in places.

'How are you really?' Denise, herself no worse for the wear, asks.

'I feel,' I start to say, 'like item nine is scratched off The List.'

What I actually say is, 'Like crap.'

11 Carbon Fiber and the Lord of the Air

Nowhere is the boundary between 'extreme' sports and 'regular' sports as clearly defined as in windsurfing. It was windsurfing, after all, that got me started, that gave birth to The List. Yet, for most of its participants, the sport of windsurfing is as benign as a day on the beach – sun-burned people on boards with brightly colored sails, put-tering across yacht basins in gentle breezes. Still, the first item on The List is 'Windsurf Big Wind.'

Tom James, the editor of the largest windsurfing magazine in the country, once told me that he majored in philosophy in college because it was something he could practice at the beach. I find myself thinking of that on the water, where I'm waiting for wind and trying to sort out this 'extreme' thing. I am starting to ride the crest of what looks to be a big wave. Extreme sports a year or so ago barely registered on the media radar; now they seem to be everywhere. MTV has led the way with *MTV Sports*, which seems to be about dudes doing dudish things. Every commercial for a four-wheel-drive vehicle involves young, healthy people attempting something life-threatening, then driving home.

I get a call one day from a sports magazine editor.

'Let me see,' she says. I can hear papers shuffling over the telephone. 'You're a . . . risk specialist, right?'

I wonder if there's a government rating, RS-1 maybe. Her call causes me to question the whole concept of *extreme*. The first uses of the word in connection with sports that I've found are from about ten years ago with the linking of extreme and skiing.

'As near as I can remember,' says extreme skier Rob Deloria, 'it was the North Face apparel company who started using the term in the seventies. Then it was *everywhere.*'

The simplest definition of *extreme skiing* is skiing where the consequences of failure are high. This is a nice way of saying that if you fall, you die. In fact, extreme was so widely used – or overused – in skiing, that by the time the word started being applied to other sports, the mere whisper of it would cause skiers to wince.

It is still, I think, a valid word.

Extremes are the frontiers of both mind and body where monsters lurk behind the trees and trails end in sheer drops. Extreme sports are different from adventure sports because of that consequence factor. You can have a wonderful adventure, for example, mountain biking some of the trails in the North Carolina mountains, but your actual risk, versus your perceived risk, is very low. The consequences of your falling or being unable to complete the ride are small – bruises and road rash. Compare that to the Kamikaze or any extreme mountain-bike downhill. The bruises become broken bones; the road rash more like the flaying of skin.

By working backwards from *extreme*, I begin to develop a working definition of *risk*. Risk is higher when the consequences of failure increase. While this may seem like a purely intellectual exercise, it's very important to anyone out there treading the edges. As I learned from the Kamikaze, the first step to getting through these things in one functioning piece is to really understand what the risks are.

In addition, sports language, like most of the rest of the English language, is going through its own escalation. To read the ads or watch the television commercials, everything is 'death-defying,' 'extreme,' 'on the edge,' 'spooky,' or 'crazy.'

Odd, seeing that our society has become increasingly ambivalent about risk-taking. On the one hand, we have traditionally venerated risk-takers, especially in sports; on the other, we have defined product liability so strictly that we would close playgrounds rather than risk someone's falling out of a swing. The opening ritual for anything on The List is the signing of the liability releases.

Sports philosopher and martial artist George Leonard writes about how the urge for risks in sports runs counter to the tendency in modern industrial society to reduce or eliminate risks from every aspect of life. 'The arena of sports,' he writes, 'has provided a place for people to take calculated risks without breaking the law.'

Nowhere is this urge as blatantly visible – or the hyperbolic language as clear – as in bungee jumping, a onetime outlawed sport turned national mania. The idea's pretty simple – tie a rubber band around your legs and jump off a high place, sort of like attempting suicide but not consummating the relationship. What began with a group of self-acknowledged crazies lobbing themselves off bridges and from balloons has become a steady stream of college students, accountants, secretaries, and executives jumping off cranes suspended over parking lots, bouncing on the tethered ends of their bungee cords like human yo-yos. Hundreds of thousands of people have now gone ahead and jumped. ('It was the best experience of my life,' a woman friend tells me after her first bungee jump. 'A lot better than sex. And probably a lot safer, too.')

While a bungee jumper might feel a certain rush of immortality ('The only thing you've truly accomplished,' sniffs the politically correct *Utne Reader*, 'is not dying.'), in fact, bungee jumping is very safe, as safe as riding a roller coaster. On my scale, that comes out to high perceived risks + low actual risk = big thrill + low medical bills. And that's good.

'Adventure,' writes author Walt Burnett, 'is a human need. We recognize it as the daring thing which makes us bigger than our usual selves. Adventure is the curiosity of man to see the other side of the mountain, the impulse in him that makes him break his bonds with lesser things and frees him for greater possibilities.'

I am starting to see each item on The List on that scale.

I also see, though, that what's missing in bungee jumping is the element of skill. Go up top; jump off. You get the rush, but not the experience, Mihaly Csikszentmihalyi's flow.

With windsurfing big wind, you not only get that kind of flow, but also the literal flow, from sailing a piece of high-tech plastic over bucking seas. Technically, I suppose, I've windsurfed big winds, but I decide that it's only fair that I sail them again for The List. At first, I chase the big wind everywhere. I hit a long stretch of business travel, so I pack a wetsuit and a windsurfing harness with me wherever I go, then rent the rest of the equipment when I get to where I'm going.

From my first contact with windsurfing, there was a simplicity that appealed to me. Windsurfing is a new sport, barely a decade old. That means not only does it not have a history, but it lacks traditions, as well. With other forms of sailing, there always seem to be guys in white jackets and jaunty, blue nautical caps, who stand ready to tell you

111

the rules. And there are lots of rules. Me, I can't even speak the language. After I'd been windsurfing a while, I was drafted onto a 'real' boat as crew by a captain who reasoned that because I was a good sailor on little skinny pieces of carbon fiber, I'd be a good sailor anywhere. How was I to know that *the lines to port* meant the ropes on the left?

Windsurfing is simple – no *lines to port* or *hold to, me hardies!* mysteries to master. Instead, there's a board and a sail. The sail is threaded onto a mast, which is attached by a flexible foot to the board. There is also a boom, which is attached at a ninety-degree angle to the mast. The idea is to stand up on the board on the water, hold onto the boom, and let the wind push you along. A lot of people find this a little like trying to chew gum and do handstands at the same time, but it's possible to master in a few weeks.

Big wind, though, changes the whole equation. The boards get shorter and shorter, with less and less floatation. In fact, if you stand on a high-wind board and there's no wind to drive it, it will sink. Like a water ski, a high-wind board is only happy when it's at speed, planing over the surface of the water. The equation gets even dicier when you add in the tipsy factor: smaller boards are less stable than larger boards. Unless they're going fast, high-wind boards have all the intrinsic stability of a greased log. The final variable in the big wind equation is the fact that you can't just stand on one of these boards and sail – you have to participate, and participate very specifically. You have to *fly* them, your body hooked into the boom through a harness and your feet pushing the nose of the little board off the wind. The board will respond like a carbon fiber rocket, only inches of it remaining in the water, while it sizzles across the waves like a drop of water on a hot, cast-iron frying pan.

It's that sensation of speed, of being able to launch this

little board into the air off the platform of the waves, that gives the sport its edge.

The first time I do actually launch a board off a wave, I perform a complex, sophisticated maneuver called an *endo*, which involves sticking the board, nose first, into the water, then cleverly following the board with the rest of my body. This maneuver is made even more hilarious by the fact that I am still attached to the boom by my harness. The result is a Rube Goldberg-like contraption made up of carbon fiber, aluminum, and flesh, pivoting around a mythical point where the nose of the board touches the water. I also get an excellent demonstration of the time dilation effects of adrenaline. My endo feels like it takes at least an hour from the time I lose control of the board until the time my head resurfaces.

The problem with catch as catch can in the wind department is that I am not catching much wind. Wind is . . . wind, by its nature fickle. The closest I come to really big wind is on a glacier-carved lake several hours north of Toronto. The water is clear and cold, just above freezing. All around the lake, the leaves are turning. While I'm suiting up, I watch a long, sleek mink steal a fish from a lethargic fisherman. The mink, stealthy as a cat burglar, first drags the line with the fish on it out of the water, an inch at a time, its eyes never leaving the dozing fisherman. When the fish is finally beached, the sharp, little mink teeth disconnect the thrashing fish from the line. The fisherman wakes up just as the mink heads into the woods with its prize.

'Heh!' the fisherman yells at me. 'Did something just steal my fish?'

There's about a thirty-five-mile-per-hour wind – nothing compared to the big winds in Florida. But the six-foot, wind-driven waves stand to make the afternoon interesting. Ocean waves come in sets of three; if you can count, you can usually get out even on a day with big waves. But the wind-driven waves on the lake just keep pounding. I angle my rental board – I would have preferred my own shorter board – off the wind and run smack into a neck-high wave, which sends me and the board back into the rocks. This makes me glad I don't have my own equipment. After about three tries and three trips back to the rocks, I get the hang of it: I have to sort of jump about three waves to get under way.

What follows is a great afternoon, jumping waves and making long carving runs across the lake. The wind is steady and cold, but practically the only uncovered parts of my body are my eyes and nose. When I crash and burn, I can feel the cold of the water gnawing at me, a huge mink with a tiny black-suited fish.

It is a wonderful afternoon, but it's not . . . extreme.

Toweling off, looking for the mink, I make a decision.

I'm going to have to go to the Gorge.

The Columbia River thunders through the gash between Washington and Oregon, its roar echoing along the Victorian logging towns that line its sides. About an hour and a half from Portland, on the Oregon side of the mighty Columbia, is the town of Hood River, stapled up the sides of the mountains leading to stately Mt. Hood. Once Hood River's livelihood was linked to the trees, the huge forests of the Pacific Northwest. But the logging industry died, and Hood River seemed destined to die along with it.

But miracles, as Willie Nelson once noted, occur in the strangest of places. In addition to the huge volumes of water passing through, the Columbia River Gorge has a huge volume of wind, fueled by the imbalance of temperature between the waters of the Pacific and the miles of green forests. Throughout the summer and into the early fall, the wind screams down the river at anywhere from twenty-five to sixty-five miles per hour every day, without fail. In the early 1980s, as the sport of windsurfing was being born, a few hardy pioneers discovered the wind machine of the Gorge and the quaint – and cheap – Victorians on Hood River's hills. By the time I get to Hood River, it is the windsurfing equivalent of a ski town. Every car has a roof rack, a stack of boards, and a bumper sticker that reads 'Pray for Wind' or 'Welcome to Oregon. Now Go Home.'

It is autumn; the wind machine less reliable than summer blasts. As I drive along the riverside highway, I stop high above the river over a sailing spot. Far below me, in the gold-washed autumn light, sails move like dragonflies, darting along the water, then soaring on the gust, hanging motionless over the river. Sometimes a half dozen boards launch at the same instant, at different angles, a complex equation of molecules and force. I feel the wind against my face and imagine the marshmallow shove of the wind, the lift as the board begins its run. The wind and the water have the jagged rhythm of good rock and roll, the sharp edges and the reprises, the steady backbeat that blends with the pounding of your heart. Even now, as I write this, I can close my eyes and still see those sails dance, Mylar leaves in the autumn sun.

In Hood River, I hole up in a cheap no-tell motel, pressboard paneling and a lumpy mattress. It is, however, twenty-two dollars a night, which I figure will leave me enough to rent about five days' worth of gear. The morning dawns sunny, cool, and still as a tomb. The flags hang listless against their poles.

Uh oh.

More on faith than anything else, I rent equipment and take it down to the marina to set up. All around me other people in wetsuits are rigging gear, taking no notice of the fact that there is no wind. I decide that everyone else knows better, so I hurry to get everything rigged. Then I sit on a picnic table and wait. At around nine in the morning everyone begins checking their watches and looking west toward Portland, as if waiting for a train to arrive. And from the west, up the Gorge, something is coming – wind.

'Show time,' someone says.

The river lists and quivers. The flags flutter, then snap. And the wind hits like a fist. Trees bend, leaves swirl and blast away. From the shore, a dozen boards launch into the river, dancing quickly into the mile-wide current. The morning sun holds the Mylar sails in sharp relief, Kodacolor sharp. I wrestle my own gear to the water, wade into the cold river, then step onto my board.

And we are gone away, flashing into the channel. I raise up, do a little hip curl, and hook my harness onto the lines trailing from the boom. Then I settle back, my butt a foot off the water, and let the board run. I am sailing sloppy now, the little board bouncing off the tops of the waves. Ahead of me and to my left, I watch a board launch high into the air, the rider just missing a complete 360-degree loop and splashing into the water. Then I blow past.

The wind is gusty that first morning, the sail a living thing in my hands. It fights to escape, and suddenly I am snatched forward by the invisible hand of the wind. I miss my turn and fall into the cold water. I lie on my back and maneuver the sail so the leading edge is into the wind. The lift is there, waiting. I push up and kick with my back foot, and with a snap I am back on the board, flying again.

I only leave the water long enough to eat and rest. Like everyone else, I don't leave until the great wind machine powers down in the afternoon.

For the next four days, I sail. I catch the big wind, and

for a moment am weightless, formless over the river. I race the sluggish barges, filled with logs destined for Japan. In the evenings, I drink brown ale, eat grilled trout, and talk about sailing big wind with people I don't know. Many of them have walked away from the 'real world,' rebuilt their lives, to stay close to the great throbbing wind machine of the Gorge. It is as if the concept of *flow* lies on the town like a benevolent tide. I talk to Eric Stanford, a photographer, mountain climber, and world traveler whose house overlooks the river on the Washington side.

'Where else would I want to be?' he says. He came to windsurfing after years out on the edge. One ride across the river, and he was hooked. I talk about the feeling, the fleeting sense of flow, and he just smiles.

12 Waterlogged

'Ta-da!' says my instructor Jonathan Derksen, proudly. 'This is your duckie!'

My duckie doesn't have webbed feet or quack, but it does float. *Duckie* is slang for an inflatable kayak. When you think kayak, you usually think of those garishly colored one-person plastic boats usually seen tearing down rivers on Mountain Dew commercials. Inflatable kayaks came by their moniker during low-water years on the East Coast, claims Eugene Buchanan of *Paddler* magazine, when rafting wasn't feasible.

'Instead, a guide would paddle out in an inflatable, and all the clients would follow behind him,' he says. 'Everyone thought it looked like baby ducks following the mommy, and the name stuck.'

In the last few years, duckies have gone from the status of pool toys to high-performance watercraft, largely because of their shorter learning curve.

Kayaking is not a skill to be learned overnight, because of a little maneuver called the *Eskimo roll*. Kayaks, not being the most stable of watercraft, occasionally roll over. Experienced kayakers can easily right themselves with an Eskimo roll, a move that involves twitching the hips like Elvis-run-amok while shoving in just the right way with the paddle. Inexperienced kayakers who fail to master this maneuver get to stare at fish and contemplate drowning, a situation made worse by the inescapable fact that a kayak is more likely to roll over in high-speed, whitewater sections of a river (exactly the kind of sections where your head is most likely to become an unfortunate twelve-pound keel) than when it's sitting at the dock.

Actually, I prefer paddler Jeff Bennett's definition of duckies: '[Inflatables are] to hard-shelled, whitewater kayaks what mountain bikes are to road cycles; they provide access to thrills that might otherwise be impossible to gain without years of practice.'

In other words, they're perfect for someone pursuing The List.

I'd sort of left the whitewater List item on the back-burner, mostly because it seemed, if not easy to do, at least easy to find an opportunity. I figured when a waterfall and a kayak presented themselves, I'd take the next obvious step. As it happened, I landed a whitewater raft trip to Central America, to Honduras.

Aha, I thought. *Opportunity knocks.*

The exact point when I know I'm not in Kansas anymore comes New Year's Eve at the airport in San Pedro Sula, just a hop, skip, and a jump from Miami International and the main point of entry for the aging banana republic of Honduras.

San Pedro Sula is a shock for deplaning Americans, unless of course said Americans are fond of salsa music and speak fluent Spanish. The plane lands uneventfully enough, but where I expect to find immigration or customs, there is a salsa band playing at heavy metal volumes for the hordes of baggage handlers and apparently their assorted significant others. The walls of the tiny room shake with the music, and some of the yellow-shirted baggage handlers sway to the rhythms.

Every baggage handler knows exactly two words of

English: 'No problem,' which is the inevitable answer to any question.

'Where can we catch the plane to La Ceiba?'

'No problem.'

'Does anybody need to stamp these papers?'

'No problem.'

'I seem to have misplaced my Uzi.'

'No problem.'

No problem indeed. Of course, I've come to Honduras not so much for the ambiance as for the whitewater, a crashing torrent that flows down from the eight-thousand-foot peaks of the Nombre de Dios Mountains only eight miles from the gulf coast.

The trick to finding the connecting airplane is to wander out of the airport, past men with guns, past assorted black-market money changers who can turn your dollars into *lemperas* – known locally as *lemps* – to a different entrance. What looks like a darkened, deserted terminal is actually where you find your connecting flight to La Ceiba.

I have to tell you the truth here – La Ceiba is not, perhaps, the garden spot of Central America. One of the rare Honduran guidebooks we were able to find put it this way: 'La Ceiba is not a particularly attractive town, and there's not much to see in the town itself . . . It's difficult to find postcards anywhere on the North Coast . . .'

Luckily, postcards weren't a critical issue. Early on in the history of The List, I'd met Dick Eustis. He was a well-known, well-respected river guide in Colorado when he got sick of being cold and decided to head south – far south. Eustis and several of his cohorts from the Rocky Mountain Outdoor Center in Colorado had stumbled into Honduras while looking around for challenging new rivers to run.

'We'd been hearing a lot about Costa Rica when we met

a Honduran, who kept talking about these great rivers,' Eustis says. 'It was getting to be winter in Colorado, so we loaded up and headed south.'

After a nine-day trek across the southern United States and through Mexico in rickety trucks with kayaks strapped to the top, the crew arrived in La Ceiba.

They immediately headed up a narrow dirt 'highway' dubbed La Culebra (the snake) by the locals, along the Rio Cangrejal, the river of crabs, which feeds into the gulf at the north end of town.

Eustis was amazed.

'It was one set of rapids after another,' he says. 'The farther up the road we went, the tougher the rapids got.' Also, the more spectacular the scenery and wildlife – wild parrots, iguanas, even jaguars make their home in the Honduran rain forests. Just to keep the unwary traveler jumping, there are also six-foot-long fer de lances, among the deadliest snakes in the world.

'Locally,' adds Dick, 'they call them "two-minute snakes", 'cause that's how long you have if you get bitten.' There's plenty of antivenom, though. Unfortunately, it's all in Costa Rica.

'The short story is, avoid snakes,' Dick concludes. 'Especially ones that look like they have a purple beard.'

No problem.

First thing the morning after our arrival, we load the rafts and head up La Culebra. I've already filled Dick in on The List and my need for kayak instructions, and he laughingly agreed.

The road, La Culebra, was originally a banana road, carved out of the jungle to allow fruit shipping between the port and the interior railhead. The further into the interior we go, the more the road resembles a donkey path. In sections, huge chunks of fallen hardwood trees

121

have been cut away to allow the passing of a vehicle by the narrowest margin. Several months before my arrival a vicious flood scoured away the rain forest – along with hundreds of hapless villagers – from the sides of the Cangrejal. The waters ran so fast that even the granite boulders that line the river have been scrubbed free of decades of moss and left shining and white as skulls.

The river is fast – as billed, one set of drops after another. After a certain point, rafts can't put in, and the upper reaches of the river, including some spectacular drops, belong to the kayaks.

The river is rock and roll from the start. Unlike a lot of American rivers, where sections of rapids are punctuated by long, calm floats, the Cangrejal is in a big hurry to get to the gulf. The sets of rapids are close together, the breaks short. The river offers whatever your fancy, from mild Class II to unrunnable Class VI. The raftable section of the river is like an hours-long roller coaster, with bumps.

I decide it is probably a good idea to mention to Dick that I've never been in big whitewater before.

'Oh,' he says.

Actually, I've never been in a raft before. Denise has assured me that Dick won't think of letting me row down a big river given this fact.

'That's okay,' says Dick. 'We'll just give you a crash course in rowing. Do exactly what I say and you won't drown. That's a joke.'

No problem.

'Okay,' Dick shouts over the river, 'we're just going to blow over the boulder . . . Whoops!' The raft teeters on a boulder until we rock it back into the currents. Waves crash over our heads, and we seem to be constantly on the verge of getting tossed out of the boat. Dick's instructions are crisp, explicit, and, unlike some sailboat captains, not delivered with the threat of a keelhauling. Of course, given that at any point we seem to be headed for certain disaster against a rock face, there's a spectacular incentive to pay attention and do exactly what Dick says. The water boils, and we slam, bang, and buck. The river is warm, eighty degrees or so, and over our shoulders we see clouds building at the top of the Nombre de Dios range. Parrots fly in circles above us. We pass Hondurans on the banks of the river, celebrating the new year. The night before, we'd drunk Salva Vida beer and listened to automatic-weapons fire. Happy New Year. No problem.

We pass iguana hunters on their way up La Culebra, stalking and shooting the big lizards out of the huge rain forest hardwoods. A charcoal smuggler drifts past us on a raft made of lashed-together logs. He steals wood from the forest, a national preserve, cooks it to charcoal, and sells it for a few pennies for cooking. He stands and poles his raft across the river, studiously ignoring us. The logo on his shorts reads 'Nike.'

There is that jarring conjunction: our high-tech rafts and kayaks mirrored against wash day on the Cangrejal, where the city's women come to the broad delta to wash their clothes in the river and drape them over the stones to dry. New Firebirds and horse-drawn carts. The open thunder of the river and the mysterious darkness of the rain forest.

'I think we can get you up to speed in a duckie,' Dick Eustis tells me the morning after our first raft run. 'I don't want to try it in a hard-shelled kayak, since you'd probably drown.'

I agree that drowning seems like a bad idea.

'Any idiot,' Dick says, 'ought to be able to learn how to boat in a duckie.'

'No problem,' any idiot says.

My plan is simple: I will spend the morning in the impossibly blue waters of the Gulf of Honduras paddling

123

around in my duckie, learning the four main strokes, discovering the secrets of climbing back into the thing when I fall out – in general, playing around like a kid in a very big bathtub. In the afternoon, we'll haul the duckie up the mountain, and I'll run as much of the Rio Cangrejal as Jonathan thinks is prudent, or however much I can convince him to let me do – whichever comes first.

It is a flawless Caribbean day. Men lounge aimlessly in the thatch-roofed bar on the beach, watching us with humor as we unload the light-blue duckie from the back of one of Rios Honduras' (Dick's company) battered Toyota trucks. An old man with a horse-pulled cart made of a truck transaxle and cracking gray timbers, loaded to the brim with green bananas, stops to watch. We shove the duckie into the water, and Jonathan wades in for the lesson as I ungraciously crawl into the rocking kayak.

'This is really simple,' he says. 'There are a total of four strokes – forward, backward, sweep front, sweep back. That's it – all you have to remember. Anybody can remember that much.'

I keep my opinions to myself, as I have a history of forgetting my address. The duckie, though, is great fun, much like sitting on a rubber raft in a pool. The gulf water is warm, and the swells are slight – we'd actually hoped for surf, but nature refused to cooperate. The strokes are self-explanatory. Using a double-bladed kayak oar, forward is forward, backward is backward. The sweeping strokes are like reaching to the side with a broom and sweeping, forward and backward. In little time I am puttering around the gulf like a veteran, much to the amusement of the men on the shore, clearing into their second – or third or fourth – Salva Vida ('lifesaver') beer.

The other critical maneuver is *self-rescue*, or how to get back in the boat when you've fallen out. That's another plus for duckies – if you do fall out, you have a nice, fully-inflated salva vida, lifesaver, of your own. Rule 1 is stay with the boat. I find I can easily stay with the boat, but getting from the water back into the duckie is a little like climbing a rope ladder – harder than it looks. At one point, after about fifteen minutes of watching me struggle back into the boat like an injured walrus, Jonathan has his own suggestion: 'Try not to fall out.'

Then, we're ready to head for the river. As we're towing the duckie in, some of the local fishermen in brightly-painted, wooden *cayugas* – one of the boats the word *kayak* comes from – cruises by.

'Give me thirty minutes and I could improve that guy's stroke,' muses my teacher. 'On the other hand, I don't have to paddle out on the ocean for ten hours a day. More I think about it, maybe he could teach me something.'

As we bounce along the rutted dirt road paralleling the Cangrejal, Jonathan is saying, 'The thing about duckies, is that they're not sexy. People use duckies instead of kayaks on first descents of wild rivers, because you can pack them in. But to say you've done a first descent in a duckie – well, it just doesn't have that ring to it. Maybe we should start calling them *shredders* or something.'

We put in at the edge of what amounts to a private park, a few scattered tables in a clearing carved in the rain forest, where the owner of the closest shack charges a few pennies to visit. Jonathan picked this particular spot because of its calm eddies as a place to give me a crash river orientation before lobbing me downstream.

'The other thing about a duck, as opposed to a kayak, is that it's slow,' says Jonathan, 'so you've got to compensate by paddling like a crazy person.'

The river in a kayak is a very different creature from the river in a raft. For one thing, you're lower in the water, so even small rapids loom large. The boat is less forgiving than a raft, more able to magnify your small errors into major screw-ups. Jonathan explains the proper way to enter the current, at forty-five degrees, and I make a few tentative passes from the quiet eddy into the main stream of the river. I quickly retreat. In contrast to the warm womb of the gulf, it's quickly obvious that the river means business.

'You're supposed to be having fun,' says Jonathan.

'I always look like this,' I reply, and we head out into the baby rapids.

I'm stiff as a board, sloppy with my forwards and backwards and sweeps, but the duckie – I've begun thinking of it as *my* duckie – is surprisingly responsive. Flying through the rippling, Class II rapids is like being on an out-of-control amusement park ride.

'First rapids!' shouts Jonathan over the sounds of the Cangrejal. 'Now are you having fun?'

In fact, I am – huge fun. Around the bend, though, is the next set of rapids, short, but a steep drop, with waves cresting over my head. From my vantage point at river level, it looks like I'll be trying to sail an inflatable raft into a washing machine.

'Don't think,' Jonathan says. 'Just follow me through.'

The amusement park ride suddenly turns into a hairy roller coaster as the duckie noses over the edge of the drop, then sails into the river and waves crash over my head. My butt hits something hard as the hydraulic pressure of the water forces the duckie away from the looming rocks and shoves it off another small cliff. And, suddenly, I'm through, back in the calm, large amounts of the Cangrejal running out of my mouth and nose.

'You got off line a little there,' Jonathan says, 'but you made the right moves. When in doubt, paddle like hell!'

He paddles his kayak over and looks at me closely.

'Honest,' I say, 'I'm having fun.'

'Relax,' he says. 'The worst that can happen is you can drown. Ha-ha.'

126

The next set of rapids comes up quickly. These are bigger, with multiple drops studded with huge granite boulders, and they're much longer, requiring something that passes for skill. The waves blasting off the rocks would be considered big at a surfing beach. Branches hang down from the rain forest, obscuring part of the right side of the river. I follow Jonathan into the action.

Within seconds, I'm sucked toward the overhanging branches. The duckie is bucking wildly, and it's all I can do to keep my butt anchored and keep paddling like hell. We skate along the right-hand bend, I duck desperately around chunks of rain forest the size of my leg. Most of the time, all I see is water, the waves over my head obscuring my vision. And then, as before, I'm through, equal parts adrenaline and river water draining from my body.

'You recover well,' says my teacher. 'I'm surprised, though, that you decided to take such a harder line down.'

Ha-ha.

We beach the kayaks and walk up ahead to scout the last set of rapids, a long steep section called *Lava*. I am uncomfortable with rapids that have their own name. It seems ominous to me.

'This is a significant section of rapids,' Jonathan says as we climb over some boulders. It was scary as hell in the raft, which we'd used the day before. At the beginning of Lava, the Cangrejal begins funneling into a narrow granite gorge. In places, the rocks overhang the river. There are car-sized boulders, boiling holes in the water, and a steady pounding of huge waves. From the top of a nearby boulder, the rapids seem to go on forever.

Jonathan sits down on the rock and starts pointing out landmarks.

'Start where you want to end up,' he says, pointing at

the calm water far downstream. 'See that black rock sticking up just before you get to the pool?'

I nod knowingly.

'You want to be just to the right of that rock when you go past it. You're going to be traveling pretty fast, so try to fix a picture of what it will look like in your mind.'

He methodically works his way back up the rapids, reading the water like some Apache reading the prairie. To him, the line through the rapids is perfectly obvious. To me, it's an obscure vision, lost in the thunder of waves, the boiling haze thrown up by the churning waters. I need, he stresses, to see that invisible line that stretches from the top to the bottom of the rapids. I need to hold that line in my head and make sure the duckie tracks along that line – right of this rock, hard left around the hole, swing to right to avoid the suction under the rock. I think about that string as we hike back down to the boats.

'You don't have to do this,' he says. 'I've taught good kayakers who've taken a pass on this one.'

I shrug it off. A duck's gotta do whatever it is a duck's gotta do.

'Well, don't worry about falling out,' he says optimistically. 'One way or the other, we're all going to end up in the same place.'

With that Zen thought in mind, we head into the river.

The current snatches the duckie out of the eddy, and I'm into the first drop before I have time to finish worrying. From then on, it's crazy time, my shoulders screaming as I fight to keep the duckie on the invisible line. Rocks loom up out of the spray like glistening white ghosts, appearing hugely, then disappearing, before my mind grasps what has happened. I pass the first marker to my left as a solid wall of river water passes over my head. The nose of the duck edges right, to the overhanging rocks with their vicious suction. *Paddle like hell . . . paddle like hell.* And I'm back on the line. Time seems frozen as my body pumps chemistry into my bloodstream – flee or fight time. I nose into a huge hole, and I seem to be looking at the bottom of the river for a second. *The line . . . hold the line.* I'm paddling, but my left paddle is pulling air, since that whole side of the boat is no longer connected to the river. I pass the next marker slightly to the right, dead on the line. The funnel narrows now; the holes are deeper; the waves higher. The duckie slopes to the left, but I manage to coax it back to center. I drop into one last wall of water and I'm through, into a calm pond overhung by rock. The duckie bounces off the rock wall and is still. I am, I discover, shaking.

Jonathan, on the other hand, is grinning.

'So,' he says. 'Want to do it again?'

Amazingly, before I can stop myself, I say yes.

The question though is, have I fulfilled the whitewater off a waterfall item on The List? Denise says yes; I say maybe.

'You've done big water in a kayak,' she says. 'That ought to count, don't you think?'

I agree, but there's still a nagging feeling that I haven't given it my best shot. After all, I did write waterfall, not big water. *Maybe,* I also think, *I'm taking this a bit too seriously.*

Six months later, though, another assignment takes me to New Zealand. One of my activities there is something called *river surfing,* which involves pitching one's self into whitewater on a Styrofoam bodyboard, the type happy children might use for bodysurfing on a day at the beach.

It is when I stand two hundred feet over the snapping, clawing rapids of the Karawaga River outside of Queens-town, New Zealand, that I am struck with how far I've gone, both literally, in miles, and spiritually, in my head. *When*, I find myself wondering as the dark, bitterly cold water torrents beneath me, *did The List take over my life? When did I first notice a normal, everyday existence giving way to some mad dash around the world, chasing . . . what? And does it even matter?*

'Feel like doing it, mate?' my guide, twenty years my junior, asks with an inflection that says, 'If, that is, you're able to stumble your old bones down this cliff.'

'No problem,' I say.

Imagine being caught in a cosmic washing machine in the agitate cycle. Imagine being lifted out of your crib by your mommy and shaken hard while your daddy turns the full force of a fire hose on your body. Make that an icy fire hose – the water temperature is just above freezing; my wetsuit feels more like a T-shirt.

You cannot 'fight' the river. You are in it, a part of it, being acted on by not just what you can see on the surface, but surging, racing currents below the surface. They pull you in contradictory directions, shove your legs apart and together. The river is unimaginably strong, and you are so very, very small.

The boulders, when they appear, are monstrous, house-sized. You see rounded curves and jagged edges. You distantly feel the impact on your lower body. You ride the waves, crash over the edge, feel the pressure drawing you down, down, down; shaking you hard; turning you loose. And then you can breathe again; your legs cramp as you kick your way into an eddy, hunched onto the cold rocks, staring back into the living, breathing lair of the river gods.

The river draws you on, the cold working its insidious way into your very bones. There are other rapids, strange swirly things that suck you into holes, spin you, spit you out. To borrow an old cliché, you are caught in the coils of a massive snake, tossed by the rippling muscles while

130

hypnotized by the beauty of its scales.

Here is where I finally get it, where, I think, 'risk' becomes more than an academic exercise:

I am sitting in a restaurant, staring at a plate of smoked salmon pasta. I am holding a glass of red wine in my left hand. I sip it; it's a dark, smoky merlot. I don't know where I am. I don't recognize the people around me. It is as if I have just been born, on the edge of a plate of pasta, holding a glass of wine. Pieces come back, but with agonizing slowness. I hold the wine, look at the people, remember the river. Part of the river. I don't remember, for instance, the last set of rapids. I don't remember how I got out of the river. I don't remember climbing the steep cliffs to the car, shucking my wetsuit, drying off, riding to a nearby winery. Talking. Carrying on a conversation. I don't remember ordering the wine, but it is one of my favorites.

My god, I think, chills dancing up and down my spine. *What have I lost?*

The Lake Taupo district of the North Island is unquestionably beautiful, but it chafes at Queenstown's smug title as the adventure capital of New Zealand.

You can do anything in the Lake Taupo district, Denise and I are told, so we immediately go looking for anything to do. That's how we come to be, once again, donning wetsuits and climbing helmets, only a couple of miles from the thermal boles of Tokaanu Thermal Park, in the shadow of the old cone of the Ngaurahoe volcano. Dave Stott of Plateau Outdoor Adventure Guides meets us with a bevy of guides-to-be, unemployed city youth the government is paying to learn a trade – river rafting.

Today, though, we aren't rafting. We're going to take an inflatable kayak off a seven-meter waterfall ('Actually,' says Stott, who, up until two years ago, was a bicycle messenger, 'it's closer to eight meters. I measured.'). To put this in perspective, it's sort of like paddling off the roof of a two-story building. *That, I think, is definitely a waterfall.* I resolve not to think about it.

'You don't have to do this,' Denise says. She's been especially worried since the Karawaga rapids. I have been at times distant, rattled, worrying about the lost minutes like a cracked tooth, trying to find what's missing in my head.

I shrug off her concern and tell her it is not that bad.

Suited up, we haul the specially built duckie down a narrow trail. The duckie has been reinforced to take the impact: There's a flat plywood bulkhead for me to set my feet firmly on, and there are added airbags for extra floatation in the nose, the idea being that there are certain situations in which I might want to get back to the surface as quickly as possible.

It's a cold and crisp morning, and in the distance we can see a ski resort perched on an old volcano cone. We turn a corner and are confronted by torrents of water, crashing a long way down into a pool.

'Oh, shit. No way!' says one of the guides-to-be.

'The water's a little up,' says Dave diplomatically.

I take one look at the waterfall and decide I'd better get myself together. *Mikey blow bubbles,* I think.

We hike the boat to a beautiful spot just above the waterfall. It's so pristine that I keep expecting Bambi to step to the edge of the stream for a sip. I stick my hand into the water, and my fingers go instantly numb.

'Well,' says Dave, 'time for a safety briefing.'

This briefing is comprised of: make sure your feet are flat on the kayak's bulkhead ('so your ankles don't break on impact, don't you know?'); paddle hard (so you've got some speed when you go sailing off the edge of the world); get your oar over your head (so you won't eat it on impact); and down you go.

'You know this is at your own risk,' says Jason, one of the guides-to-be.

'Isn't everything?' I reply. Before I have time to really think about it, I slide into the kayak, splash a little of the ice-cold water on my face to, hopefully, take some of the edge off my imminent immersion, and get shoved into the fast current.

'Arms up! Arms up!' shouts Dave as I rocket toward the edge. I raise my arms, and time begins slowing down. The nose of the kayak is thrusting into air, not water. The nose of the kayak begins pointing downward, and we are falling, falling, falling. It takes about two forevers (my old friend adrenaline twists reality) to hit the impact zone. I see stars from the shock of the cold, and then we are *sinking, sinking, sinking* toward what Dave calls the Green Room, the cold, calm water deep underneath the waterfall. From the Green Room, I look up and see the kayak is between me and the surface.

Time to bail, an alarm goes off in my head, and I'm out of the boat. The hell with the duckie. The pool isn't that big, and I don't want to get blown down the next set of falls, which don't look all that – how to put this, *survivable*. And then I'm back on the surface, in a world of light and air, swimming for the shore, my kayak following along behind me like a wet puppy dog.

Whitewater off a waterfall.

No problem.

13 Claustrophobia Check

The feeling is butterflies – definitely butterflies.

Butterflies that flutter around my stomach and threaten to make a permanent home in the back of my head as I slowly circle the crystal-clear, year-round, seventy-two-degree water of north Florida's Ginnie Springs, looking down. There's a hole in the bottom of Ginnie Springs, and in a few moments, I'm going to glide into it, through the looking glass, down into a dark, dark world of smoothly sculpted limestone walls and ceilings, where cold currents rush out of tiny openings and air pockets shimmer silver, puddles of mercury trapped on the low ceilings, caught in my lights.

Time for a reality check.

In the palmetto-scrub flatlands of north central Florida, below the grazing pastures of the gray Brahma cattle, not that far from the Disney-spawned suburbs, is an awesome underground world – a collection of springs and rivers and caves to challenge even the broadest imagination. The 'doors' to the labyrinth are the springs, where the underground water has erupted through to the surface, and the sinks, where the ground has literally fallen away. I've traveled to Ginnie Springs to come to grips with that proverbial hole in the ground, because the springs sit smack over the heart of underground Florida, Mecca for cavern and cave divers from around the world.

In all honesty, of the thirteen items on The List, cave diving is proving to be the hardest nut to crack. Unlike most of the other items on The List, scuba is primarily an intellectual, rather than a physical, exercise. The intellectual challenge is driven by the fact that even basic scuba is insanely equipment intensive; the challenge is to become knowledgeable in and comfortable with a self-contained underwater life support system.

The other challenge is that scuba is fairly rigidly structured. In order to be issued a *C-card*, a certification that allows you to fill scuba tanks with air, a person has to complete a course offered by one of several certifying agencies. The courses aren't particularly hard, but they are time-consuming and, once the equipment is factored in, expensive. I sail through the basic scuba course, then move quickly on to the more advanced offerings.

After a series of classes that includes diving to below one hundred feet, underwater navigation, exploring wrecks, rescue, and other specialties, my instructor asks me what I really want to do.

'I want to dive caves,' I tell him.

'Idiot,' he says.

Like most people in Florida, I first heard about cave diving from newspaper headlines announcing yet another death in the caves. Eventually, I run down John Orlowski, who, with his wife, Shelley, is one of the top cave diving instructors in the world.

'It's like this,' says the ultra-low-key Orlowski, who moved to rural north Florida to be close to the caves he loves, 'underwater caves are the most unforgiving environment on this planet. It's like being in space – the consequence of a system's failure or a mistake in judgment is swift and brutal. You die, and you die hard.'

For years, cave diving was a sport that stayed out of the limelight. It has recently, though, come out of the closet.

'When the diver is properly trained and using the proper equipment, cave diving is probably one of the safest forms of diving,' says Orlowski. He and Shelley exchanged their wedding vows in a legendary underwater cave system in Mexico. 'When the diver isn't trained, it's probably the most dangerous.'

Orlowski himself helped to boost the visibility of cave diving when he and his partner, Steve Gerrard, raced to Venezuela to rescue a diver trapped deep in a cave, an event chronicled on television's *Rescue 911* and in the pages of *Reader's Digest*.

'Actually, we thought we were going in to retrieve a body,' says Orlowski. 'The diver was lucky enough to find a large air pocket, and he was waiting for us after thirty-six hours.'

It's easier to talk about cave diving than it is to do it. For a species that spent many of its formative years climbing trees to escape animals with big teeth, the concept of going down in the dark sets off all kinds of alarms. I've managed to arrange a tour of some of the systems in Ginnie Springs, all that's possible for a non-cave-certified diver, and even that's pushing the envelope. Finally, however, I'm in the water.

I'm not going in there, I think, hovering over the entrance to a small cave, one of the gateways to the huge underground world. A voice – my voice? – keeps repeating, 'Not me.' The hole in the bottom of the springs seems like some kind of leftover from a particularly grim Grimm tale, just waiting to snap me up. I talk calmly to myself as my partner gestures downward. Then, with my heartbeat more or less under control, I drift through the entrance.

Once inside, there is the inescapable knowledge that the clock is running – every exhaled air bubble that becomes pooled mercury in the ceiling crevices is another minute gone. The logic of the air bottles on your back is simple and absolute: you don't want to still be underwater when the air runs out.

Divers began penetrating Florida's underground world almost as soon as Jacques Cousteau and his partner perfected the Aqualung in the early 1950s. With the earliest penetrations came the first deaths. More so than their dry-land counterparts, underwater caves are totally unforgiving. A simple equipment problem that might be an inconvenience in open water, where the diver has a clear shot to the surface, can be a death warrant in a cave. The floors of many underwater caves are covered with the silt of ages, a silt so fine that, when stirred up by an unwary diver's fins, it can completely obscure the way out. More than one diver has spent the last air in the bottle looking for the hidden way home.

After grim years in the 1970s, with more deaths and more and more caves being closed off to protect uneducated divers, the statistics began to turn. The secret was, not surprisingly, knowledge. Caves could be dived safely, but only through the rigorous application of painfully learned techniques. Divers developed a training procedure, taking an open-water scuba diver through a four-step process to full cave-diver certification.

'First and foremost, there has to be a certain attitude and mental preparedness,' says Orlowski. 'Cave diving may not be more physically demanding than open-water diving, but it is mentally much more strenuous . . . With open-water diving, the theory is that if you have a problem, you can always go to the surface. Cave divers don't have that option. You have to handle the problem right there, on the bottom.'

And the problems can be many – equipment failures, rocks taking their toll on fragile gear, the occasional cramp, numbing cold. Or The Fear, the simple knowledge that there are tons and tons of rock and water between you and the world above. Your pupils dilate; your breathing becomes rapid and shallow; you are sweating inside your wetsuit which, up until a moment ago, was barely keeping you warm. Your brain says, simply, one word: 'Out!'

There's a question I hear welling up out there, and it boils down to why?

With cave diving, that's a tough question to answer. Orlowski talks about how beautiful, peaceful, and relaxing the caves are. I speak with Michael Madden, another top cave diver. He's camped out in the jungles in Mexico, getting ready for another expedition into the Nohoch cave system, the longest cave system in the world.

'I've got twenty divers in there now, and I'm heading back as soon as I finish some computer mapping here,' Madden says through a crackling phone connection. 'I mean, the classic description for cave diving is "The Star Trek Syndrome" – to boldly go where no person has gone before. I think that's what stimulates most of us.'

Madden first began cave diving after instructing for a couple of years in Mexico.

'I'd take my students for their training dives in these freshwater sinks, and I'd see these black holes leading back into caves,' he remembers. 'I'd just be staring at these holes, thinking, "I wonder where that goes?" '

There is that, but the Star Trek syndrome hardly captures the haunting beauty of the smoothly twisted stone walls, the rooms, the narrow passages. I remember one diver talking about 'flying' through a cave system, as close as you can get to visiting another world and still be on Earth. I think it is that other-worldly quality that resonates with some people; the closest I can come to describing the feeling of cave diving is as a space walk, extravehicular activity in a hostile environment.

I float through the easiest cave system, entranced. The fear that was so strong when I followed the fixed line into the cave has vanished, replaced by wonder. As a pre-planned experiment, we shut off our lights for a moment, and it is dark beyond imagining, womb-dark, a world without a word for light. We flick back on the big cave floods, and in the crevices see small fish. There are many denizens in the cave; the deeper you go, the less use for unnecessary appendages like eyes. We move downward, the passage narrowing until my tanks touch the ceiling, my body inches above the floor. The first time my tanks touch, a shock wave ripples through my body – *it's so very narrow.* The animal in my head, which up until this point has been silent – largely, I think, out of shock – starts rattling the bars.

And this cave is huge, by cave standards.

I decide then and there that a tour doesn't fulfill the cave diving entry on The List. I will have to learn how to cave dive on my own.

This proves to be harder than I originally anticipate. The first instructor I talk to listens patiently, studies my log of dives, and suggests I 'come back in a couple of years.'

Eventually, I turn to Shelley Orlowski. I figure anybody who gets married in an underwater cave might be sympathetic to my pleas.

'We can work something out,' she says.

What working something out means is that I continue to take dive classes, one after another, whenever I can scrape up the money and the time. What I'm leading up to is John's Full Cave course, eight or nine days of intensive training in the north Florida cave systems. Before I can be certified as a cave diver, I have to have a minimum of fifteen cave dives in at least five different cave systems. And of course I'll need to have my own equipment, which is totally different from recreational scuba equipment. Of course.

When I finally meet the Orlowski's standards for training, I head to Live Oak, Florida, the Orlowski's home, for two weeks at the $22.95-a-night No-Tell Motel. It's $25 for the deluxe room with a remote control for the television, so I pull out all the stops and pop for the deluxe.

After a long drive, I turn left down a sand road to the Orlowski's trailer. There are horses, dogs, cats, a vegetable garden, a fountain, fish, and dive equipment all over the place. There are also, in the middle of the menagerie, the Orlowskis. John is tall, with an emaciated rock star look; Shelley short and dark, but also with the rock star look. Pierce their noses, and they could pass easily on Melrose Avenue in L.A. While Shelley heads out to teach another class, John and I talk. Rather, I talk; John coaxes. What he's looking for, I finally decide, is motivation – am I here on a whim or am I really committed. This is actually a pretty good question, so I answer honestly.

'I don't know,' I say. 'We'll see later.'

As it gets later and later, I figure we're not going to do any diving. But just before sunset, John abruptly stands.

'Let's go do a little diving,' he says.

We load up his cluttered dive van and drive to Peacock #2, a hole in the limestone strata with an entrance into the underground world. This time, however, we're not going to be entering that world. We're just going to drop down around eighteen feet in the cool lake so I can practice following a line.

In the caves, lines are life. They're your umbilical cord to the outside world, the way home. Famous caves, like those of the north Florida system, have permanently attached mainlines, laid by explorers like the Orlowskis. The lines are color-coded and intricately mapped. Where there aren't any fixed lines, I'll lay my own, using one of a number of reels that I'll have to get used to carrying.

That's rule 2 of cave diving: always have a continuous line to the surface. Rule 1, by the way, is always be trained.

We drop into the cool water as the sun sets, and John runs a long circle of nylon cord off his main reel around the bottom of the little lake. First I get to follow the line with my eyes open. The next lap, I follow by feel, with my eyes closed. Not that it matters; with the sun down and the lights off, the little lake is as dark as a tomb. Finally, I take off my mask, stow it, and follow the line by feel again. Masks have a way of becoming diver safety blankets, a little piece of dry land to hang onto. A surprisingly large number of divers panic when their masks are knocked off or lost.

When we surface, the north Florida sky is alive with stars.

The first days are easy. I follow John through the cave systems at Peacock #1 and Telford Sink. As before, The Fear quickly gives way to an enchantment, caught in the lure of a totally alien environment. It is like entering a Giant's Lair, stealing through some part of a Great Game, played out in the flooded labyrinths below some long-dead castle.

John works patiently on my skills – learning to kick without stirring up silt, adjusting my buoyancy to compensate for the almost two hundred pounds of dive gear I'm carrying. Telford is silty, with visibility reduced to a few feet. I feel my heart rate increase, the animal in my head pounding on the walls.

The line! The line!

But the line is there, just within my reach. I stifle an overwhelming urge to grab the thing.

'You'll want to hang onto the line, but you're going to

resist that impulse,' John has told me. 'Panic is a strange thing. It affects different people different ways. One of those ways is to clamp down on the mainline and not move. You sort of freeze up. Of course, it makes your body easy to find.'

It is amazingly hard not to grab the line. The world is reduced to a soft, brownish-grey ball, around two feet in diameter, centered on my nuclear-powered cave lights. The mainline drifts in and out of that glowing sphere, like a dream, an image caught in a fading, too-grainy photograph. I become better acquainted with the animal in my head, always on the verge of emerging in its screaming, mind-numbing glory.

'Of course I'm scared,' John tells me before the dive. 'Anybody who's not scared is a complete fool. But fear doesn't have anything to do with how you act. Even if you're going to die, you might as well die doing the right thing, which is trying to get out.'

The mythology of cave diving is full of stories of lost divers methodically searching for a way out until all the air is gone. One of the most experienced cave divers, hopelessly trapped in an underground avalanche, continued digging until the very end. He died, but his partner was able to make it to safety.

'When faced with dying or achieving the impossible,' writes Orlowski in his manual for cave diving, 'some people choose to live.'

There is one tunnel that John doesn't like to go into, since a woman cave diver became separated from her fiancé – and the mainline – panicked, and just kept swimming down a long dead-end tunnel. Her frantic claw marks are etched into the silt of the currentless tunnel, maybe into the limestone itself. Finally, John says, the claw marks stop.

At first, I am put off by this macabre talk. Then it dawns

on me what is happening: Cave diving is a deadly sport, with no margin for error. The people who train new cave divers want that point driven home so deeply that there can be no question of misunderstanding, no question of, 'why didn't you tell me . . .' Every cave diver I meet can name someone – a friend, an acquaintance, a spouse, an instructor, a student – who has gone in, but not come out of the caves.

Every one.

The next morning we drive to another cave system, Madison, whose two entrances are in a beautifully landscaped private park for cave divers. It is bright and sunny, and the sink itself is a clear, crystalline blue. In our extensive pre-dive briefing, John says that because there's a substantial flow of water out of the cave, we'll go in the smaller, side entrance to avoid the big flow.

And, oh yes, the 'smaller' entrance is a lot smaller. Just big enough to shove yourself through, tanks scraping on the rocks, chest in the silt.

'It's not far,' John says. 'Ten or fifteen feet. I'll go through first, and you follow my light.'

Another test, I think as my stomach knots and the animal in my head goes stark raving crazy.

Once under water, John slips through the little hole in the wall like an eel. I peer in and see his light beckoning. *It's not far,* I think. *Ten or fifteen feet.* I put my mind somewhere else, bury my chest in the muck, and start pushing my way through. What seems to work best is crawling on my fingertips. I can feel my tanks scrape on the rocks above me – *the rocks above me . . . tons and tons of rocks above me . . . crushing me crushing me crushing me.* I move like an inchworm for fifteen feet, then pop out of the tunnel. John signals okay? I signal okay back.

We do endless drills – take off mask; put mask on; shut

143

off the right tank; shut off the left tank; turn lights off and do it all in the dark. The purpose of the drills is to, as John puts it, make sure my brain keeps working, no matter what.

'The one piece of equipment that can't fail is your brain,' he says. 'As long as your brain is working, you have a chance.'

The Madison cave is, for me, what cave diving is all about. I feel like I'm flying, through the tunnels, into the rooms. We fly along the top of the caves, through upside-down valleys and mountain ranges in miniature. When my gauges read that I've used up a third of my air (rule 3: one-third going in, one-third coming out, one-third in reserve), I turn sorrowfully. I can't wait to come back.

Midweek, we pick up another student, and the training gets progressively tougher. We practice following mainlines out of caves with our lights off, moving along the lines as they twist and turn from the caves, only the lightest touch connecting us to the way home. First above ground, then underwater in the dark, we practice finding a lost line.

In a dark that is darker than dark, the pure absence of light, I disconnect my reel, loosen the tension knob, and tie off the end to a knob of rock I have located by touch. Now, I know where I am, and I can get back to my reference point. I feel the rock wall behind me, and in my mind, I visualize a straight line away from that wall. Crawling along the rock bottom of the cave, I follow that line, until I reach the far wall. I add a bit of air to my buoyancy wings and begin climbing up the wall. Without light, with no visual clues at all, up and down have no meaning. I add more air and start climbing back across the ceiling, reeling out line. When I get back to my reference point, I have captured the mainline in my loop. I now know the way home again,

In one drill, John drops behind us, and suddenly he is gone. The other student and I frantically search the dark surface of the sink, but no John. As we prepare to resubmerge, Shelley walks to the water's edge.

'Where's John?' she asks.

'I don't know,' I say.

'Great,' she says casually. 'You guys killed my husband. He's not much of a husband, but he's all I got.'

At that moment, John's head pops to the surface.

'Anybody want to explain how I got dead?' he says. My face burns crimson in the dark.

The drills get harder. We practice out-of-air drills, moving with the lights out and only touch contact between divers. We practice swimming through *restrictions*, narrowings in the tunnel, without our regulators, holding our breath. A swim of twenty-five feet – not even an effort swimming along the bottom of a pool – is a lifetime of anxiety. Most of our drills are in Cow Sink, a small, beautiful jewel-like cave. There are numerous rock formations, strange shapes, perfect little rooms. When I think of cave diving now, I think of little Cow.

John often tries to trick us. Once, he and another instructor jump from the mainline to a side tunnel with its own line. The other student follows, but I refuse. I stay on the mainline and use my light to signal down the other tunnel. After a few minutes, the other three divers turn around and return to the mainline.

When we get out John asks, 'What would you have done if we hadn't come back?'

'I would have left you a message on the mainline with my writing slate; then I would have exited,' I say nervously.

'That's correct,' he says. 'It's easier to get a new partner than a new life.'

'But you're the instructor,' the other student blurts. 'I

followed you because you're supposed to know what you're doing.'

'What did I tell you on the first day?' John replies calmly. 'Following anyone blindly can get you killed, along with whomever you're following.'

'But . . .'

'There aren't any buts . . .' John says, again mildly. 'You'll only get one mistake. This is the hardest dive training you'll ever do, and we have a reason for making it that hard.'

I have been in the caves for nine days, diving two, three, sometimes four times a day. The fear doesn't really go away, but I find myself looking forward to each new cave system. Technically, John says one morning, I've completed the course, but if I'd like to hang around and dive awhile, feel free. I jump at the invitation.

We do one last set of drills, lights out. I pretend I am out of air, and the other student hands me his *octopus*, a separate breathing regulator on a seven-foot-long hose. We then begin the long, dark swim out of the cave. Most of the mainlines have some sort of surveyor's marks or tags, and I have counted marks going in, so I'll have some kind of reference coming out. We move slowly; I'm in the lead, breathing off the long hose attached to my partner's tanks. I have an *okay*, a very light touch on the mainline, but my fingers are locked tightly together, so the line won't slip away. My partner is touching my leg and maintaining his own light hold on the mainline. Every minute or so, I see a brief flash of light as John monitors our position. John picked this cave because the mainline goes through all sorts of contortions, around, over, down, and through. At several points, the mainline runs through narrow constrictions, blocking forward movement. I get stuck briefly several times.

I got in, I think (the animal screams and shouts and beats

146

the bars of the cage), *I can get back out.* About halfway home, there is thrashing behind me. My partner has lost his hold on the mainline. He still has my leg, but he's thrashing, feeling for the lost line. With each thrash, he jerks the regulator in my mouth. I am like a hooked bass. I decide to give him thirty seconds, then I'm turning on my lights and going back to my own regulator. I start counting ... *lollipop one* ... *lollipop two* ... *lollipop three* ... let the air out of my wings, and sink a foot to the stone floor of the cave. Keeping a solid hand on the mainline, I make sure my own regulator is handy and that I can easily reach the light switch. Then I wait. At lollipop twenty-five, I feel my partner's hand groping up my leg.

Good, I think. *He's connected to me; I'm connected to the line. Follow my arm, and pretty soon, he'll have the line back ...* Which is exactly what he does.

When we emerge, the Florida night is cool. There is just enough of a breeze to keep the mosquitoes at bay. We shuck the tons of equipment and sit in the night.

'You like this, don't you?' John asks me.

'Yep,' I say.

'Like it enough to keep doing it?'

'Yep.'

'Good.'

14 Air

I am hanging, securely wrapped in a canvas cocoon, strapped in above and behind the bed of a bright red Japanese truck. I am wearing a blue helmet and swaying in the wind. To my left is a county prison, which I can see out of the corner of my eye when the wind 'weather vanes' me around. To my right is a windsock, which is sticking straight out and looking like it wants to rip free of its moorings. Above me is a brightly colored kite; ahead of me is a runway. It ends in a stand of trees.

'Comfortable?' asks Dave Glover, my companion sausage creature and pilot of the aforementioned kite.

I nod. Trussed up as I am, as long as I don't see Sharon Stone with an ice pick, I'm as good as I'm likely to get.

'You know, there's never been a fatality involving tandem hang gliding,' Dave says, as if this is supposed to be comforting. He has the bedside manner of one of those family doctors in Norman Rockwell paintings, warm and fuzzy. We hang together under the single, dragonfly wing of the kit, and he runs through the basic instructions: Push the bottom bar forward to slow down; pull back to speed up; hips to either side to turn.

'Gentle, small motions,' he cautions. 'No need for a death grip. And when in doubt, let go. The kite wants to fly. Really.'

I nod and attempt to look happy. I am actually practicing

deep-breathing exercises, which I continue while Dave runs through his preflight check.

We are hooked in, all set, the kite ready for the sky.

'Ready?' he asks.

I nod, jauntily, I think.

'Hey, this is going to be great!' he says. 'One other thing – if you feel like you're going to hurl, don't turn your head toward me to tell me, okay?'

I nod. And we are rolling down the runway, the red truck gathering speed.

'It's going to be a little bumpy going up,' Dave says, his helmeted head next to mine. 'Nothing to worry about.'

I nod. *Bumpy. That's always good.*

There is a tiny *ping* as Dave frees the hang glider from the embrace of the speeding truck. And then . . .

I am falling . . . up.

I am in an elevator, cut loose from its cables and falling wildly toward the thirty-third story. I am trapped in a reverse bungee jump . . . a Nightmare on Elm Street movie, where undead Freddy snatches you up through the ceiling . . .

Below us, the red truck has gotten very, very small, a scuttling beetle to which we're attached by a reinforced cord. The beetle careens off the runway, heading toward the stand of trees. Tugged by the inexorable cord, we keep climbing.

'Whew!' shouts Dave. 'I love it every time!'

I attempt to nod, but am unable to complete the maneuver, due to my heart, which is apparently lodged in my throat.

I have ambivalent feelings about flying. Part of me feels the pull that the Wright Brothers must have felt, that reverse gravity that causes one to stare longingly and lovingly at birds in flight, to feel the pull of a kite in the wind and think, Why not?

Balanced against that longing is the pure rat-scrabble fear of a species that evolved out of the trees – that of taking the long fall, arms flailing, clutching at nothing but pure air, an endless primeval scream ripped from an unwilling throat. Okay, maybe I've seen too many bad movies, but I am honestly afraid of heights – although my co-sausage, Dave, has a theory that no one is actually afraid of heights; what we're all really afraid of is the loss of control that falling brings. Ironically, as I will later learn in the mountains, he will prove to be exactly right.

John Harris – the person responsible for strapping me to this particular kite – got all of the first part – the longing for the air – without the downside fear of the long fall. He grew up on a farm in Missouri, watching kites drift in the winds of hot, midwestern summers. He even managed to get a degree in engineering and head for a career as an oceanographer before he stumbled on a grainy wire service photograph in a Winston-Salem, North Carolina, news-paper. The picture was of a fledgling hang glider. That was in 1973.

'Your own personal wing,' he says today, still with an element of awe. 'No airport. No engine. No launching strip.'

He began an almost frantic search for information on the hang glider and finally traced the maker down through the newspaper. Once he found the kite maker, he did the only thing that made any sense – Harris bought one and, armed with a poorly made eight-millimeter film of *How to Fly* and a tremendous amount of faith, carted the flimsy thing to the high dunes of Kitty Hawk, where the Wright Brothers found their wings, and jumped off.

'It flew, more or less,' he says. By the end of the first

hike back up the dunes, he was 'hooked on the idea of a personal, portable flying machine. I thought everybody ought to be able to fly one of these things.'

Exit John Harris the engineer; enter John Harris the hang gliding evangelist. Since then, Harris and his Kitty Hawk Kites, located across the highway and slightly south of his first flight, have put 170,000 people on kites and lobbed them off the same dunes. The dunes, as the Wright Brothers figured out in 1903, are an ideal place to fly. Stand on any of the dunes along North Carolina's Outer Banks, that impossible thin stretch of sand that barriers the mainland from the Atlantic, and watch a brown pelican just hanging in the sea breeze and you'll see the first reason: The usually steady wind and the dune's gently sloping ramps make launching incredibly easy. You can start low, learn the basics, and gradually move to higher dunes. And, speaking from experience, there's a lot more give to soft sand than to, say, concrete. Plus, there's something undeniably cool about Jockey's Ridge State Park in Nag's Head, which is probably the only park with sand dunes that head south. The dunes are actually migrating to the south. They're threatening homes and roads, and the mobile sand has already swallowed a miniature golf course – which possibly proves that even a dune can have a sense of humor. On our way to the launching spot, we hike uphill past a pointed concrete cone, the top of the golf course's castle, an artifact for future archeologists.

My first experiences in launching off the dunes in a fluky, gusty southwest wind the previous summer, helped me learn what *lawn dart* means in hang gliding: a tricky maneuver that involves cramming the nose of the kite – and in this case my nose as well – into the soft sand.

'Uh-oh,' said my instructor, after my first launch. 'Lawn dart time.'

Sand and all, though, hang gliding retains that sense of

adolescent fantasy, of stepping off a cliff and miraculously going up instead of down. Flight, breaking free from gravity for the tiniest part of a second, is a powerful drug, one that is not easily forgotten.

Training fledgling flyers, however, is more prosaic.

A hang glider is amazingly simple: a large kite with an aluminum trapeze slung underneath it. That's all, folks. Of course, today's gliders represent more than twenty years of evolution, sleek flying machines that share few handling characteristics with the first clumsy kites.

'We say that gliders will fly themselves,' Harris adds, 'and that's the literal truth. Part of learning to fly now is learning a light touch, so you don't disturb the glider.'

Controls, learned in ground school, are simplicity in themselves. The pilot hangs suspended ('like a sack of potatoes,' says Kitty Hawk Kites chief instructor Bruce Weaver) underneath the center of the wing in a harness. Hands rest on the *control bar*, the lower leg of the aluminum triangle under the wing. Pushing forward on the control bar noses the glider up into the wind, which slows it down. Pulling back on the control bar has the opposite effect, pulling the nose down and increasing speed. To turn the glider, you shift your weight in the direction you wish to turn, which involves a sort of push-pull movement on the bar to get your hips going the right way.

To land, you push the bar all the way forward – this is called *flaring*. To get an idea of how it works, watch any bird. When the wings flare, birds (and good hang glider pilots) land gracefully on their feet.

The next steps involve the Sisyphusian task of walking up the dune (which will remind you that you're not in nearly as good shape as you think you are), hooking in, and performing a *hang check* to make sure your precious sack of potatoes is securely attached to the glider. Then, standing with the control bar held securely to your thighs and the glider nosed into the wind, you start running toward the edge of the dune. If there's any sort of wind at all, within about three steps you'll notice an interesting phenomenon – you're running, but your feet are no longer touching the ground. With your instructor running alongside shouting instructions – 'Shift your weight right! No, your *other* right!' – you sled through the air down the face of the dune. You fly – 'Flare! Flare! Flare!' – And, ideally, seconds later, you land on your feet.

'It's not hard,' says Bruce as we wrestle the ungainly butterfly back up the face of the dune. 'You just have to dial the movements into your body. You might also want to consider not having a death grip on the control bar. The kite'll fly itself.'

To prove his point, one of the other instructors takes a pink-winged Eaglette, the training gliders Kitty Hawk Kites uses, runs to the edge of the dune, and flies. His hands don't touch the control bar until it's time to flare.

'See?' says Bruce. 'Overcontrol – not undercontrol – is the problem.'

The most recent training wrinkle is tandem training – the student and an instructor fly together on an oversized kite launched from a truck, a boat, or even pulled aloft with an ultralight aircraft (basically a powered hang glider).

'Think of flying as a sandwich,' says Dave, one of Kitty Hawk's top tandem instructors. 'The bread of the sandwich is training on the dunes, learning takeoffs and landings. But you don't really get to fly much while you're learning. The baloney of the sandwich is tandem instruction, where you really get to fly.'

Item 8 on The List: Skydive, and whatever those kite and parachute thingies are . . .

Item 8, as might be obvious, came after a pitcher of beer

had been consumed. Afterwards, I decided that, on the balance, skydiving might be the easiest thing on The List to accomplish, because it seemed to be a case of 'you pays your money, you jumps out of your airplane.' And living in Tampa, I also figured the proximity to the Zephyrhills Sport Parachute Center north of the city wouldn't hurt. In fact, the local telephone book is full of skydiving academies.

The only drawback to quickly knocking off item 8 is that just the thought of jumping out of an airplane makes me sick to my stomach. I have this persistent vision of being scraped off the field, the *drop zone*, with a spatula, my mortal remains crammed into a sandwich-sized baggy. Everyone shakes their head sadly: 'Chute didn't open, but he died like a man . . . we guess.'

I finally hit on a strategy that I think will work. I will give my buddy Denise a gift certificate to a skydiving academy for her birthday, as she has at least demonstrated a passing interest in jumping. Then, out of humiliation and fear of being drummed out of the Guy Corps, I will jump with her.

Before I can think of the thousands of reasons this is a stupid plan – after all, 'stupid plan' has been my theme song – I start making phone calls.

The first calls aren't very promising.

'This week only,' the female voice on the telephone, probably belonging to someone in the sixteen-year-old range, says, 'we're offering discount skydives.'

Discount skydives? Is this smart?

'For example,' she continues relentlessly, 'if you sign up no later than Friday, which is tomorrow, I can offer you fifty dollars off your first jump. . . . Can I have your credit card number?'

I say I'll call her right back.

The next academy is only a phone call away.

'Your good luck, man,' the operator (an instructor himself, he informs me) says. 'We're in the middle of a price war. Our war is your good fortune . . .'

Price war?

I make another call to speak to a friend of mine who writes books about skydiving. As a rule, he says, price breaks aren't really important in a sport where they can scrape you off the drop zone with a spatula.

'Ask them whether their instructors are on salary and how long the instructor you get has been working there,' my friend says. 'Ask how many jumps your instructor has. Since you're probably going to be doing a tandem jump – that is, you'll be attached to the instructor – ask how long the instructor has been tandem rated and how many tandem jumps he or she has. Other than that, just have a good time.'

Sure.

By about the fourth phone call, I get the First Right Answer: 'We don't do sales,' the person says. 'And we don't offer discounts. In fact, we're about the most expensive school around.'

I sign up before I lose my nerve.

The next weekend, Denise and I are on the way to Zephyrhills. I don't know what I expected. I guess I had some sort of television vision of guys and girls in air force khakis, starched and creased, running around neat, immaculate classrooms with clipboards while powerful airplanes roared overhead.

'This is it?' asks Denise incredulously when we pull up to the Zephyrhills – Z-Hills – drop zone.

It looks like a Grateful Dead concert, only without the stage. The drop zone itself, a couple of football fields worth of treeless Florida cow pasture, is surrounded by a motley collection of aging, paint-flaking school buses, campers, pick-up trucks, beat-up cars, brightly colored tents, lean-tos made of military surplus canvas, quilts scattered on the ground, campfires, longhairs in tie-dye holding babies of indeterminable sex, wandering dogs, loud music, and, incongruously, people falling out of the sky on brightly colored parachutes, all under the blaze of a Florida sun that would melt lead.

'Do we have backstage passes?' Denise asks innocently.

Instead of the neat, immaculate classrooms of my imagination, there are a series of prefab, partially-constructed buildings, raw plywood and torn strips of tar paper, plus the occasional trailer. A number of people of all ages, and judging by the languages being shouted all over the place, from a variety of nations, wander from building to building. Others, shielding their eyes from the brutal Florida sun, stare into the sky, watching parachutes open.

And the plane ... Suffice it to say that if an aging Volkswagen bus could be morphed into an airplane, that vehicle is sitting in front of us. It looks like a 1952 Airstream travel trailer with wings. All it needs is a Ford Fairlane station wagon with fake wood paneling to pull it around.

'I am not filled with confidence,' Denise says.

'It's not as bad as it looks,' I say confidently – a confidence I don't, by the way, even remotely feel. 'But if I hear "Dueling Banjos" from *Deliverance*, we're out of here.'

Eventually, we find our academy, which is a wooden building with three of the usual four walls, a roof, and a VCR.

'You guys gotta watch the film first,' the receptionist

says, wiping sweat off her face. 'Then sign all the liability releases.'

I like the film.

'No parachute is a hundred percent safe . . . No airplane is a hundred percent safe . . . You could be killed . . .'

The video shows an ambulance and a bunch of people, presumably with spatulas, clustered around a nondescript lump on a drop zone.

After about ten minutes of video explaining that anyone who would willingly jump out of an airplane doesn't have the sense of a can of peaches, we are presented with liability releases, which say the same thing – the death part in uppercase letters.

'You know,' says Denise, who is a lawyer, 'I believe these things will hold up in court. Not that it would matter to us . . .'

After signing away our lives, we start 'ground school,' which is getting fitted for a parachute harness and meeting our instructors, the guys who are going to be strapped to our backs for the jump.

'The plane is leaving in a few minutes,' says a woman who sticks her head in through a missing wall. 'You guys gotta go.'

We're quickly fitted, then hustled to the *jump simulator,* which is a shed about two feet off the ground, with an open door built to simulate our airplane's door – in other words, a large hole covered by a blanket. We hurry in through the side door, connect to our instructors, and duck walk to the faux airplane door. Outside, we can hear the 'Volksplane' cranking up. It sounds as if one of its rubber bands needs rewinding. Arching our backs, we jump gracefully two feet to the ground.

'Perfect,' my instructor says. 'Let's get on the plane.'

I look back and see Denise grinning a grin usually reserved for particularly bad situations in rock climbing. I wave, and we race toward the Volksplane.

'I don't mean to sound stupid,' I say as we wait to clamber into the empty belly of the beast. 'But what about landing?'

'I'll explain on the way down,' my instructor says.

'Oh.'

As the plane lumbers down the grass runway, we get the short history of Z-Hills, which is one of the premier drop zones in the world. For most of the year, skydiving gypsies from all over make their temporary homes in the trailers and tents around the Z-Hills drop zone, living off savings or working around the academies to scrounge up enough for flights. The camp is called The Dark Side of the Moon. Pink Floyd would approve, I suspect. Some of the gypsies never leave, staying to become instructors or settling into the shaky central Florida economy with other refugees.

I make the mistake of looking out the airplane window.

Oh, shit.

As Denise will say later, the very worst part is taking off in a plane you know you won't be landing in.

The plane grinds like a Volkswagen bus heading up a steep grind, and I wonder if there's any chance I can talk my way out of this. I am sick to my stomach, sweating, and rank with pure animal fear. The animal in my head is comatose with shock.

'You're doing great,' says my instructor, which is good, since I'm still sitting on the floor of the plane. Denise waves. She looks green.

And then we're at 13,500 feet, above the cow pastures, our destination. There are fleecy clouds around us. The sliding door in the rear of the Volksplane is slid up by a bunch of happy jumpers who, laughing and talking, throw themselves out the door into the whipping wind.

'Okay!' my instructor yells over the wind. 'Let's go!'

In a daze, I assume the waddling duck position, with my instructor clipped to my back. I check and recheck the clips. After all, he has the parachute. I have him. We waddle back to the door of the Volksplane, and for the first time, I look *down, down, down,* right into the pit of my nightmares.

What, I think, am *I doing here?*

'Okay, Michael!' shouts my instructor as we crouch in the doorway, the wind blasting around us. 'Take your left hand and grab the right side of your harness!'

Moving slowly, like a Volkswagen through molasses, I accede to his request.

What does he really want?

'Okay, Michael!' *He is so damned enthusiastic.* 'Now grab the left side with your right hand! That means you're going to have to let go of the door, Michael!'

Let go of the door?

Slowly, with a great act of will, my fingers come away from the warm metal of the Volksplane's door frame. As soon as my hand clears the frame, my instructor falls left . . . and down.

He shouts something enthusiastic, and for an instant, I see the door frame and the Volksplane falling away from me and then the ground out of the corner of my eye. I am falling, free falling.

Months later, Nick diGiovanni, a twenty-year skydiving veteran who specializes in jumping off buildings, will give me the best description of the free-fall experience I have ever heard. It is like, he says, your mind is an index card file. Every one of those index cards contains an appropriate response to various outside stimuli, from current ones – like your boss is mad at you – to older, darker ones – you are being chased by a hungry saber-toothed tiger. When faced with a situation, your mind rapidly flips through the card file, looking for the appropriate response. But there is no appropriate response for falling at more than a hundred miles per hour from a couple of miles in the air. And there's no way for you to 'create' that card on the ground.

'You gotta do it,' Nick says.

In the first few hundred feet, my mind goes stark raving crazy flipping through the card file, looking for something that matches brain-numbing noise, incredible speed, and the ground rising below you. Not surprisingly, it can't find the card, so it takes the only other option available – it throws its little mental arms up in the air and shuts down.

'Is this great or what!?' my instructor, who I notice is still attached to my back, shouts above the roar of the wind.

He's asking me?

I manage to engage enough brain cells to arch my back and assume the flight position, my arms out and slightly ahead, like Rocky the Flying Squirrel. A few feet away, I see Denise, whose face is frozen by the speed and the wind into a rictus of a grin. She appears to have achieved a hamsterlike flight position. She waves, and I think I wave back.

We fall from 13,500 feet to 4,500 feet in approximately fifty-five seconds. It is, up until this day, the longest minute of my life. At 4,500 feet, there is a slight bump, and all of a sudden the noise and the speed are gone. We rock gently below the parachute.

'Let's talk about landing,' says my instructor.

'Good idea,' I think I say.

A couple of minutes later, we land on our butts in a Florida cow pasture. A few feet away, Denise and her instructor turn a half-gainer, then skid to a stop. I wonder if kissing the ground would be appropriate.

But the kite thingies are better, or maybe free fall has given me a different perspective, a new set of index cards.

We are really flying, about a thousand feet above the runway, about forty-five minutes north of the dunes. From underneath our glider, I can see far out into the Atlantic to the east; south all the way to the dunes themselves. We make lazy circles, searching for *thermals* – columns of heated air spiraling up. We catch a small one, and the kite climbs another couple hundred feet.

'Look at that hawk over there,' says Dave, pointing downward to a huge, red-tailed hawk making lazy circles in his own thermal.

'His thermal is better than our thermal,' Dave says. 'Birds know these things. Next rotation, we're going to slide over to his thermal.'

With a slight shift of weight, the kite slips across the sky into the neighboring column of air. We rise again, but not nearly as fast as we were rising. A quick glance shows us the hawk has faked us out and grabbed our thermal, and is headed for the stratosphere.

'Okay,' Dave says. 'Maybe birds are smarter than people.'

The flight is hypnotic, everything you might have imagined flying to be in those summer afternoon daydreams. The glider responds quickly to gentle movements – and, as billed, we take our hands off the control bar, and the glider flies on. But the wind is dying and the miniature cyclones of the thermals vanish, leaving us back in the thrall of gravity. We slowly spiral down toward the runway.

I would like to report that we landed as gracefully as the aforementioned hawk touched down. But actually, thanks to the last gasps of a small thermal and my own innate clumsiness, we landed like Bruce Weaver's proverbial sack of potatoes, breaking pilot Glover's winning streak of perfect landings. Then we quickly reload the kite back on the truck, and it's reverse bungee time again.

Months later, I will actually become certified as a paragliding pilot, flying the soft wings, parachute-like, as opposed to the hard wings of the hang gliders, off the gentle hills around Boulder.

I will crash only once, smacking Wile E. Coyote-like into a cactus.

Ouch! the imaginary cartoon balloon over my head will say.

15 The Zen of Ice

The plastic boots – double plastic mountain boots; white, like oversized Mickey Mouse feet – crunch in the old snow, the sound muted by the wind. My instructor came to New Hampshire seven years prior with a newly minted degree in political science, intent on spending a summer away from the books before she started work. ('Any day now,' she shrugs.)

'There are two things to remember about ice,' she says. 'One, ice is not a solid, like rock. It's a liquid, a thick liquid. The second important thing flows, so to speak, from the first, and it is, *don't fall*.'

The ice we are talking about is not cubes in glasses. It is the curtains of ice that stretch along a cliff face in New Hampshire, just outside the town of North Conway, nestled in the White Mountains. North Conway is best known for its seemingly endless string of factory outlets, which draw shoppers even on bitterly cold afternoons in January from as far away as Boston. But North Conway's attraction for me has nothing to do with discounted Calvin Kleins or Bass Weejuns. It has everything to do with these frozen cliffs, the Frankenstein Cliffs, one of the legendary ice climbing areas in America – and, for me, the best place to cross item 7 from The List.

I arguably know less about ice climbing than I do about

rock climbing, which is little indeed. But ice, with its hidden flaws and traceries of fault lines, carries with it something that rock does not – the true and ineradicable stench of danger, of risk. In rock climbing, they say, protection is pretty bombproof: A steel nut slipped into a crack, or a mechanical camming device with its hardened teeth dug into the rock, or even a bolt driven into the wall, offers a relatively secure place to attach your rope. Fall and, in all likelihood, the protection will hold you.

On a frozen waterfall, however, the protection is usually an *ice screw*, a giant, almost foot-long screw with a hollow core. Where the pointed end of the screw would be is a ring of jagged teeth, which look sort of like the mouths of mutant leeches in old science fiction movies. The teeth chew away at the ice until the threads can catch. Then the climber finishes screwing the screw into the ice, the excess ice driven out through the hollow core, and clips the rope into the screw's head.

So far, so good. But ice, remember, isn't really a solid. Cranking a screw into a frozen waterfall is not the same as screwing a lag bolt into a four-by-four pine post. Pine is . . . pine, but the nature of ice is hidden, cloaked. Ice can be hard as steel or as soft and mushy as a snow cone. It can be as brittle as old glass or as malleable as a plastic sheet. Its hard surface can hide an even harder interior, or it can hide a spider web of tiny fault lines, waiting to splinter at the slightest tap of a hammer. It's a safe bet that a pine post is pine post for its entire length. But even the smallest frozen waterfall is a topographical map of different ice states, each with its own characteristics, its own natural laws.

Tomorrow, pine will still be pine, but ice may be something different. Ice is crystals in flux, growing, shrinking, changing states, melting, driven by pressures from within and without, by subtle shifts in temperature and humidity, by gravities we do not completely understand. Even the word *ice* isn't enough – climbers might refer to snow ice, granular ice, glacier ice, soft white ice, rotten ice, rime ice, hoarfrost, *neve*, *firnspiegel*, water ice, brittle ice, green ice, blue ice, black ice, *verglas* . . . live ice. Ice is a mysterious animal in a lair we can only approach at our own risk.

Before my trip, I run into a serious rock climber, a professional on the indoor climbing circuit. I ask him whether he's excited about climbing this winter. He looks at me as if I am a not-very-intelligent bug.

'I buried three friends last winter,' he says. 'I want nothing to do with ice.'

On my way to New Hampshire, I stop in a climbing shop in Nashville to buy a pair of expedition-quality climbing gloves for the ice. The clerk takes my money and stares at the bright blue gloves.

'Going on an expedition?' he asks.

'Ice climbing,' I say, shrugging it off.

'Been climbing twenty years,' the clerk replies, bagging my purchase. 'Only fools climb ice.'

'Teaching ice is different from teaching rock,' my instructor is saying as we hike along the cliffs. 'We can take pretty much anyone and get them up the rock. But ice is so much more physically demanding, that we insist the student be in very good shape before we'll teach them.'

'Why is ice more physically demanding than rock?' I ask.

'You'll see,' she says.

It is seriously cold, below zero, a nasty, wet, New England cold, with a wind whipping through the valley to add insult to injury. I am stuffed into borrowed ski clothes. I'm warm, but I have the mobility of an eight year old bundled up for the first snow of winter. We have spent most of the morning introducing me to the concept of *self-arrest*, that is, using my ice ax to arrest my slide, should I fall on a shallow ice slope.

I first have to meet My Friend The Ice Ax. Imagine a long-handled pick with a long, curving nose, serrations on the underside of the curve. When the long nose of the ax is driven into the ice, the under serrations grip tightly. The other side of the pick can be either a hammer or an adze. I'll climb with two axes, one with an adze, the other a hammer. But whenever I'm on an ice or snow slope, I'll always have an ax in the uphill hand, using the spike on the end of the handle as a walking stick, or using the long nose for self-arrest.

We practice arresting on an iced-over gravel road, frozen hard and as slick as those oil-soaked test pads in television car commercials. My first fall, I quickly slide all the way to the bottom.

'That is,' my instructor says, 'what happens when you *don't* self-arrest.'

For the next hour, I practice falling, then rolling over and jamming the nose of the ax into the ice. I fall face forward; I fall backward; I fall feet first; and each time, I practice twisting, rolling, and jamming my body weight onto the ax.

'Self-arrest has to be a reflex,' she says. 'Below the conscious level. If you fall out of your bed at night, you should automatically self-arrest.'

'Will it work?' I ask. 'Will it stop a really bad slide?'

'Depends on how steep it is and how hard the ice is,' she says. 'Even if it doesn't work, it gives you something useful to do in those closing seconds of your life.'

The first frozen waterfall we approach hardly qualifies as a cliff. It's more of a gentle slope, coated with a meringue of hard bluish green ice.

166

'It's harder than it looks,' she says.

I don my climbing harness and *crampons* – spikes that clip onto the bottom of my Mickey Mouse boots – while she talks about the 'dance' of ice.

'You're going to find this hard to believe at first, but ice is about elegance,' she says. 'Guys especially like to slam that ax into the wall, kick those crampons in like a rampaging bull. But ice is about using a minimum effort to move the wall. You'll catch on soon enough.'

Ice climbing is the ultimate Spiderman fantasy. At its most extreme, your axes are tethered to your hands, and you step up using only the two forward-facing spikes – the front-points – of your crampons. Set the axes, step up, set the axes, step up. You are a spider on a windowpane, moving up.

Ice climbing has always been a part of mountain – alpine – climbing. Obviously, much of the great mountains is ice and snow. But sport ice climbing, climbing frozen waterfalls, is relatively new, dating back to the late sixties and early seventies and driven by Yvon Chouinard, dubbed by *Outside* magazine as 'the godfather of ice climbing.' Chouinard refined the alpine techniques and modified the mountain climber's equipment for waterfall ice.

We practice the beginner techniques, the flat-footed French technique, *pied à plat*, which involves twisting the ankles into all sorts of strange contortions to get the crampons flat against the ice, and front-pointing, facing the ice wall. We practice using only our hands, then one ax, then both axes.

Finally, we're ready for the first short climb. First, my instructor will climb to the top of the cliff and set her anchor for the top rope. Along the way, she'll protect herself with ice screws, and I'll be belaying her from the ground. As she gets ready to climb, she stops and moves her face close to mine.

'You are the most important person in the world,' she says. 'And I love you very much. Don't drop me.'

We both laugh, but the point is made.

Once the anchor and the rope are set, she rappels down. We exchange places, and she picks an easy, short waterfall a couple of feet to our right as my first climb.

It is, in short, incredibly hard.

What looks so simple, so easy, when an accomplished ice climber makes the moves becomes a clumsy nightmare for me. For one thing, my ax seems determined not to catch on the brittle ice. I pick my impact point, drive the ax into it, and, presto, ice cubes.

'Gently, Michael, gently.'

I move up, but slowly, raggedly. My worst sin (which haunts me throughout The List) is an urge to move before I'm in balance. I need three points anchored in the ice to be in balance. I set one ax solidly (well, more or less solidly); then, leaning my weight against the ax, I step up on my crampons. Once I move my full body weight up, I adjust my feet to give myself a solid platform to move from. When this works, it is an amazing feeling; when it doesn't, my primary feeling is an urge to throw up.

The experience is compounded by the fact that ice is cold!

It is below zero and windy, but I am already sweating profusely, a combination of fear and the fact that ice climbing engages major muscle groups of the arms and legs, generating heat. The combination of sweat and ice quickly seems to soak everything; my gloves soon squish.

I finish the first short climb and am deemed ready to climb to the top of the cliff.

'Remove the ice screws on your way up,' my instructor says.

This route is steeper, and I quickly feel the heat in my

triceps from the steady hammering with the axes – it's like hammering nails in as high above your head as you can reach. We have not trained our bodies to work this way. The more I front-point, the more my calves, which have the unpleasant duty of holding up my body while the points are attached to the ice, start lighting up. I imagine my calves looking like some sort of cartoon container, rapidly filling up with lactic acid and fatigue poisons.

'Is it supposed to hurt this much?' I shout down.

'Imagine,' she shouts back, 'wearing high heels all your life! Ice climbing is revenge!'

But I finally make the top, and it is one of the most sublime experiences I remember having, about the most fun you can have while freezing.

Over the next couple of days, we move to harder and harder routes. I am beginning to understand that concept of elegance. The cold, the wet, the fear, the effort suck strength at an incredible rate. In rock climbing, when arm muscles start flaming out, you can usually find a place to rest, to recover your strength. You can find a place to rest on the ice walls, but that doesn't make the cold go away. In fact, it makes it worse. As soon as you stop moving, you stop generating heat. Instead of a net heat gain, there's a net heat loss. One minute, you're thinking how hot you are; the next, your teeth are chattering.

Our climbs get longer, from one *pitch* – the length of the rope – to two pitches – two lengths of the rope.

'Again,' my instructor says, 'unlike rock climbing, on ice, we don't want to fall. We don't want to test our protection unless we absolutely have to. Most of the time, the screws will hold. Most of the time.'

The fear is that if the ice screw pulls out, the added momentum of the longer fall will 'zipper' all the other screws out of the ice. There are other equally good reasons for not falling. For starters, there are the twelve sharpened steel points on each of your feet, plus the two ice axes tethered to your hands. That means in even the smallest fall, there are a total of twenty-six knives flailing around, looking for something to stick into. Sort of advanced, psychotic juggling.

My instructor climbs the first pitch while I stay on a shivering belay. She sets three screws into the waterfall, just above a tiny ledge about sixty feet above the ground, anchors herself, then places me on belay. The climb is easy at first, and becomes increasingly steep. As the second climber up, I also have to pull the ice screws that my instructor used to protect herself on the way up. The first screw practically pops out – had she fallen against it, the screw probably wouldn't have held. The second screw, though, about twenty feet higher, seems to have been screwed into aircraft-grade titanium, then welded into place. My calves are quivering – *sewing machine legs* – while I try to find a balanced spot on the nearly vertical wall to wrestle with the frozen screw. I find a little chip of ice that lets me place my left foot almost flat against the waterfall. Then I set the front-points of my right boot. I stand up, hammer my left ax into the wall, then loosen the tether, and slide my left arm through to the elbow. This gives me the stance of a quick-frozen subway rider and allows me to use the ice ax in my right hand to chip away the ice around the screw. Then, as any self-respecting male would do when faced with a recalcitrant physical object, I use the butt of the ax to pound the screw head until it starts turning.

I have gotten the screw to back out a couple of turns, but there are clearly ice trolls underneath the waterfall holding onto the other side of the screw. I am looking down over the screw, and I can't figure out where the water is coming from that keeps pooling, then refreezing, around my screw. I realize, finally, that it is my sweat. 'Oh Michael,' my instructor shouts. 'It's getting cold up here. How long do you plan to stay there at that screw?'

Just then, I crank the last turn, grab the screw with wet gloves, and attach it to my climbing harness. Then I hold my glove up to let the sweat trickle out.

Once I make the ledge, we perform the same maneuver – she climbs; I belay. She belays; I climb. On the second pitch, though, my nonathlete's body finally makes a few connections. The face is steep, and I front-point my way along easily. The screws act like screws ought to. The axes tap gently into the ice and catch solidly. At one point, I tap gently and about seventy-five pounds of ice sheer away from the waterfall next to me and fall into the valley, shattering into a million crystal pieces.

I pause then and look out across the White Mountains. They are indeed white, with the afternoon sun fracturing off the occasional frozen waterfall across the valley. The wind is sharp, almost metallic, and tastes of ice crystals. When I exhale, I can feel not only my calves, but my triceps and the muscles in my neck quivering with exhaustion. The only sound is the wind. *What an odd place,* I think, *to feel so peaceful.*

'As long as you remember ice is thick liquid,' my guide is saying as we trudge along the cliff face, 'you'll be okay.' She points out different ice formations, different kinds of ice, different strategies for each icefall, but she keeps coming back to The List.

She is a parasailer, as well as a rock and ice climber.

'Those are the parachute thingies?' I ask.

'Yep.'

What she is wrestling with herself is life after the frozen waterfalls, the 'real world,' always scratching on the edge of her consciousness.

'When I'm climbing,' she begins, 'when I'm flying . . . it's so hard, but there's this feeling of, I don't know, accomplishment? But it's not accomplishment exactly. It just feels good, you know, like magic or something.'

I nod.

'I'm familiar with that feeling,' I say.

'So the question is, if I quit doing this stuff, does the feeling go away forever?'

'I don't know.'

We walk for a while longer. The sun is setting, the wind rising out of the valley.

'So, I think I know where you're going, Michael,' she says, unstrapping crampons and clipping her ice axes to the day pack. 'But how do you plan on getting back?'

Ice, I think, *haunts me*. Since I walked along the Frankenstein cliffs, I have climbed ice in fairyland box canyons in Colorado, on towering icicles above ski towns, in piles of frozen froth in Alaska where you have to beat away the meringue to get to the solid ice underneath. I have been scared – no, make that terrified – and cold and wet, sworn to myself at least five times that all the fires in hell couldn't get me, miserable ice climber that I am, to set foot on another frozen waterfall. Yet, somehow, item 7 never seems to get completely crossed off The List.

16 Over the Edge

The world changes, but The List is the same. After much agonizing, I have left Florida for the foothills of the Rockies – Boulder, Colorado. I have told myself that the move is based on sound business judgment, but underlying that judgment is the simple fact that it will be easier to train for the remaining items on The List in the thin air of the mountains than in Florida's muggy winters.

I lay out a training schedule for the last three items: the Iditabike, the deep dive, and Denali. The logistics are simple – for the next six months, I'll be traveling every two weeks, doing something life-threatening. It doesn't look so bad, written down in black and white. *At least,* I think with more than just a touch of gallows humor, *it's a different life-threatening event each time.* To have one's life threatened by the same thing every two weeks would get boring, I suspect. Instead, many things will have the opportunity to kill me – avalanches, rock falls, drowning, moose stompings, freezing, simple exhaustion. What more could I ask for?

'I hope you're happy,' says my best friend. 'You managed to really get yourself out there this time.'

I agree that I've finally gotten over the edge a bit.

'You understand, don't you?' he persists. He is a scuba diving instructor and an expert on the cold, dark wrecks of the north Atlantic. When he talks about risks, he is not talking hypothetically.

'Understand what?'

'Understand that you can't fuck up at all,' he says. 'You've used up all your margins. If your head isn't together, if your focus wavers just once, you're going to die out there. One of these things is going to kill you.'

I have this reflexive urge to minimize The List, to explain that it's not as bad – or as spooky – as it looks. My friend, though, is having none of it.

'You almost died in that river in New Zealand,' he continues. 'By your own admission, you're lucky you weren't scraped off the mountain in that mountain-bike race. That's the problem, buddy. You got lucky once or twice. But you can't keep getting lucky. I *know* what I'm talking about.'

My friend is not the only person who's worried. I start getting calls from other folks I've met along the way. More than a few of these calls contain the phrase, 'Do you understand that you can die? Do you understand how far you've pushed this?'

Frankly, I am weary of being told I can die. I know I can die, and I know it on a level they can't imagine, a gut level, a cellular level. Some nights I wake with a lurch, covered in sweat, grabbing for an ice ax or a breathing regulator that isn't there. I dream of losing the mainline, my hand slipping off the line as my cave lights flicker and die. I feel the dark in the back of my throat, and, suddenly, it is swirling snow and I am stumbling, lost, lost, lost . . .

I am afraid of the cold and the dark and the heights and the depths, but I have come too far, given up too much.

'A step at a time,' Denise counsels me. 'Concentrate on what comes next, just like rock climbing. Take each move as it comes.'

I talk to John Orlowski, my cave instructor. One of the absolute rules of cave diving is that any dive can be called by any of the divers at any time, and caver etiquette demands that no questions be asked. He proved that to me one day as we were descending into a deep cave system. The dive had been going perfectly, and there were no problems that I could perceive when John called the dive and signaled a return to the surface.

When we got out, I didn't ask, but John offered an explanation anyway.

'The deeper we went,' he said, 'the more certain I became that someone was going to die. So I called the dive.

'If you feel bad about anything,' John says, 'you've got to be man enough to walk away from it. Out here on the edge, if it feels bad, we can't risk doing it.'

Just nerves, I say. *Too much, too quick.*

'Well,' he says, 'when I call a dive, I figure those caves will be here tomorrow. The same goes for mountains.'

I get another call from my best friend.

'I've been asking around,' he says. 'And I can't find anybody who has gone up as far as you're going up or as far down as you're going down. I think you're out there on your own on this one; sort of George Plimpton from Hell.'

'Thanks,' I say.

17 The Intensive

'I think you need to come for an Intensive,' Steve Ilg tells me over the telephone one night.

'An intensive what?'

'An Intensive,' he reiterates. 'A one-on-one training session with me. Frankly, I'm worried about you, Michael. The time frame for this "big finish" isn't realistic. Your body doesn't have time to get ready.'

Frankly, I'm worried about me, too. It's all very well and good to announce you're planning on doing three major events in six months time; something else again to do them. The key problem is the prerequisites. Neither Denali nor the deep dive are walk-ons; both require an extensive series of prerequisites to get on with any reputable guide. The truth is I have neither the mountaineering nor the diving prerequisites, which means I'm going to be hustling back and forth between up and down for several months.

My first bump against those prerequisites comes while I'm searching for a guided group on Mt. McKinley. There are many ways to climb a mountain. You can, if you so elect, pick a mountain and start up by yourself, which, if you happen to be a world-class climber like Alex Lowe, works just fine. I'll later run into Alex in Talkeetna, the little town at the base of Denali, and he'll talk about taking his skis, grabbing a plane up to Base Camp, and seeing if he can make the summit while he's waiting for his climbing partner for a much more 'serious' climb to arrive.

'It would be,' he tells me, 'sort of fun.'

If you don't happen to be among the top ten climbers of your generation, another way of getting up a big mountain is to form a climbing team and create your own expedition. On a mountain like McKinley, where there's a constant danger of falling to deep, bottomless crevasses, a team roped together makes much more sense. If you fall into a crevasse, there's someone to help you get out. But a team requires that all the team members know what they are doing, and in all honesty I don't.

Up until McKinley, everything on The List had been an individual activity – I was the sole person at risk. But mountaineering is a team endeavor, something I really hadn't given a lot of thought to when I wrote The List. Heck, the movie *The Eiger Sanction* is still my mountaineering bible – manly men, driving spikes into the Death Wall of the Eiger, hauling themselves up by thin ropes and sheer force of will.

Of course, I know now that was nonsense. I also know that with my lack of experience, putting together my own team is pretty farfetched.

'Finding people to go to McKinley with you is no problem,' said Nancy Prichard when I first broach the subject. 'Do you know what to do when you get there?'

The answer to that question is a resounding no!

Which means that I am a major liability.

That leaves the third option, a guided climb. A guided climb is, essentially, a package trip. The guide company provides an experienced guide or two, team climbing equipment such as ropes and sleds, food, and a measure of security. You pay your money, and away you go.

Not hardly.

Guiding on Denali began in the mid-1960s with the

legendary Ray 'Pirate' Genet, a brilliant, driven climber who saw his fortune in guided climbs to the windswept summit. And who could pass up a wildly bearded, Hemingwayesque adventurer whose motto was To The Summit!? But Genet died on Mt. Everest in 1979, and the National Park Service, hurting for cash, decided to open up the mountain to other groups. They awarded seven franchises, which have become increasingly hard to retain as the park service has tightened standards. No more than nine clients can be taken up at one time, and the client to guide ratio can be no more than four to one.

I pored over the six remaining franchisees. Ironically, Genet's operation lost their franchise for several reasons, not the least of which was the death of a client. I didn't like that, 'death of a client.'

No matter how you approach it, Denali is daunting. Despite the number of climbers who come to the mountain, despite the stunts – the youngest, the oldest, the first blind climber to summit – Denali kills roughly one out of every hundred climbers who try for its summit.

One in a hundred?

If the New York Marathon, with 15,000 runners, ran those risks, there would be 150 dead people at the end of every race. Even a modest local race, with 500 participants, could expect five deaths. No other endeavor carries that kind of risk, and the Denali guide services are deadly serious about what they do.

I decide to go with the American Alpine Institute (AAI) of Bellingham, Washington, a small company dedicated to alpine climbing. Their wordy brochures cover climbs around the world – they don't do 'tourist' trips, or 'adventure travel.' They exist to climb. AAI also has a reputation for flawless instruction in mountaineering techniques, and the best record of any company for getting clients to the top.

AAI has also never lost a client, which I find very promising.

I call Dunham Gooding, the founder of the company, in Bellingham, explain what I'm trying to do, and ask about his four annual McKinley trips.

'No,' he says.

'No, what?' I reply.

'No, we won't take you up the mountain,' he says. 'You're not qualified.'

Keep him talking, I think. I blather about climbing, about risk sports, whatever.

Dunham listens.

Finally, I pop the question. 'What do I have to do to be qualified?' I ask. 'You tell me what I have to do, and I'll do it.'

'Let me think about it a few days,' Dunham says. 'I'll get back to you.'

In the meantime, I call Steve Ilg in Durango. What I need, I tell him, is a training program aimed at riding the Iditabike, climbing Mt. McKinley, and pulling off a deep dive.

'Let me see,' says Ilg. 'That's long-distance biking, steady high-altitude hiking carrying a heavy load, and, I'm just guessing here, but a little swimming thrown in so you'll be comfortable in the water.'

I say that sounds right.

'The problem here is that these things are mutually exclusive, exercisewise,' Ilg says. 'I think you need to come to Durango.'

Durango sits nestled in the San Juan Mountains, a former mining community reeling under the impact of a flood of sudden émigrés drawn by a flawless outdoorsy lifestyle.

Ilg, though, is an original Durango boy, come home to make his mark. And he is calmer than when we first met in Santa Fe – which, given how laid back he was then, is pretty scary. He outlines a three-day intensive, a one-on-one workshop designed to keep me moving in the right direction.

The problem, he has outlined by telephone, is the old bugaboo of specificity of training. The best training for hiking up a mountain is hiking up a mountain. The best training for riding a bicycle long distance is riding a bicycle long distance. If you want to do many sports, you're going to have to do some complex juggling. If you want to do many sports in a short span of time, something has got to give.

On paper, Ilg's plan is simple – he'll put me through the paces of weight lifting, stretching, bicycling, and other cardiovascular activities, then spend some time using his own special body work to make sure I'm aligned – all the usual things a person might do to a '56 Chevy truck to keep it running.

Ilg, as usual, beaming like he knows some universal secret, meets me at a small health club in downtown Durango. As is also usual with Ilg, the workout is as much talk as lifting.

'We have,' he says, 'come through the physical to the kingdom of the mental.'

I nod.

Ilg frowns. I'm not getting it. He can shift gears faster than I can.

'I can train you for the physical, despite the problems,' he says. 'But the physical is only the very tip of the iceberg. The question is, are you going to be ready in your head?'

I shrug, irritated. The hardest thing about approaching the mental aspects of extreme sports is not standing up and shouting, 'Bullshit!' It's so much easier to run or bike or climb, to spend hours in the gym watching cast-iron weights go up and down, feeling the stretch and flex of muscles, the dripping of sweat, and the burn of the lactic acid. Weight lifting for the head is too solitary, too lonely, too . . . *nonempirical*. I've learned too well about adrenaline and beta-endorphins and the rush-rush-rush of blood through my heart. I know how to create charts and graphs, measure the steady strengthening of my muscles and the second-by-second improvements of my running. I crave the feel of the burn, of hanging on the very edge of athletic performance. I hurt, and recover, and hurt again.

And what Ilg is telling me, really, is that these hard-fought gains are easy, are the ante of the game.

We are back to martial arts, to the dance Ilg talked about so eloquently when we first met. I think again of Bruce Lee, who once commented that *kata*, the ritualized, dancelike martial arts motions taught to every student, don't matter. Unfortunately, that insight is only fully realized after years of learning *kata*.

'Turn into a doll made of wood,' Lee wrote. 'It has no ego; it thinks nothing; it is not grasping or sticky. Let the body and limbs work themselves out in accordance with the discipline they have undergone.'

A wooden doll it is, then.

'What,' I ask Ilg, 'do you have in mind?'

He smiles.

It's already after dark when Ilg picks me up in his truck. It's around ten degrees, and clouds racing across the moon and stars listlessly spit hard, icy snowflakes. I've already been told to dress for exertion – tights, sneakers, and a heavy shell – so I'm basically freezing.

'Don't worry,' Ilg says. 'You'll warm right up when we start running.'

He drives out of Durango to the base of a tiny ski area,

not yet open for skiing, where he parks alongside the road and hands me a pair of snowshoes.

'Ever run in snowshoes?' he asks.

'This is,' I say, 'the first pair of snowshoes I've even seen up close.'

'Great!' he says. *No one should be that upbeat.* 'This will be fun!'

We put the snowshoes on over our sneakers and start out walking.

This isn't so bad, I think as we walk up the first slope, probably an easy green run. Pretty soon I am huffing from the altitude, but Ilg sets a brisk pace. The snow is falling lightly and steadily now, muting an already silent landscape. The night has the brightness of an old sepia photo; the ambient light reflects off the snow fields. We walk for about half an hour until we reach the ridgeline where, in just a few more days, the lifts will be disgorging hordes of skiers.

'Are you warm?' Ilg asks.

'Very,' I reply. *Not so bad at all . . .*

'Good!' he says. 'Let's run.'

Awkwardly at first, I follow Ilg, running along the ridge line. The snowshoes, trick aluminum and plastic things that don't bear the slightest resemblance to those boats Sergeant Preston of the Mounties used, barely offer any more resistance than running shoes. We jog slowly, Ilg letting me get the hang of the snowshoes.

'Now sprint!' he cries, and he's off like a horse out of the gate, little white rooster tails of snow flying from each snowshoe. I chase as best I can. In a couple hundred yards my lungs are on fire. Just when I'm seriously considering passing out, Ilg slows to a jog.

'Catch your breath,' he says happily.

We slow to a walk, then go back to a jog. After a couple of minutes, he's off again, with me right behind him. We sprint, jog, walk across the top of the mountain. I remember how, just a few hours before, I was pretty smug about the shape I was in.

Wooden doll, I think.

We come to a steep slope down, steep enough that I would have to pause a few minutes before launching myself off on skis.

'Come on,' Ilg shouts. He takes huge, bounding steps, moving straight off the hill, then dropping down the slope. 'Come on!'

I head down and am immediately waist-deep in fresh powder, my snowshoes making me wallow like some great mastodon trapped in a snow white tar pit.

'Bound, Michael,' Ilg shouts from below. 'Bound *up!*'

I bound up, and a second later am on my face, rolling down the slope.

'Get up and run!' I hear from a distance, my head buried in the snow.

I struggle up, covered with powder, and run down the slope. I make it three steps before I'm on my face again.

'Bound! Graceful! Light!'

I half run, half fall down the slope, leaving a trail like a deranged garden slug through the pristine snow. When I reach the bottom, I look like some wheezing snow apparition, cold and wet.

'Good,' says Ilg. 'Now jog.'

Jog, walk, jog, sprint, jog, walk, jog, sprint, jog, walk, jog, sprint, jog, walk . . .

We come to another slope, steeper than the first one we went up.

'Up,' Ilg says. He has become increasingly more focused, less New Age as we run through the snow. His commands become brusker, the speed a little faster. I start jogging up the slope. Within a few feet I hear the blood pounding in my ears, my heart hammering so hard it threatens to rip away my shell. I focus on putting one foot in front of the other, breathing, simple things, as the slope gets steeper.

'Run,' Ilg, moving effortlessly ahead of me, says.

And I stumble, walk.

'Run, Michael,' he says.

My face is flushed, and my breathing is coming in short, painful gasps. I imagine the snow hitting my burning face, then sizzling away into water vapor.

And then we are at the top. I bend double, gasping massive amounts of the cold air.

'Good, Michael,' Ilg says. 'Now jog.'

Not good, I think, jogging at a barely moving pace along the ridgeline.

'Sprint.

'Now jog.

'Walk.

'Sprint.'

I am lying on my face on another steep slope, struggling back up, running, stumbling, sliding down.

'Good. Now jog.'

And it goes on and on, until, what seems like hours and hours later, we come to the steepest slope of them all. We pause at the bottom, and I take every second I can. I am soaking wet, from sweat, from melting snow, alternately burning up and freezing to death. *I think I am having an out-of-body – or perhaps out-of-life – experience.*

'I'm going to need you to run up this hill, Michael,' Ilg says almost sadly, as if he knows how much this is going to hurt me. 'How do you feel?'

'Great,' I say. Let the irony just lie there, like a melted snowman.

'Good,' Ilg says, and starts running up the ski slope.

I want to get this exactly right here: to say I hurt is not fair to the actual feelings running through my legs and arms and chest and lungs. Ilg had taken me to a place beyond hurt, beyond any rational concept of exercise, and there was one more hill left to climb.

Every step is in slow motion. From a distance, I see my quadriceps contract, the smaller muscles in my hips helping to lift the leg. The leg moves forward and splashes down in the powder, and the quad begins lifting the rest of me up as the next leg cycles. My lungs are beyond laboring, the cold air sucked through clenched teeth. There are bright flashes behind my eyes, as if something important upstairs is short-circuiting. I hear a waterfall in each ear, and the snow looks like white fire.

And then we are at the top.

'Catch your breath,' my tormentor says. 'Now jog.'

We jog – or, in my case, hobble – a few yards to a steep drop.

Oh God! I think, panic welling up, *do I have to jump off a cliff?*

But Ilg stops suddenly. The listless snow has given up and to the north stars glow like hard, cold stones in the bitter air.

'Feel it,' Ilg says, low and intense. The New Age exercise guru is gone now, and I look in the eyes of a man on fire. *'Denali.* Feel it. *FEEL IT!* It's out there.'

And I feel it. I feel the cold and the wind and the pain.

'And the depths and the cold. Feel it,' Ilg is saying.

My eyes close, and I feel my body sway to invisible currents, pulled by tides of blood and chemistry.

'If you make a mistake,' Ilg says, low and hypnotic, his words boring into my head, 'you are going to die.'

A wooden doll, I think, *caught in the winds and the tides, between the roof of the world and the abyss, driven by a list written on a paper napkin in a pizza joint.* The moment, caught in some elastic putty of time, stretches. I open my eyes, and the moon has come out, chasing the last of the clouds from the winter sky. I can make out the North Star, a fire in the sky. I look over my shoulder, to the south, then back to the north. *I'm coming*, I think. *It's time to finish this.*

'Well!' says the old Ilg, smiling. 'It's about time to go down now, don't you think?'

18 The Deeps

All I have to do now is keep to the gospel according to Ilg, which involves around twenty hours a week of lifting weights, snowshoeing, running, and biking, while at the same time building up some skills. I do immediately discover a basic truth, which is that no one wants to go out bicycling or running with you when it's eight degrees and snowing.

People will, in fact, avoid your phone calls, or give you some obvious ruse like, 'I want to sit in front of the fire and have dinner.'

The plus side of the Ilg Treatment is that the mountains in the winter are magic places. The trails are empty and cathedral quiet; the only break in the smooth, white surface is hoofprints of mule deer, looking for the last of the green. The first time I try to ride my mountain bike in the snow and ice, I receive an unpleasant reminder about slick surfaces and gravity. I am climbing a steep hill in the mountains outside of Boulder. The road up the hill is in the shade, and despite several inches of fresh wet snow, most of the road is ice over rock. I have let most of the air out of my tires for the climb to get as much rubber as possible on the ground, and I am chanting to myself *I am balanced . . . I am balanced . . . I am balanced.* And I am balanced, right until the point that the rear wheel sheers clockwise on the ice, and I smack, face first, into the hard snow. I lay there for a minute, then pick up the bike, and start up again. With the first push of the pedal, I am back in the snow, about six inches from my previous snow angel.

Things get better, though, after a long discussion with Tom Armstrong, a vice president at Cannondale.

'Yeah,' says Tom, who handles that company's phenomenally successful racing team, 'we get a lot of requests for bicycles to ride in the snow and ice. *Tons* of them. Let me talk to the engineers.'

The result arrives a month later, a fire-engine red Cannondale with none of the frills of a modern racing mountain bike. There's no front shock absorber or rear suspension. Instead, the bike is plain as vanilla, until I pick it up. It weighs nothing, each component selected as a balance between weight and durability.

'It's indestructible,' says Armstrong. 'It's as light as it can be without compromising durability.'

The red bike is also designed for special wheels and tires, created by a bike shop in Fairbanks for winter cycling. Two normal mountain-bike rims are welded together, then drilled for the spokes. The widest possible tire is then glued to the rim to keep it from slipping in the cold. When the aptly named Snow Cat is then inflated to all of six pounds (versus fifty pounds for a normal tire) the result is a fat, almost six-inch-wide, soft footprint in the snow. The result is a bike that rides almost as well in the snow as in the dirt.

The second part of the training equation has come in a crash course in dressing for winter. For both the Iditabike and Mt. McKinley, the challenge is the same. Temperatures will range as low as thirty degrees below zero, but because I'll be moving, especially on the bike, generating heat, I'll 'need a clothing system,' says Alexandra Cherry, whose company, Malden Mills in New Hampshire, manufactures synthetic *fleece*. For lack of a better explanation, fleece is what people mean when they say 'miracle stuff.' I learn quickly that exercising in ultracold weather has a whole different set of problems. Besides the obvious one – freezing to death – there's the not so obvious problem of overheating. On a cold day, put on a heavy jacket and run half a mile. In no time at all you'll be, to use technical terminology, sweating like a pig. So you stop running and unzip your jacket. For about sixty seconds, you're comfortable. But the inside of your jacket is soaked with sweat, and pretty soon you're shivering. Zip the jacket back up and walk at a brisk pace, and you're warmer. What's an annoyance on a Saturday afternoon jog is life-threatening when the bottom falls out of the temperature and you're a long way from home. Consequently, I begin the Great Underwear Search, juggling different weights and kinds of clothing, making sure there are zippers in the right place for ventilation and that I can get to them easily. Malden chips in with a couple of pairs of stretch tights made of something they call Polartec.

'They're awful thin,' I say skeptically.

'Try them,' Alexandra says.

And so the Ilg Treatment gets more comfortable.

The other part of the Big Finish, though, is the dive on the *Wilkes Barre*, 240 feet down off Key West. I finally catch up with wreck diver Gary Gentile in San Francisco. We have dinner at a local diner, and I outline my plans. He reacts much as Dunham Gooding from the American Alpine Institute did – 'Not a good plan.'

'Diving is not like mountaineering,' says Gary, one of the few people in scuba who also has climbed mountains. 'The focus for technical diving has to be the acquisition of skills, then the application of those skills.'

For me, Gary Gentile was one of the gurus, if you will, of The List. Long before I knew he was a diver, I'd read his science fiction novels and logged away his name as someone I'd like to meet. Later, when I read his numerous books on diving, I knew I'd found a kindred spirit. He'd come back from the crucible of Vietnam with an insatiable desire to test the limits, whether those limits were high in the mountains, in rolling whitewater, or down the untracked powder of extreme ski runs.

In 1970, though, Gary had his first dive, and his world shifted. He found an environment where he could not only push the limits, but excel as well.

'I did not seek close brushes with death, for that is foolish,' he writes. 'I did not intend to charge blindly into inextricable circumstances. What I sought was personal challenge: to pit myself against the elements of nature, but in such a way that planning and forethought offered a strong measure of control. This was the essential difference between walking point on a search-and-destroy mission and plummeting into the depths of an unknown sea. Now I was in charge of my fate.'

'How deep have you been?' Gary is asking me.

'One hundred fifty feet,' I say.

He nods.

'You're going to need to go deeper,' he says. 'You're going to need to learn how you are down there, what it's like. Then you're going to have to keep doing it, over and over.'

We finally decide that my first exposure to the abyss, the world below 200 feet, should be in a controlled, supervised situation. The next week, I make arrangements to go to the horse country of central Florida, to a 240-foot-deep hole in the ground called Forty Fathom Grotto.

The drive from Ocala, the closest town of any consequence, to the Grotto is an impressionistic montage of live oaks, Spanish moss, perfect green paddocks, and thoroughbreds

190

moving with their slow-motion gait. Appropriately, I have country music cranked up real loud, but the driving beat of Travis Tritt is not doing much to dispel my nervousness. It is, I'm afraid, much easier to talk about going where you've never gone before than to actually load up the car and head for it.

As the horse country rolls by outside the window, I review my next few days. As Gary says, it's simple – I need to get deeper if I'm going to attempt a serious wreck dive. Going deeper, though, is more than just adding a couple of pounds of lead to the wetsuit and sinking. The history of deep diving is peppered by people who did exactly that and were never seen again. Scuba at this level gets tricky. In other risk sports, say climbing, you can tell immediately if what you hope to accomplish is beyond your abilities. I've stood at the base of a rock or ice climb and thought, *No way. Too steep. Too overhanging. Too exposed.* The risk factor is visually apparent, sometimes too much so. But in diving, most times the surface of the water offers the same calm face, whether you're planning to go for 30 or 300 feet. And the limits are arbitrary, keyed to the environment and very personal.

'How deep,' says my friend Michael Menduno, the editor of the technical dive journal *aquaCORP*, 'is *deep*?'

How many angels can dance on the top of an 80-cubic-inch dive tank?

According to the big dive certifying agencies, 100 feet is deep, and 130 feet is the limit of what can be termed recreation scuba diving. Those limits have their roots back when the Navy lowered men in full dive suits with those round helmets with portholes. But the numbers are taught to every new diver, and they are, for the most part, taken as gospel.

I am really thinking about the pressure, all those atmospheres, pressing on every square inch of my body. I am thinking that a failure of the life-support system at those depths will have one single consequence. It will be dark and cold. And the pressure will squeeze me . . .

I am afraid.

I think of something Gary wrote a few years back. 'What normally keeps me out of trouble on deep air dives is fear. It keeps me from being too bold, getting too far away from the anchor line or getting out of control.'

I enter the Grotto through its small driveway with the international dive sign – a red square with a white slash – on the mailbox, then park beneath the live oaks that overhang everything. There are a couple of trailers, a small white outbuilding, and a small building with a large deck, overlooking what could pass for any small farm pond. Forty feet across; 240 feet down.

What my plan calls for is a series of increasingly deeper dives. I'll start at 150 feet. The next dive will be to 180, then 200, then 220, and finally 240 feet, the back of a cavern that drops away from the surface at a forty-five-degree angle. There'll be two other divers with me on each dive – an instructor and a safety diver. The instructor will ask me to perform certain tasks, then record the answers on my dive slate. All this has been explained to me on the telephone beforehand. It's also been explained to me that not everybody passes the course; that some divers are so spooked, so rattled by the abyss that they don't go all the way to 240 feet – or if they do, they never go back, and they don't talk much about the experience.

Forty Fathom Grotto is the brainchild of one of diving's legends, Hal Watts, who became obsessed with the deep sinkhole decades ago, when he almost died there.

Diving in the early 1960s with a bunch of surplus gear he'd traded for, and using such sophisticated diving aids as a bleach bottle, which he planned to fill up with air to

192

bring himself safely back to the surface, Watts and a friend went all the way down, 240 feet, where everything that could possibly go wrong did. While struggling with equipment and wrestling with his regulator, he actually passed out, only to come to with the regulator in his mouth at 100 feet.

'I guess you could say I've been obsessed with this place ever since,' says the gentlemanly Watts, from the front porch of his house overlooking the Grotto – the abyss is, literally, his home.

He's also been listed in the *Guinness Book of Records* for his deep air dives, and he coined one of the basic catch phrases of scuba – Plan your dive; dive your plan.

We start that morning with a classroom session about the particular monster of this deep – *nitrogen narcosis*, or The Rapture of the Deep for *Sea Hunt* fans. The deeper you go, the more the nitrogen in the air, under tremendous pressure, affects your mental processes. Perhaps not surprisingly, the exact mechanism of nitrogen narcosis isn't quite understood. It may have to do with the dissolved nitrogen interfering with the transmission of information from neuron to neuron – mental static – acting as an anesthetic gas. Think nitrous oxide here.

The result is that a diver might experience a sense of well-being, a loss of fine muscle control, euphoria (natch – that's why 'rapture'). In the television shows, a *narked* diver is always trying to kiss fish or swim to the pretty mermaid. There's even the martini rule, which states that a hundred feet of depth equals the effect of one martini; each additional fifty feet adds another drink.

Cute, but as you go deeper, you can forget the mermaids. Narcosis steadily hammers on your ability to think, to function. An activity that might be a snap at thirty feet, say doing a multiplication problem on a slate, becomes harder and harder the deeper you get. You can mentally override narcosis, I am told; but first, you've got to know what it's like.

My first dive to 150 is an excellent example of how to do everything wrong. I am uncomfortable, nervous – hey, I put the wetsuit on backward – fumbling with equipment. When I get back to the surface, Steve Hoffman, my instructor, is optimistic.

'Well,' he says, 'we got the first one out of the way.'

The second one the next day, to 180, goes better, except for the fact that my dive computer dies and starts feeding me incorrect information. At 180 feet, you don't need bad information. I also feel the first tendrils of narcosis. It's not so much an intoxicated feeling as it is a sense that someone has filled my head with thick soup. Every thought seems like a baseball thrown through that soup, moving ever so slowly toward action.

When we start down later that day for the 200-footer, I'm expecting more of the warm soup. Just below 180, though, narcosis slams through my head like a cyber freight train. Everything is spinning around me and I can't make it stop. The spinning is making me queasy and I can't think clearly. I feel the pressure, pressure, pressure . . .

I level off and signal Steve that I'm having trouble. He nods and waits for me to sort it out. I close my eyes, and that makes the spinning worse. The nausea's getting worse and I feel The Fear, the animal shaking the bars of the cage.

Think, think, think, but it's so very slow.

What did I do when I was afraid climbing? The thought moves glacially through my head. *I focused on the rock.*

There isn't any rock.

But there is the descent rope. I open my eyes and shine my light at the descent rope, a couple of feet away. At first, the rope is determined to move. But the more I focus, the steadier it becomes; the spinning in my head slows, a kid's top winding down. I blink my eyes a couple of times and my head is clear, as if the narcosis is a storm that's blown through my head and moved on.

I signal 'okay,' and we finish the dive.

'The thing is,' Steve is saying, 'it's up to you.'

We're sitting on the deck overlooking the Grotto. There is only time for one more dive, and it's up to me whether I want to go for the bottom. I don't want to go for the bottom. I don't want the dark or the cold or the 'whirlies.'

'Let's go,' I say, with something less than enthusiasm. Again, Steve will be the instructor, and Hal Watts will be safety diver. We suit up and hit the water quickly – I don't want a lot of chance to think. We have a very specific written dive plan. The last thing Hal Watts says to me is, 'Dive the plan. That's all there is to it.'

We drop quickly, the thin sunlight quickly fading into the gloom. We level off at 180 feet for a check. The plan is to stop at 220 before okaying the final drop. This time I am ready for the storm. As I start the descent, my head spins savagely, my stomach lurching.

Focus on the rock.

The spins wind down; my stomach stabilizes for the moment.

'Okay?' signals Steve.

'Okay,' I signal back.

As we go down, the pressure is like a living thing, some amoebic blanket wrapping tighter and tighter. We level off at 220, and I can tell my head wants to spin.

The rock, I think.

Perversely, instead of spinning, my head latches onto snippets of rock lyrics, blaring at full volume through my brain. Golden Earring, doing an old MTV song called 'Twilight Zone.' The noise is almost deafening.

I signal to continue down.

We've been angling back into the deep cave, and my light touches the edges of the rock walls. The last twenty feet are anticlimactic. I settle onto the silty bottom of the cave. I can see a wrecked car that locals parked in the old sink years ago. I see the rock walls and Hal Watts's yellow wetsuit. Everything is very, very slow. I look at my gauges, and one says 2 . . . . . . 4 . . . . . . 3. I want to follow each number with my finger, reading along: 2 . . . . . . 4 . . . . . . 3. I close my eyes for a moment and *think, think, think. I'm here, 243 feet. Ah.* Tied to the descent line next to me, right on the bottom, is a genuine mermaid, about eight inches long, rubber. I stare at her for a minute, then give her a squeeze for luck. *Hal Watts,* I think slowly, *has a truly sick sense of humor.* I look over, and Steve sticks out his hand in congratulations. I think for a moment, then realize he wants me to shake hands. Ah.

Are you slippin' into the twilight zone, Golden Earring sings in my head . . . *Place is a madhouse; feel like bein' stoned . . .*

I look at the gauges again. There are other numbers. My bottom timer is clicking over, thirteen minutes passed.

A good number, I think.

Where am I to go, now that I've gone too far? The music continues.

Good question, I think. *Right now, I want to go home.*

I give the thumbs up. Steve nods.

19 The Sled and I

I finally get a call from Dunham Gooding from American Alpine Institute.

He's pleased with my physical training – he's heard of the ubiquitous Ilg – but I'm definitely going to need some work on technique.

'Here's what we think,' he says, and I wait with my pencil poised. 'If you're willing to take two weeks of individual instruction in the mountains, we'll let the instructors – who are McKinley guides – decide whether you can go.'

'Two weeks?!'

'Well,' he adds, almost apologetically, 'you can split the class into two one-week sessions, if you like.'

Still, it's a huge amount of work (and not a small amount of expense).

'Do I have any options here?' I ask.

'Not if you want to get on an AAI trip,' says the head of AAI.

'Okay,' I say. 'Two weeks it is. When can we schedule the first week?'

'In four days,' he replies. 'Our guides' schedules are tight.'

Four days later, after a whirlwind pass through REI's retail stores and a visit to Boulder's legendary Neptune

Mountaineering shop for mountaineering boots ('Well, we can order them . . .'; 'What have you got in stock that fits *right now*?'), I cross the state of Colorado to the not-so-thriving metropolis of Ouray, the Switzerland of the West, just down the mountain from trendy Telluride.

Under other circumstances, I'd be looking forward to Ouray, it being the ice-climbing capital of the United States. In fact, Ouray has an ice park inside its city limits. A water pipeline runs along the top of a steep, narrow canyon, and during the winter, the city fathers allow the pipe to be opened, creating a series of frozen waterfalls all along the canyon. Ice climbers come from all over the world to climb those slabs of ice.

While I might get in a day of ice climbing, I suspect that's not what my instructor has in mind.

Mimi Borquist indeed has other plans.

'Have you ever pulled a sled before?' she asks as soon as we meet. Mimi is all of five feet tall, probably weighs the proverbial hundred pounds in soaking wet fleece. In her late twenties, she already has years as a mountain guide in Switzerland and is slated to guide on Denali this year.

'No,' I say. 'I've managed to miss sleds.'

'Well,' she responds, 'you're going to get to love your sled.'

But first, she adds, I'm going to get to love my avalanche transceiver.

'We are going,' Mimi says, 'to go through mountaineering skills from the ground up. We're going to start with how to dress, how to pack a pack, what to carry, what not to carry. We're going to hammer out the details of staying alive, then staying comfortable, at thirty degrees below zero.' I'm going to commit to memory the intricacies of crevasse rescue – pulling fellow climbers out of the huge cracks that crisscross the great glaciers – which knot is appropriate where, and how to tie it. I am going to become comfortable on a rope team, linked by a stretch of rope to the climbers in front and behind me. I will come to think of my ice ax as an extension of my body, combination Swiss army knife and survival tool.

'But first,' she says, 'time for a hike.'

After being buried under all the things I'm going to learn, a hike seems like blessed relief. We drive my hapless rental over frozen roads deep into the San Juan Mountains, parking in a snow bank just below one of the high passes. The altitude is over ten thousand feet, and the very act of lacing on the high-tech snowshoes and pulling the pack out of the car is enough to wind me.

But it is sunny and cold, and we head up into the mountains. The first thirty minutes or so are great. The southwest Colorado mountains are the most rugged in the state. They're high and lonely, and the views seem to stretch away to the edge of forever. My pack is light at about twenty-five pounds and I concentrate on getting the rhythm of the snowshoes. I haven't been on snowshoes since my hellish encounter with Ilg, but the rhythm is easy, and I'm using ski poles to help me hold my pace. By the second hour, the pack is starting to get heavier, as if someone has declared a slight increase in gravity and not informed me. We are steadily climbing up higher and higher ridges. The views are getting better, but it would help if the air were a little thicker.

As I keep learning over and over again, people – including myself, not by choice – were designed to live in a pretty narrow range of environments. As we go up or down, we quickly leave our comfort range. As we go up, the air is thinner. There's exactly the same percentage of oxygen in the air as there is at sea level – twenty-one percent – but because the air is thinner, the molecules more widely dispersed, we've got to work harder to get the oxygen we need.

Huff, wheeze; huff, wheeze.

By the end of the second hour, I'm in desperate need of a third lung or maybe a small, unobtrusive tank of pure oxygen. My body chugs and wheezes along, but it is clearly suffering decreased performance specs. My breathing has become rapid and shallow; I am sweating like a pig, alternately opening and closing zippers. None of this unpleasantness seems to affect my legs, though, which move along at about the same pace regardless of how poorly I feel. I think this is a good sign, so I resolve to ignore the missing oxygen molecules and concentrate on my legs. Almost four hours after leaving the car, when we grind to a stop for lunch, Mimi looks at me closely.

'So how are you doing?' she asks.

This is, I think, *one of the people who will decide whether I get a shot at Denali.*

'Great,' I say. 'I feel the altitude, but no big deal.'

There is, I believe, a logic to the lie. Since I began The Big Finish, I've sensed less and less distinction between the mental and the physical. We're not talking about happy talk here, not the Little Engine That Could. It's more a feeling that if you can muster the will, your body will go along for the ride. I remember talking to a Special Forces major about physical training – 'Bodies are strong; it's the mind that fails. So we train so the body will just keep going.' Trainers of world-class triathletes have exactly the opposite philosophy – the mind is strong, but the body is weak. Me, I can tell the difference less and less. There are times when my brain has turned to warm cherry Jell-O, and my body keeps moving of its own accord. There are other times when my body feels like it has been doing rounds in a dryer, but my brain pulls me through. As the Ilg-Man teaches, I'm beginning to suspect we are indeed

200

integrated systems. If I keep *saying* I'm okay, I'll probably *be* okay.

Maybe.

After lunch we begin my love affair with the avalanche transceiver. An avalanche transceiver is a little radio you wear in the backcountry, so if you happen to be buried alive by an avalanche, your friends can find you. When you're hiking, everyone's transceiver is set to *send*. Should you be caught in an avalanche, the people above ground will set their transceivers to *receive*, track down our signal, and dig you out.

This is not as easy as it might seem. The signals are weak, and you find the right direction depending on whether the signal is getting stronger or weaker, which can be amazingly hard to tell. I learn this the hard way, wandering around snow fields looking for a transceiver Mimi has buried.

The first time, it takes me fifteen minutes to find the buried transceiver. Had the transceiver been, say, me, I would have become a Popsicle in fifteen minutes.

'Good start,' she says, 'but we're going to need to pick up the speed a little bit.'

The drills progress from with eyes open to with eyes closed to blindfolded. I like the blindfolded drills best – being totally focused on the high-pitched hum from the transceiver while holding a picture of a perfect search grid in my head. After a couple of hours of blind man's bluff, we head up, hiking. Eventually, I get to crawl home.

'This is your sled,' Mimi says proudly. The sled is a couple of feet wide and about four feet long, created out of a pair of skis and a complex aluminum frame – sort of like the bastard mating of a cross-country ski and a lawn chair. The sled connects to my climbing harness at my waist, and for the rest of the week I will carry a full pack on my back and Mimi's gear in the sled. This is not just Dunham Gooding's idea of a good time for me. On McKinley, we will not be able to carry all our gear on our backs. Each member of the team will have his or her own sled, which will follow us most of the way up the mountain. If there is a single, critical requirement of the big mountain, it's the ability to pull the sled, day in and day out.

The first day of pulling the sled is a little like learning to ride a bicycle with one hand tied behind your back. The sled has a mind of its own and it's malevolent. The sled wants to pull to the right, but only if you need it to go to the left. If you need it to go to the right, it pulls to the left. The steeper we hike, the more the sled becomes a dragging boat anchor, fifty pounds of lead that seems determined to get back below sea level. Plus, a climbing harness was designed as just that – a harness to take your weight when you're hanging. As a harness for pulling a sled, it's sadly lacking. I notice this when I feel the first cold wind creeping around my butt.

'Your pants are falling off,' says Mimi helpfully.

We – rather I – pull the sled up a frozen highway for what seems like several forevers, until we come to a steep gully filled with ice that heads up to the right.

'Rope practice!' says my guide, who is altogether too excited about having me carry her load.

Rope practice consists of learning how to move up a rope that has been fixed in place by other climbers. It's really pretty simple. You have a device called a *Jumar*, an ascender, that locks on the rope. The mechanical lock allows the Jumar to slide in only one direction. As you climb up, you push the Jumar up the rope. Should you fall, the device locks and catches your fall. I like it, because my fear of heights vanishes when I'm connected to a rope.

'Then you're not afraid of *heights*,' says Mimi practically. 'You're afraid of *falling*. There's a difference.'

As I move up the steep slope on a rope Mimi has anchored, I come to a small, frozen waterfall, about six feet high. No big deal. I set my crampons a few feet up on the waterfall, then drive my ice ax in at eye level. Just as quickly, my ice ax blows back out, driven by the water pressure behind it. A perfect tube of freezing cold water arcs out of the hole, hitting me squarely in the face, running down my chest into my pants. Behind me, I can hear Mimi giggling.

Soaked, I continue on.

At the top, she has yet another surprise. About twenty-five feet over my head at the top of the gully is a *capstone*, a huge boulder that has tumbled down some time in the ancient past. Mimi has climbed to the top and attached another rope around the boulder, leaving me a length of rope.

'You're going to climb the rope,' she says, propping her pack in the sun. 'I'm going to sit in the sun.'

The purpose of this drill is using *prusiks*, little loops of ropes with a special knot that, like the Jumars, only slide in one direction. One of the greatest dangers on McKinley will be the crevasses. A glacier is a living thing, a moving river of ice. As the glacier pushes its way up a hill, all those tons of ice compress. As the glacier continues to move, tops the hills, and heads down, the ice expands and cracks. Or the friction of some unseen obstacle on the ground may cause the layers of ice to move at different speeds. The result is the same, a crack in the glacier. Ideally, a climber's route should avoid crevasses altogether. On McKinley, that simply isn't possible. There are too many and no alternate routes. So McKinley climbers are constantly crossing crevasses on unstable bridges of ice or snow. Crevasse rescue, the ability to get yourself or another climber out of these cracks in the world, is the most basic survival skill on the mountain.

Getting yourself out is where the prusiks come in.

Climbers on the mountain move in rope teams, everyone's climbing harness tied to a single rope. Each team member has their two loops of rope attached to the main climbing rope in a prusik knot. Should a member fall into the crevasse, they can use the two one-way knots to inch back to the surface, one loop attached to the climbing harness, the other with loops for the feet. Stand up in the foot loops, then slide the waist loop a little higher. Hang on the waist loop, and move the foot loops up. Sort of your basic inchworm scenario.

'Up you go,' Mimi says.

Forget climbing – it takes me fifteen minutes to get the stretch out of the rope. Eventually, I inch my way up (and *inch* is the operative word here). Each inchworm move gains me about three inches. An hour of steady inching gets me about three-quarters of the way up the rope. I take a break, the rope spins, and I can see hundreds of feet down into the valley.

'Are you afraid?' Mimi shouts from her sunny perch down below.

'Nope,' I say, spinning.

'See!' she says triumphantly. 'I told you you weren't afraid of heights!'

I reach the top and start to pull myself up and over, when the voice from down below alters the plan.

'Prusik down!' she shouts, then goes back to sunning.

Prusiking down involves hanging upside down to get the knots to release, then doing a sort of hanging abdominal crunch to reach the knots and move them. About halfway (and a million crunches) down, the knots tangle and refuse to move.

'What do I do?' I shout down.

'Untangle them,' says Mimi.

Great. First I'm a sled dog; now I'm a bat.

To try this at home, put a bar across a doorway; hang by your ankles; then try to untie a piece of string you've knotted around your belt buckle.

Eventually, I once again reach the ground.

'Good thing, too,' says Mimi. 'I was losing my sunny spot. And your sled's waiting.'

The week passes. Whether on frozen waterfalls or back up the gully, my sled is never very far away. I set up tents when my hands are frozen, knock them down when I'm exhausted, find the hidden transceiver, climb up and climb down and climb back up again. Once, my sled and I race to the top of a peak well over 13,000 feet, beating another team on skis. I listen to the groaning of the snowpack and learn to avoid – as much as anyone can avoid – the avalanche slopes. One afternoon, moving up the side of a steep hill with my trusty sled, I put my foot down in the snow and watch a foot-wide crack run like chain lightning from my footprint for a hundred yards along the ridgeline, the snowpack shifting, sliding, then stopping of its own accord.

'The lesson is,' says Mimi, 'that we just don't know. The mountains are mysteries, and all we can do is be as sharp as we can and try to stay alive.'

At the week's end, at a coffee shop in downtown Ouray, I pop the question. 'Did I pass?' I ask.

'I'd climb with you,' Mimi says.

Two weeks later, American Alpine Institute calls and tells me to send money. I'm on the team.

20 Mushing the Bike

Before I know it – and well before I'm ready – it's time to head to Alaska for the Iditabike.

I won't say I was exactly deluged with information from the race organizers in Anchorage, but each little bulletin from the Frozen North causes me to worry a little more:

'The biggest threat to life on the trail is hypothermia, commonly called exposure,' reads one such bulletin. 'If you get hypothermia, you will be too stupid and clumsy to help yourself. If you don't get help, you will likely die. Stay on the trail where you will be found.'

My particular favorite is on moose. After explaining that moose are large, intractable animals with a temper and a predilection for stomping people into bloody place mats (newspaper clippings enclosed), the bulletin includes a handy passage on how to tell if a moose is attacking you. 'If a moose is moving toward you, it is probably attacking you.'

The solution? 'Get out of the way.'

More words to live by.

Following Ilg's ongoing psychotic training schedule, I've been spending hours alone in the mountains, riding the red Cannondale over untracked snow. I've also been sprinting the bike up hills until, as Ilg so vividly puts it, I am 'coughing blood.' I am also aware, though, that the Iditabike is not really about bicycling. It is about Alaska in

February, where there's barely a two-story building between you and the North Pole and there's enough snow to bury your condo.

I forget where I heard about the Iditabike the first time – the organizers don't exactly knock themselves out publicizing it. But word seeped out of the last frontier about a bicycle race on the Iditarod Sled Dog Trail, in the dead of winter. What I remembered most was the race's slogan: Cowards won't show, and the weak will die.

That's what got the race added to The List.

Later, I learned the truth behind the race, which is every bit as weird as whatever I might have imagined. It was conceived in 1983 by Joe Reddington, Sr., the father of the Iditarod Sled Dog Race. His idea was a human-powered marathon, and the first event included skiing, snowshoeing, and a running division. Four years later, Dan Bull added bicycles.

The race has alternated between epochs of wilderness survival and relatively uneventful rides on hard-packed snow. Temperatures have ranged from a balmy forty degrees to a nippy forty below zero, and winds from nonexistent to howling, nightmare blizzards. But no matter what the weather, the race is always run.

'The course is doable under any weather conditions,' says one of the members of the Iditasport board, Janelle Matz. 'There will be no cancellations . . . so be prepared.'

Two years before, Sam Case, a professor of exercise physiology from Western Maryland College, conducted psychological and physiological studies on the race participants. Instead of the usual jocks, Case found a bunch of 'creative and independent introverts,' scoring on their psychological tests closest to stunt pilots and rodeo cowboys.

'Come on up!' says the ever jovial Dan Bull, the official

race organizer, when I call about signing up. 'You'll freeze, but we haven't lost anyone . . . yet.'

He sends me the entry form and a dense, two-page liability release that reads, in part:

I fully realize the dangers of participating in a winter skiing/bicycling/running/snowshoeing race held in the Alaska wilderness during winter conditions, and fully assume the risk associated with such participation, including, but not limited to, the following dangers: hypothermia, frostbite, collision with pedestrians, vehicles or other racers and fixed or moving objects, dangers arising from surface hazards, equipment failure, inadequate safety equipment and weather conditions; and the possibility of serious physical and/or mental trauma and injury, including death, associated with winter athletic competition . . .

I sign the release in front of a notary, send my two-hundred-dollar entry fee, and agree to show up in Anchorage with a bicycle, a sleeping bag rated to twenty degrees below zero, an insulated pad for under the sleeping bag, a *bivy sack* – a one-person tent – to stuff myself and my sleeping bag into, a stove, fuel, waterproof matches, a pot, two quarts of water, an extra day's supply of food, a headlamp with extra batteries and bulbs, a bicycle pump, spare parts for the Cannondale, and a lot of aspirin, all of which I will strap to various parts of the bicycle. Normally, I'd carry packs alongside the bicycle wheels. But I'm dissuaded from that idea by the bicycling guru of all-weather sports in Fairbanks. The Iditarod Trail can be so narrow and deeply rutted, the guru says, that the side panniers would drag. Instead, all twenty-two pounds of mandatory survival gear (three more pounds than the weight of the bike) have to be mounted up high,

over the wheels – making, the guru adds, the bike handle
'like a pig.'

It is almost dark when I arrive in Anchorage. In my
mind, I know there are almost as many daylight hours
in Alaska in February as there are in Colorado. But
Alaska seems to have this long, lingering dusk, as if the
sun itself is equivocating, trying to decide whether to sink
or not.

Turn up the lights, I think. *Let's have some real daylight
around here!* My Cannondale's transport box looks as if it
has been drop-kicked all the way from Colorado to Alaska,
but when I take the bike out, all the pieces seem to be
there and the gears are working.

There are a couple of other passengers uncrating
bicycles, and we look at each other with undisguised
curiosity. *What sort of idiot . . .*

The Iditabike has sort of gotten away from me mentally.
Denali has been in my mind every waking moment, and
in a lot of my dreams. Its hulking mass orbits the edges of
my consciousness like some huge moon, its gravity steadily
pulling the tides of my mind. From the first black-and-
white picture I saw so many years ago to the most recent
book I read *(Mt. McKinley: Icy Crown of North America)*, I've
encountered hundreds, maybe thousands, of images of the
great mountain. Now I feel almost like a high school kid
on his first date. Or maybe, more appropriately, a prisoner
waiting to meet his executioner.

On the way from the airport, my friends and I stop
along the bay. To the north, in the dim, pinkish light,
Denali towers over the landscape like the avenging god of
my nightmares. The mountain is just visible in the
distance, its twenty-thousand-foot crown punching above
the mists. It's freezing cold, but as I stand on the edge of
the frozen bay and stare at the mountain, I feel a haze

of sweat break out on the back of my neck.

I've come, I think lamely.

The mountain says nothing.

The next morning I start hammering out the on-site logistics of mounting all my gear on the bike, an event I'd entitle The Miracle of Duct Tape. When I'm finished, the once-sleek Cannondale looks like the pig it will ride like. The bulk of my twenty-below sleeping bag, now compressed into the shape of a giant aspirin tablet, is bungeed to my handlebars. It's taken roughly an hour to come up with the right combination of straps, duct tape, and bungee cords to make the six-pound tablet sit relatively still, but every time I turn the handlebars, it bobs up and down like a turn signal dog from a '62 Chevy Impala. Next, I strap my bivy sack, a long tube containing my tiny stove, an extra pint of fuel, a pot, matches, food, and what have you on the rear rack. The food is actually a supply of PowerBars, compressed carbohydrate bars, which many people claim can hardly be called food. One of my friends argues persuasively that PowerBars are, in fact, compressed sawdust. While I know that the below-zero temperatures will turn the bars into some organic compound with the consistency of an iron pipe, I figure I'll be able to stuff them in my armpits until they thaw enough to chew. This is the kind of keen survival planning I know will get me through.

As soon as I finish strapping everything down, I give the bike a shake, and of course everything falls off.

Several hours and rolls of duct tape later, all the gear is attached to the bike, and even my headlight is duct taped to my helmet. I look like Mickey Mouse about to go caving. On my first fully outfitted ride, all that weight high up makes the bike feel not like a pig, but as if a small child is trying to walk back and forth along the top tube of the bike. Thanks to my superior bike-handling skills, though,

I am able to quickly fall into the nearest snowbank. My giant aspirin tablet pops off.

Back to the duct tape.

The race itself is the soul of simplicity. Get on your bike, your skis, your snowshoes, your sneakers, or a combination of the above and ride, run, ski, or slog 85 or 155 miles, through frozen swamps, rivers, hills, and moose patties. There are no rules per se. Stray too far from the course and get in trouble – you're not going to be found until the spring thaw. You must hit each checkpoint by a certain time or you're disqualified. After that time, the checkpoint, usually a tent, is dismantled. I have gone over and over the course on paper, gaming it out, but now that I'm in Alaska I'm struck by the foolishness of that strategy. It's lower-forty-eight thinking and planning, whereas the actual race will be determined by the weather.

The weather has been warm, which is not good. Warm means the snow is slush and the ice is covered with a layer of water. But, at the mandatory meeting before the race, we're told the 'good' news.

'It's getting colder,' the ever effervescent Dan Bull announces. 'Much colder. Expect temperatures around forty degrees below zero the first night.'

That's colder, all right.

We are warned again about moose – are given yet another newspaper clipping about the most recent moose stomping – and the survival equipment is checked to make sure that we are not trying to shave a few pounds off the mandatory fifteen pounds. I would have been happy to be able to get the weight of all that gear down to fifteen pounds.

The other eighty or so racers are a strange mix of athletic gods and aging hippies. The legendary John Stamstad, who's won the race numerous times and is heavily favored to win again no matter what the weather, looks as if he's wandered in from 1968. He's an emaciated-looking protohippie who has just returned from almost dying in the Australian desert while riding across that country. He is telling me about his race footwear, which he has crafted himself. Unlike my winter mountaineering boots with insulated liner and three-sock system, he has a pair of ultralight cycling shoes with a light insulated liner.

'Don't your feet get cold?' I ask. He looks at me as if I've recently arrived from Mars.

'They freeze and go numb,' he says. 'It's not a big deal.'

My conversation with Stamstad makes me think that perhaps there's some kind of graph of the mental states of extreme sports participants. It's a geometric curve, getting steeper and steeper as you go up it. As you head up the curve, the definition of *extreme* keeps changing. What looked psychotic a couple of years ago now looks like a good Saturday afternoon workout.

It's good, I think, *that The List was drawn up when I was at the low end of the curve.* I suspect I wouldn't like John Stamstad's list.

The morning of the race dawns clear and very cold. The bike is strapped and taped together, and I'm dressed in layers of long underwear, thin fleece, and jackets with lots of zippers. I've eaten a bland breakfast of bagels and something called GU, a semi-liquid food that comes in little packets and tastes like cake frosting. I've used it before in the backcountry, and I've noticed that no matter how cold it gets, it never seems to freeze. I have consciously decided to ignore the implications of this fact.

The race starts on the appropriately named Big Lake, a long frozen stretch of ice. I survive one quick pre-race crisis, a flat tire and frozen pump. I get an air fill from a loaner pump and stuff mine inside my jacket to let it thaw.

Before I have time to really think, the gun goes off and we're under way.

The real racers are off like hares, leaving the others of us at the rear to pick our way across the rutted ice. There are about five or six inches of snow over most of the lake, and the rear wheel of the Cannondale dances all over the place. I know it's 'only' twenty-seven miles to the first checkpoint, and assuming everything goes right I expect to be there in five or six hours.

I am about to get a lesson about assumptions.

My strategy is to cruise – as my old bicycling buddy John Rodolf would say, 'Start slow, then taper off.'

I'll pedal easily, save my strength, I think, as I watch the other cyclists pull away. *I wonder why they're pushing so hard?*

The lake is uneventful, even fun. You have to kind of steer around looking for the hardest packed snow, but the surface is solid and the fat tires have plenty to grab hold of. After an hour or so on the lake, we head into the woods and I'm greeted with the first of the *whoop-de-doos*. The rolling terrain is cut with numerous creeks and streams, creating a roller coaster ride – up and down and up and down and up and down. As it happens, the roller coaster's track is covered with ice. My first approach is tentative; I baby the bike down the steepest part, lightly feather the rear brake, steer carefully. This results in my sprawling on top of the bike at the bottom of the whoop as both wheels spin out from under me.

I fall a couple of times trying to disentangle myself from the bike, which I then push up the next whoop.

Forget conservative. The next whoop, I fly down, the bike shaking and quivering on the ice. We arrive at the bottom upright.

Okay, I think. *That works.*

After a period of time in the woods whooping, I come

to a fifteen-foot drop into a frozen swamp. Ahead of me is a mile or more of smooth, flat snow, rutted by bicycle tires.

Time to make some time, I think, and head into the swamp.

I go about fifteen feet, and the bike sinks up to its axles in loose snow.

That's odd, I think. I get off and push the bike to a set of ruts made by other riders, then remount the bike. The Cannondale and I get about five feet before we're in knee-deep snow.

Every so often I can ride for a couple of minutes, but for the most part I'm pushing the bike in deep snow. Crossing the mile of frozen swamp takes just over an hour. I stop in the woods before the first whoop-de-doos, eat some GU, drink some water from the pack on my back, and refigure my time to the first checkpoint. I am not yet in trouble, but things are not going swimmingly. It's too cold to stop for long.

I run into a friend from Boulder, Monique Cole, an athlete and author who is writing the official history of the race. We're able to ride along together through the woods where the snow is harder packed. We drop out of the woods to cross a wide frozen stream. On the other side, struggling up the steep fifteen-foot-high frozen bank, is the hapless Italian team. Hapless, because their bikes are equipped with normal tires instead of the wide, flat snow tires the rest of us are using. In the increasingly softer snow, they can't ride at all. They've come all the way from Italy with an Italian television film crew, to push their bicycles across these swamps. At the moment, they're stuck at the foot of the bank, trying to get up the pure sheet of ice.

'Use your bike like an ice ax,' a rider shouts from the top of the bank. 'Shove your bike ahead of you, and take a step at the same time!'

Halfway up the bank, one of the Italian riders loses his

footing and slides back to the bottom. This happens to one after another for many minutes, with the rest of us waiting our turn to look like idiots. Monique gets most of the way up when the Italians, ever the gentlemen, realize it's a woman on the slope and extend a helping hand. I have a couple of good falls on my own, the bike bouncing and sliding back down, until I figure out the secret, which is shove the bike in the deep, loose snow to the side of the worst of the ice, then crawl up on your hands and knees. Pure fun.

When we hit the next swamp, I'm on my own again. Monique's lighter weight lets her pedal on the loose snow while I sink in.

The situation is getting progressively worse. The longer the sun shines on the swamps, the looser the snow gets and the deeper I sink. By midday, when I expected to be past the first checkpoint, I am pushing the Cannondale through ankle-deep slop. Except for shorter and shorter periods in the woods, I have given up riding altogether. As the snow gets looser and I sink deeper, it becomes harder to even make the bike roll. For long periods of time I am forced to pick the bike up and carry it, my own little snow anchor.

The hours pass with excruciating slowness. I try to turn my brain off, to disassociate from the whole experience, but it is obviously lodged in *record*. My arms and shoulders begin to ache from the effort of shoving the bike along. I respond by alternating sides, so at least my right arm and shoulder can hurt as badly as my left arm and shoulder. I occasionally start to drift off and get my ankles tangled up in the pedals – twice, I fall on top of the bike.

Mostly, I think about how even wasps learn from running mazes, but that I, unfortunately, keep forgetting to take these events seriously enough. I get on the bike and ride about three feet before we sink again.

I now understand totally why the other bikers were pushing so hard to get across the lake – to get across the swamps before the snow crust melted.

Perfect time for this revelation.

I occasionally sing songs to myself, carry on long conversations with old friends, try to remember passages from books or obscure movies.

I resolve not to look at my watch, because it's not good for me. I reflect on how time ought to be more linear than it is. In deep diving, time passes so quickly, the computer logging minutes at a frenetic pace. Out here in the swamps, time moves like an insect caught in hardening amber, agonizingly pulling each leg out of the golden resin, only to be trapped again . . . I give up and look at not only my watch, but the computer on the bicycle. I have been out for five hours and I'm only halfway to the first checkpoint.

I am, in a word, screwed.

I resolve to pick up my walking pace, and as soon as I hit the woods I ride hard to make up time. I also know that it's impossible to make up time. All you can do is keep going and time will run at whatever pace it chooses. I occasionally see other racers, but most of the time I'm alone. My brain moves ahead in fits and starts, misfiring and starting again. Unlike a long event in which you can just shift into autopilot, the Iditabike is hard, the riding is tough, technical, demanding. I have to be in the *here*, all the time.

On-line, real time, I think, again on my bike and heading into the next whoop-de-doo.

Not on-line and real time enough, however. The fifteen-foot drop looks vertical, and before I even have time to think what to do, I am pummeling over the edge. At the bottom, I gracefully continue over the handlebars – an *endo* – and smash my right shoulder into the steep ice heading up. I lay there for a full minute, my eyes closed, waiting for the stars to stop spinning around me. Then I raise my right arm slowly, sending spasms of pain into my shoulder. *If my shoulder were broken*, I reason, *I couldn't lift my arm.* This is mentally reassuring, but my shoulder still seriously hurts. I spend a few minutes massaging it, eat a handful of aspirin and a couple of tubes of orange-flavored GU, then push the bike up the whoop. I ride stiffly to the next swamp, where I promptly sink.

Time passes, and one swamp looks pretty much the same as the next. A pink glow begins to suffuse the western sky – *toward Japan*, I think – and I can feel the temperature dropping. Pretty soon, I'll be on my headlight, with its battery pack hung under my jackets against the skin of my back where it's warm.

And I notice that I can't feel my feet.

I stop and begin the foot-swinging ritual designed to get things going again down below. I swing my legs back and forth, trying to wiggle my toes, although no toes appear to be home. I stamp out a place in the snow and stomp around like some Iron John seminar participant. All I need is a spear. After another bout of swinging my legs, the feeling begins to trickle back, and I immediately wish it *would go away*! It hurts, stings. I curl my toes, and they burn.

I begin moving again. I made the decision at the start of the race to cache my gaiters, those insulated, waterproof leggings that stretch from the top of the boot to just below the knee, at the first checkpoint. My reasoning was that I'd probably be riding steadily for the first few hours, and I wouldn't need either the extra insulation or the waterproofing. In fact, I thought the extra insulation would cause my feet to sweat too much and I wanted to avoid wet feet at all costs.

Using my twenty-twenty hindsight, I see that I made a

fundamental mistake. Now, my feet are wet, cold, and the temperature is probably already below zero. My Cannondale's computer reads just twenty miles. I've got seven more miles of shoving my bike through frozen swamps.

Seven more miles!

I consider sitting down and crying, or at the very least demanding that Scotty beam me back up to the *Enterprise*. Instead, I start pushing my bike through the swamp.

Here is where it starts to get weird. The sun has gone down and I've flicked my headlight on – more for the security of the light than a need to see. The snow seems to glow, and I can clearly see the outline of the next set of woods ahead of me. I am cold, but not shivering; my feet are more or less constantly numb. A depression as deep and as smothering as the snowpack has settled on my brain and my right shoulder aches and aches. I am almost across a swamp when I hear a voice.

It startles me so badly I drop the bike. I spin around 360 degrees, looking for the person talking, but there is nothing but the snow.

'What the *fuck*!' I shout.

Nothing. But the voice is still there.

I can feel the chemistry set of my body start pumping adrenaline, my muscles gearing for flee or fight there on the frozen swamp. Then I listen to the voice, which is talking about me. It is my friend Sandy back in Florida, and she appears to be praying.

I know he thinks he's alone out there, and I know he's tired and he probably hurts, the voice is saying, as clear as if Sandy were standing next to me. *But remind him that he's not alone . . .*

I am dumbfounded. I plop down on the bike in the snow and just sit there as the voice fades, some cosmic radio signal drifting into the background static. I sit there for about ten minutes, then I get up and push the bike. I am cold; my feet are numb; my shoulder pulses; but I feel better.

With less than a mile left to go on the computer, I come to a steep drop out of the woods onto a frozen river, the Big Susitna. I make a couple of false starts at getting down the fifteen feet of ice to the river, but decide instead to throw the bike into the waist-deep snow alongside the trail. I wade through the snow to the edge, then drop the bike as gently as possible to the river. It bounces once, then slides to a stop. I then climb down to the river, using tree limbs and roots for handholds.

Once on the ice, the wind is screaming and I figure it must be far below zero. I push the bike the last half mile, a blinking strobe in the distance marking the checkpoint. It takes me forever to reach the strobe. No – longer than forever.

I'm shivering when I get there. Their thermometer, hanging outside of one of two tents, reaches twenty degrees below zero. But there's hot water and sympathy as the last of us straggle in. One of the tents is for the *refugees*, frostbite victims and people suffering from exhaustion or broken equipment. There are five people in the tent, including my friend Monique, along with an old cast-iron camp stove. The tent is warm, probably around ten degrees. I pull off my boots and start massaging my feet in front of the stove. It is like massaging a piece of steak. My toes are white and lifeless, and I feel nothing.

Monique says she's going on as soon as she warms up.

'If you don't go on, Michael,' she says, 'you'll never make the next checkpoint in time. They'll disqualify you.'

I know she's right. But my will dissolved somewhere back in those frozen swamps. I am afraid for my feet, afraid in general. I am tired – no, exhausted – and I hurt.

It is twenty degrees below zero, and everything has gone to shit. I massage my feet and wait for the pain to come.

Monique waits for my answer. I wish my brain were working faster. I wish I weren't so cold.

'I'll stay a while,' I hear myself saying. She nods, then leaves to pack her bike. I think I have never hated myself quite so much as I do at this very instance. *Quitter! Quitter! Quitter!* the animal in my head shrieks, but I can no more go outside than I can fly. It is as if I have been inhabited by an alien being, who won't let me get on the goddamned bike, go back into the goddamned cold, get back on the goddamned trail. I break out my camping gear and claim a corner of the tent nearest the flap. I stuff my sleeping bag into the bivy, unroll my pad, then lay the whole thing on the ice. Finally, I stuff a handful of chemical heaters in the end of the bag and climb in, shucking my outer clothes as I do. It is two hours before the pain in my feet eases enough to let me fall into a dreamless, restless sleep.

'You Bane?' The first words I hear around dawn are from a race official.

'I'm Bane,' I say, sticking my head out of the bag. The cold is enough to take my breath away. I breathe shallow, holding each breath in my mouth to warm it.

'You can't make the next time point,' she says, checking her clipboard. 'At three o'clock this afternoon, you're going to be disqualified and evacuated off the course.'

I nod.

'Three choices, no actually four,' she continues. 'You can finish the race on your own, but there'll be no support, no checkpoints, and you'd better be an expert at winter camping. Are you?'

I shake my head no. It's shaping up to be a great morning.

'Three choices then,' she says. 'We can evac you from here, you can ride back to the start line, or you can just keep riding until we disqualify you and a bush pilot flies you out.'

'What the hell,' I say. 'I'll just keep riding.'

'Good choice,' she says, and goes on to the next person.

I get dressed, I saddle up the red Cannondale, drink a cup of cold instant coffee, and hit the trail. This time, my feet are surrounded by chemical heat packs and safely laced into insulated gaiters as well as three pairs of socks and the mountaineering boots.

But I needn't have worried. It is bright, sunny, and bitterly cold. The hard freeze the night before has turned yesterday's mush into pure white concrete, and the bike flies along the Iditarod Trail. Twice I pull off to let sled dog teams pass, the huskies' breath steaming in the cold air. I am actually making up time – not that it matters. The longer I ride, the better I feel mentally. My shoulder still aches and there's no feeling in most of my toes, but I think I'll learn to live with decisions made at twenty below. In a sense, I'm free to concentrate on the frozen countryside, the mountains in the distance, their ridgelines, razor sharp in the cold air. For miles the trail is lined with huge wolf tracks, crisscrossing the bicycle ruts.

They're watching me, I think, and that thought is comforting rather than threatening. I see a moose on the trail ahead of me, and I pause for a snack until he ambles away into the frozen woods.

Almost before I know it, it's afternoon, and I emerge from the woods onto another frozen river. There's a plane on skis parked there, an antique Cessna, with a huge 'Cyndi Lou' painted on the nose.

'You Bane?' the pilot asks, same question as this morning.

I nod.

'You're outta here,' he says. 'Take your bike apart and we'll bungee it to the plane.'

The plane is parked next to a house, full of people, heat, and cans of Coca-Cola. I step inside for a minute, then head back out to disassemble the Cannondale. The pilot comes and without another word pulls out a snake's nest of bungee cords and begins tying pieces of the bike to the little plane – the rear wheel here, the frame there, the front wheel on the other wing.

When he's all done, he says, 'Climb in the backseat.' I look in.

'There isn't a backseat,' I say.

In disgust, he points to what appears to be the gas tank. I climb on top. The plane rumbles and shakes and shudders, then starts down the frozen river. Suddenly, we are airborne, wind whipping through the partially open Plexiglas windows. For just a moment, as we bank away, Denali is suspended in the red frame triangle of my bike. I feel my stomach knot.

You're not good enough, the great mountain whispers. *This time, you go home. Next time, I'll grind your bones into powder. You'll die here.*

And then we are headed back to the start line, where I will catch a ride back to Anchorage. It will take four days for Monique to finish, and the trail will be strewn with thousands of dollars of mountain bikes, discarded by the owners in an attempt to just get to shelter. Later, another racer will ask me a strange question.

'Did you,' he asks tentatively at the race banquet, 'hear any voices out there on the trail?'

'What kind of voices?' I ask.

'You know,' he says awkwardly. 'Voices. Sometimes . . . people *hear* things out there.'

'I guess it happens,' I say.

21 Denali

'Hey you guys,' the driver of the small van is saying, 'There's your mountain!'

All eight of us – six climbers and two guides – lean to the left, giving the van the aspect of a small boat sloshing on open water. Out the left-side windows, shining in the May sunshine, is the towering bulk of Denali, still a hundred miles away.

'It's sumthin', huh?' says the driver.

We all agree, it's sumthin', all right.

After years of expectations, months of slogging through the Colorado backcountry pulling a sled, thousands of dollars on my battered credit cards, I'm in Alaska, on the way. Leading the way will be the main American Alpine Institute (AAI) guide, Steve Dunbar, who spends most of his summer doing search and rescue in Antarctica, and thusly has an interesting definition of cold. With him, on her first trip to Denali, is Angela Hawse, formerly of Outward Bound.

Talkeetna, in the shadow of Denali, strikes me as, say, Dodge City around the turn of the century. It's drizzling – common, since a mountain the size of Denali makes its own weather patterns – when we get to town. The few hundred 'real' residents of the log cabin slab front stores and bars are swollen by what appears to be a fashion show straight out of the pages of the Patagonia and North Face catalogs.

In the short season, from late April until the end of July, Talkeetna is filled with climbers from around the world. Everybody looks exactly like we look. Well, that's not quite true. There are actually two flavors. One group of climbers, *the newcomers*, looks exactly like us – brightly colored climbing shells, yellow and red predominating; matching pants; fetching fleece hats and sneakers for around town. The second flavor looks like us, except with all the happy edges sanded off. The color is faded from the shells; the pants patched with duct tape; the fetching fleece hat ragged and stinking of sweat and old sunscreen. Instead of excitement and plans, flavor two just looks tired. They eat a lot, too. In other words, it's not hard to tell whose been up and who's waiting to go up.

Our first stop is K2 Aviation, one of the several flight services that shuttles climbers between Talkeetna and the Kahiltna International Airport, where the landing strip that serves Base Camp is located. We're hoping for a chance to get to the mountain today.

Base Camp, though, is whited out, as the drizzle in Talkeetna has given way to screaming snow at eight thousand feet.

Our next stop is the ranger headquarters, a claustrophobic log cabin in 'downtown' Talkeetna, where we pay our $150 mountaineering program fee, sign in, and watch a short film that tells us 1) Denali is dangerous as all hell, and 2) to pick up after ourselves on the mountain.

Then it's back to K2, where we spend hours on the runway, checking and sorting gear, dividing bags of food and common gear, checking the tents, the medical equipment, the emergency radios, and assembling the sleds. It is one last chance to race to the mountaineering store in Talkeetna for the one last thing we forgot (which we will, in all likelihood, discard higher up to lighten the load on our sagging shoulders). It is one last chance to stock up on

Snickers bars (which are carried in amazing numbers at the Talkeetna general store); another chance to call home and assure spouses and friends that everything is fine.

If this sounds like a major undertaking, it is.

The difference between going up a big mountain, one of twenty thousand feet or more, and hiking in, say, the Rockies, is more than one of just degree of difficulty. It's possible – just barely, if you're a top mountaineer – to treat a twenty-thousand-foot mountain as a hike, but you do so only with dire risks. A big mountain is a world unto itself, a microplanet with its own atmosphere, its own gravity, its own natural laws. What works at sea level, what works at five thousand feet in the Blue Ridge Mountains, even what works at thirteen thousand feet in the Colorado Rockies, will not necessarily guarantee your survival on a big mountain. As befits a smaller planet, the weather is violent and wildly unpredictable, as if a visitor to that planet can run through spring, summer, fall, and winter in a single afternoon. Hurricane winds routinely scour the frozen landscapes, and they will remove a human presence as easily as a two-ton boulder.

Perhaps the greatest danger of the big mountains is the subtle blurring of subjective and objective dangers. As I've gone through The List, I've come to rely on the *subjective* and *objective analysis*. If you're walking down the street and a chunk of building lands on your head, that's an objective risk. Nothing you could have or should have done would have prepared you for being hit in the head by a flying gargoyle off a building. If, however, you are walking down the same street listening to your Walkman, not paying a bit of attention, and step in front of a bus, that's a subjective risk. You're just as squashed, but on the subjective risk you had some control. The game I've painfully learned is to access both risks, then focus my attention on the subjective ones, the ones I can change.

On a big mountain, the list of risks reads like a *Who's Who* (or *What's What*) of ways to die. There is the weather – the storms, the cold, the wind – avalanches, crevasses, climbing falls, failure or loss of equipment, diseases of altitude and exhaustion, and a host of minor horsemen. All of these are aggravated by the undeniable fact that, as you climb higher, you are not thinking quite as clearly as you are at sea level. As with diving deep on air, just when you need your brain to be the clearest its ever been, it is slogging through a marsh of poorly understood chemical reactions, misfiring and sputtering. The greatest threat of the big mountains is that first they blunt our most important survival tool.

And Denali is more dangerous still.

Like the Florida alligator the neighborhood kids feed, Denali's accessibility has bred, if not contempt, at least complacency. After all, the Himalayan peaks are off in some mysterious, mythical country; the South American giants are buried in the heart of the rain forests. But on a good day, you can see Denali from downtown Anchorage. Every climbing season is full of Denali firsts – the first summiteer under thirteen years old; the first blind climber; the first All-This or All-That team to make the summit. At times, in fact, the great mountain has almost a circus air about it, with Talkeetna and the McKinley Base Camp jammed with people from all over the world, partying heartily, while the summit smiles down benignly from 20,320 feet.

That belies the simple fact, as restated by *Anchorage Daily News* reporter Craig Medred, who has made a career of observing the mountain and its people, 'On the average, one out of every 100 people who head up McKinley die.'

That particular number refuses to go away.

In the cold drizzle of Talkeetna, I pause at the Climbers' Memorial, a tiny graveyard to mark the names of the climbers lost on the great mountain. Some of the names are familiar to me; some just names inscribed in stone. The newest name, from a week ago, has yet to be added, and it is a given that by the end of the climbing season, there will be more. Before I come down from the mountain, there will be more.

'Subarctic Mt. McKinley, 63 degrees north of the equator, rises out of a sprawling web of glaciers whose tongues push into the lowlands to an elevation of 1,000 feet,' writes Glenn Randall, in *Mount McKinley Climber's Handbook.* 'In the Himalayas, at the latitude of Miami, the glaciers extend only down to 13,500 feet. The climate only halfway to McKinley's summit is as severe as the North Pole's. Nighttime temperatures two-thirds of the way up McKinley frequently hit 30 degrees below zero during May, the peak climbing season. Not until Himalayan climbers are nearly twice that high do they experience such extremes. The northern latitude means that the oxygen content in the air on McKinley's summit is equivalent to the oxygen available on the summit of a Himalayan peak that is 800 to 1,500 feet higher . . .'

On the other hand, as Frances D. Chamberlain, the second woman to climb the mountain, noted in 1963, 'There are no mosquitoes . . .'

The six of us climbers – Tom Walker, Roger Kubly, Rich Davidson, Tommy Cary, Jimmy Chandler, and myself – spend what's left of the evening exploring Talkeetna, which takes about twenty minutes. Then we start our waiting game, watching it drizzle and periodically checking with K2 for conditions on the mountain.

Our plan, taken at its most general, is simple. As soon as there's a break in the weather up top, we'll load into K2's blood-red ski planes with all our gear and head for 7,200-foot-high Base Camp and the famous Kahiltna

International. Then, over the next two to three weeks, we'll walk the roughly 16 miles and 13,120 vertical feet to the summit.

Accomplishing this 'simple plan' will involve building five camps as we move up the mountain – Camp 1, at 8,500 feet; Camp 2, at 10,000 feet; Camp 3, at 11,000 feet; Camp 4, at 14,300 feet; and finally High Camp, Camp 5, at 17,200 feet. Ideally, this system will give us time to acclimatize to the altitude, and, just as important, to acclimatize to the mountain and to each other. We're carrying enough food, gas, tents, and miscellaneous supplies to last a team of eight people a month. Because the supplies weigh so much, we'll often spend days ferrying loads from one camp to the other, then returning to the lower camp to sleep. From the moment we leave Base Camp, our lives will begin narrowing in focus. Our individual identities as writer, doctor, engineer, pharmacist will give way to being either a member of rope team one – Steve's rope – or rope team two – Angela's rope. Our daily rhythms will become simple: carry, move, rest, wait.

After a day in Talkeetna and a last, long shower, Angela comes out of the wooden offices of K2.

'It's clear,' she says. 'Time to go.'

What follows is a frenzy of disassembly, stuffing, restuffing, and outright cramming as our disgusted bush pilot, who once flew F-16s, jams pieces of equipment into the four-seat, red Cessna that will ferry the first half of our party to Base Camp. Before I have a chance to clearly think, even start to put my thoughts in order, I'm crammed, complete with my survival gear should we crash, into the right-hand rear seat, and the little plane is sluggishly snarling and growling its way down the runway, then shifting its aim to the gray-clouded sky.

'Where y'all from?' the pilot asks perfunctorily as the little plane pops through the cloudbase into the bright sunshine at 10,000 feet. We answer – 'Colorado,' 'New Mexico,' 'California' – but we're not paying attention. Instead, we are all riveted on the jagged whiteness of the Alaska Range, literally the shattered edge of a continent, pushed up by the cataclysmic collision of the Pacific continental plate and the American plate sixty-five million years ago. Through the front windscreen, off to the right, Denali stands above Mt. Foraker and Mt. Hunter. Soft snow, spindrift, curls in a long comma from the summit.

'Blowin' up there,' says the pilot. 'Not a good day to be on top.'

I try to imagine what it must be like on top, the screaming winds approaching hurricane force, creating a chill so low that it no longer makes any sense – *thirty below, forty below, sixty below.* I try to imagine the wind pulling and tearing, scouring and biting, looking for the tiniest piece of exposed, fragile flesh. But the images fade quickly – insufficient data. Instead, I just stare at the Great God of the North, its massive ice floes the color of hammered gold in the afternoon light.

I've come, I think, incredulously. I can't take my eyes off the mountain.

The pilot points out a dot at the end of one of the glaciers.

'Kahiltna International,' he says.

The dot rapidly disassembles into a ragtag collection of multicolored tents, bamboo pendants, and a line of cones marking the 'runway,' an uphill icy slope.

'Hang on,' our pilot says, and he noses the red plane toward the first cone. At least the afternoon light is good. Sometimes, the pilot has mentioned, when the light is really flat, it's hard to know exactly where the ground is. So the plan is then to get the plane to where the ground more or less has to be, then cut the power. This makes for, he says, an exciting landing. The engine screams as first one ski, then the other hits the ice, and the plane skates to an uphill stop, turning 180 degrees for its downhill takeoff.

'Hurry,' the pilot says as someone outside takes off the right-hand door. We clamber out and start stacking equipment to the side of the plane. As soon as the last ice ax and ski pole are out, the door is put back on, latched, and the little red plane heads downhill to a shaky takeoff.

Within minutes, the plane is gone, and the only sound is the wind.

Sixteen miles away, the summit of Denali, surrounded by a crown of light, beams down at us. It is, says one of my partners, like being in God's own cathedral. That particular illusion is dispelled quickly when a huge chunk of Mt. Hunter, just a few miles away, lets go, tons and tons of snow tumbling onto the glacier. Within seconds, the echoing thunder of the avalanche reaches us.

'That was a good one,' says Angela.

Up the slope is the ragtag collection of two dozen or so tents that forms Base Camp. A couple of the tents are permanent, but most are expeditions either waiting for the next plane off or waiting for the weather to calm so they can start up. All the tents are partially hidden by walls made of snow blocks. In the center of camp are the *caches*, holes dug deep and marked with the ubiquitous bamboo poles. The caches hold extra food for the return and gear that doesn't go up the mountain. The bamboo poles marking the caches are also marked with the name of the expedition and the expected return date. If your cache has been sitting around for a couple of months unclaimed, people start to get worried.

The caches are dug deep because of the ravens, huge, magnificent black birds with the ability to dig deep and rip canvas haul bags to little pieces. More than one expedition, we are told, has come back looking forward to extra food and extra clothes in the cache, only to find shreds of 'miracle fibers' and the empty wrappers of candy bars littering the snow. If you don't presently believe ravens are messengers from the underworld, you will after an incident like that.

We begin hauling the gear from the hill to an abandoned tent platform.

'Level it out,' says Steve. 'Then let's build some walls.'

Thus begins a routine that will eventually become as reflexive as walking into a room and turning on a light. The leveling is easy enough – shovel and ax; chip the ice and use the shovel to take off the rough edges. Stomp around until the platform is flat and level. Next we take handsaws, find an area of firm snow, scrape off the powder, and begin cutting roughly two-foot-by-one-foot blocks in the snow. We use a shovel to pry the blocks out of the snow. Then we build a wall, just like a New England farmer tracking stones.

It is bright and sunny, and in no time we are stripped to T-shirts and long underwear bottoms, sweating like pigs, building a snow fortress. The walls rise quickly, and when they get a little more than four feet high, Steve calls a halt to the quarrying, and we begin pitching tents.

At first, I am self-consciously clumsy. Of the team, I have by far and away the least experience. Everyone else has at least one big mountain, and most members have several under their belts. Pitching winter camp is second nature to them; for me, it's trying to visualize the instruction sheet I used to put this exact same tent together on my front porch, with the temperature a bitter seventy-two degrees.

But eventually the tents are set; my dreadfully expensive Marmot down sleeping bag, which I came to believe in during the Iditabike, is *lofting*, fluffing up after being compressed all day, and our first dinner on the mountain is done.

This is not so bad, I think to myself, crawling into the bag as the temperature heads toward the big zero.

Shows what I know.

We wake early, both from anticipation and the drone of the ski planes landing more climbers. It is still sunny and bright. I hike up to one of the great conveniences of Base Camp, a plywood throne toilet, built over a deep hole in the ice, where you can do your business while looking across the camp at some of the most spectacular real estate on the planet. There are a couple of us waiting in line, tactfully staring in the opposite direction, when a Korean climber hikes up. His jacket is patched with a long stretch of silver duct tape, his hair matted to his head, his lips burned from the sun and festering. He looks like he's been in a war. We step off the trail and let the climber make his way to the front of the line.

'How was it?' another person in line asks.

The Korean climber stops for a moment as if pondering, then resumes his hike to the toilet.

'Cold,' he says back over his shoulder. 'Very cold.'

We begin breaking down camp and loading our packs and sleds for the first day. Base Camp is almost empty – most of the teams have taken advantage of this break in the weather and headed up. A few teams make their way down from the higher camps to Base Camp. As we watch, one team struggles up the nasty, small hill to Base Camp until they're within about a hundred yards of the first tents. Then they just stop, as if the batteries have all finally run down to zero. Some people from camp hike down to them with energy drinks and warm water to get them restarted for the final steps.

My rope includes Angela, the guide, who will lead; Tom Walker, an engineer for an oil company in California; Rich Davidson, yet another engineer, this one from Los Alamos,

New Mexico; and me. Tom, in his early thirties, has been on big mountains in South America, and Rich – forty-five, my age – has climbed throughout the world for the better part of two decades.

Basically, we line up like sled dogs. The main rope is knotted and clipped to our climbing harnesses around our waists. Our two prusiks, in case we fall into a crevasse, are attached to the climbing harness and the rope. The sled has its own harness, connected to it by five-foot aluminum poles, which go on over the climbing harness. My sled has somehow arrived without poles, so it's tethered to my climbing harness with lengths of parachute cord. For this first day, we'll be carrying everything – all the food, fuel, climbing gear, bamboo poles to mark our way, stoves, spares, everything – the six miles uphill to Camp 1. My share of 'everything' comes to around eighty or ninety pounds in the sled. My personal pack, a giant expedition pack from Lowe Alpine, is also stuffed to the gills with my own gear and whatever joint gear I can cram in. It weighs in at sixty pounds. Between the sled and the pack, I feel as if a high school student is perching on the small of my back.

'Well,' says the ever-cheerful Steve, 'let's go.'

It's hard to explain the feelings that come with actually stepping off. The anticipation mixes with the low-level buzz of the fear, all dwarfed by the gargantuan scale of the Alaska Range. The further you hike, the smaller you get, as if you have entered a room built for giants. Around us, the sun sparkles off the snow. The ice falls shade through all the colors of semiprecious gems, the deep, clear blue of amethyst or the amber, cat-eye yellow of topaz, a hint of pale green emerald. The snow crunches under our boots, and often in the distance avalanches thunder.

I would like to tell you the hours pass quickly in this

great cathedral, but the fact is the hours pass a slow sixty minutes, one at a time. The sled inexorably pulls at the waist, while the straps of even the best-adjusted pack gnaw into the muscles of the shoulder. It is blistering hot in the sun – all our exposed skin is slathered with sunscreen, the consistency and thickness of latex paint. And, when the sun drops behind a cloud, it is freezing cold. Sometimes I listen to the radio, tuned into an Anchorage headbanger heavy metal station that seems to defy the mountain. Sometimes, I just walk, concentrating on shutting my brain off.

Six or seven hours later, dizzy with exhaustion, we see a small cluster of tents off to the right of the trail, at the base of a steep hill.

Camp 1.

It takes two hours to dig our tent platforms, reinforce and build walls, and get the tents, including our cook tent, erected. It had started snowing a few hours back, and by the time we finish camp, it is seriously coming down. After a quick supper, we dive into our tents and bags. I close my eyes, and in my head I'm still walking. I walk until I finally fall asleep.

The next day is a carry day. Camp 2 isn't that far away in miles, but it's almost two thousand feet higher. To acclimatize to the altitude, and to ease the load on our bodies, we'll take a majority of our supplies up to within a few hundred feet of the campsite, bury them, then return to Camp 1 to spend the night. The next day, we'll strike camp and move to Camp 2.

We harness up early, the snow having broken in the night, and move out.

Somehow, I imagine that the lightened load, probably a hundred pounds total (a *junior* high student on my back), will make a substantial difference in the day's overall pain index. I have, of course, failed to factor in the increasing steepness of the trail. We are, after all, climbing a mountain, and by definition the trail goes *up*.

So does the pain index.

A member of a rope team doesn't have the luxury of a solo hiker. A solo hiker can control the pace, slow it down to a barely moving crawl or plop down on a rock and wait for either breath or inspiration, whichever comes first. A rope team, though, has to keep moving, even if it's at the pace of the slowest – me – member. On any big mountain, and especially Denali, good weather is a gift. No, make that a *loan*, to be withdrawn by any whim at any time. As long as the weather holds, we need to move, and move as quickly as we can. Breaks are measured out like water in the desert – at least, it seems that way to us, slow climbers that we are.

'Does this seem worse than yesterday?' Rich, my tent-mate, asks during a break. I am too tired to speak. I just nod. 'I thought so,' he says. 'I'm glad it's not just me.'

At 9,700 feet, Steve takes a look at the two ropes, then points out a cache site. In record time, we dig the holes, stash the supplies, stick in the bamboo markers, and head back down the hill. After a quick supper, we're asleep in record time, as well.

Things, including our spirits, begin picking up the next morning. I think it's the mental realization that we all are actually stuck on this mountain, and we have the proverbial long way to go. It has taken a few days for all the concerns and worries of day-to-day life in the lowlands to be scrubbed away by the snow. From my own point of view as an avowed nonathlete, it has taken my body a few days to get used to the idea that this pain is going to last a long time, so get used to it. Everything else on The List has been an event of a relatively short duration. I've become confident negotiating with my body – *Okay, guys, we're going to need six hard hours of output, then it's Snickers and beer* ... The mountain is different. Each day's output has been low intensity, but relentless, the extremes of heat and cold, the altitude, the heavy load – the fear – conspiring to sap strength. But I am constantly amazed by the body's ability to adapt and to persevere.

We move quickly to Camp 2, carry the next day, then move to the 11,000-foot camp the following day. Superlatives fail in the great cathedral of the mountain. We hike alongside ice falls of shifting colors, through landscapes carved of rock and hard blue ice. We're still using ski poles; it's not steep enough for the ice axes yet. At one point, I place my pole, then lift it, and look down through the hole into the dark green caverns of a huge crevasse. We hike on bridges of snow and ice, the summit of Denali emerging from its cloudy crown for minutes and sometimes hours. We hike along with other teams, talk about preparations, other mountains, plans. The mountain seems benign, even friendly, and we are lulled by its beauty.

We arrive at Camp 3 in the bright sunshine to find a stupendous series of five tent platforms unoccupied. It looks like a bunch of kids have created snow castles, connected by mazes. There's even a 'bathroom,' a small room walled on three sides. I promptly dub the camp Fortress Denali and we set to work digging in the camp. Rich and I decide to take the farthest platform, near the edge of a crevasse. Although the walls are a sturdy three feet high, we decide (fueled by the fact that it's a beautiful day) to dig the platform a little deeper and get the walls up to at least five feet. After a few hours of work, Fortress Denali is something to behold. Our platform has five-foot walls, benches for seating, plenty of room inside the walls for gear, and a convenient side entrance to the bathroom. We decorate Fortress Denali with minarets of carved snow blocks, the entrance minaret festooned with a happy face of M&Ms. We finish just in time for the afternoon snowstorm, the clouds rising up from the lowlands like some huge flying saucer. We talk about the coming climb.

The great rock headwall of Denali, the steepest part of the climb, is just above Camp 4, only a few days away. I have thought about the headwall for years, its fifty- to sixty-degree slopes of snow and ice, climbers moving slowly, a step at a time, up the ropes fixed in place. I have imagined myself stepping onto the top of the headwall, the world below me, the summit just an arm's length – well, a day – away.

'I'm worried about the headwall,' says one of the other climbers. 'It scares the hell out of me.'

We'll spend three days in Fortress Denali, including a rest day. We're just pleased as punch.

The weather is deteriorating.

Up high, we're told by a passing ranger, it's a nightmare of high winds and stunning cold. Only four people have summited so far this season, and, as we know, one has died on the way down. Teams are trapped higher on the mountain, waiting for a weather break to move up or down. Worse for us, a weather system is forming around the mountain. The eight o'clock evening weather report, delivered by Annie, the flight controller at Base Camp, is for more of the clear, cold weather we've had, but even Annie calls the weather report 'bogus.'

The weather gets progressively worse during our rest day; the mountain starts to show its teeth. The snow approaches whiteout conditions for a while, then lets up. Steve decides that it's critical to carry to Camp 4, a much tougher climb than the hikes we've been doing, the next morning if the weather breaks at all.

Even worse for me, my tentmate is running a fever and starting to cough badly. It is, he thinks, a respiratory infection he has brought with him to the mountain that has blossomed in the thin air. Dr. Jim, Jim Chandler from Alabama, on Steve's rope, concurs. It goes without saying that the higher you go, the less your body is able to repair itself. Instead, the body has to throw its not insubstantial forces into maintaining heat and acclimatizing to the altitude. Listening to Rich cough scares the hell out of me. I know I'm susceptible to acute mountain sickness (AMS) – I found the unfortunate proof of that during my débâcle bicycling on Mammoth Mountain at a paltry twelve thousand feet. Because of Denali's reduced oxygen because of its position near the Arctic Circle, we are at the equivalent of 12,000 feet already.

While the symptoms of AMS – fatigue, headaches, insomnia, lack of appetite, and nausea – are bad enough in and of themselves, to me the real danger is that AMS is often a precursor to the high-altitude killers, pulmonary and cerebral edema. In the pulmonary variety, there is an increase in the fluids in the lungs; in cerebral edema, there is an increase in the fluid surrounding the brain. The pulmonary variety is by far the most common.

'The unpredictable nature of HAPE, high altitude pulmonary edema, is that anyone sleeping above 12,000 feet is a potential victim,' writes Jonathan Waterman in his classic book *Surviving Denali*, which we have all just about committed to memory. '[It] is dangerous because of its rapid onset. Because if it isn't diagnosed in its early stages, HAPE often reaches life-threatening proportions within hours.'

The only cure is to descend, and descend quickly.

There is one other fact that we have all learned: chest infections predispose a person to HAPE.

Rich coughs steadily all night.

The weather breaks in the morning, but Steve is still worried.

'We're going to have to push the pace a little,' he says.

'We have to be through Windy Corner before the weather turns.'

Windy Corner is exactly that, a rocky corner, jutting out like the bow of a ship, at around thirteen thousand feet. In a storm, Windy Corner, with its high exposure and howling winds, will be just about the worst place to be.

We have, I think, *crossed a threshold here*. The trail from Camp 3 to Camp 4 is steeper, more exposed. A fall along parts of this trail can have serious consequences. Instead of ski poles and snowshoes, we'll be moving on *crampons* – spikes that lace to the bottom of our plastic mountaineering boots – and carrying our ice axes. The axes are the mountaineer's last-ditch survival tool – we've practiced over and over again falling, then jamming the sharp tip of the ax into the ice or snow, to catch the fall.

Self-arrest. I remember my ice climbing instructor's comment on self-arrest, when I asked her how well it worked on hard blue ice. 'Well,' she said, 'if it doesn't, at least you've got something to do in those closing seconds of your life.'

The terrain between the two camps is heavily crevassed. 'If we're going to have a crevasse fall,' says Steve, 'we're probably going to have it here.'

We rope in and head up Motorcycle Hill, just outside of camp. How the hill got its name is a little vague, but I would give just about anything for a motorized trip up it. It's about as steep as a black diamond ski run (*Thank you, Ilg!*) and covered with a thick layer of powder over ice. We crunch our way up at a slow pace, but one that's more of a toll on us than any of the previous days. The hill is deceptive. Each time we get to what looks like a flat spot – a respite – the trail gets steeper. I finally manage to shut off my brain and concentrate on putting one spiked foot in front of the other, staring down, watching the rope ahead of me move.

After a minor lifetime, we crest the hill, only to see the trail turn, every bit as steep.

'Guys, over the next section we're going to be on hard ice,' Steve says. 'I'm going to need you to move fast, but move very, very carefully. Some of these places, it's a long way down.'

We start up again. The trail is now hard, blue ice covered with snow. Each step is deliberate – *set the ax, step, step . . . set the ax, step, step . . . faster now, but no less deliberate*. It's still sunny when we finally round the corner that gives us a view of Windy Corner, but there are clouds building.

'Quick break,' says Steve, 'then back to it.'

The hours drag on as we start the steep hike up to Windy Corner. At one point, the trail runs near high ridges, their tops thick with snow. Angela points at the accumulation of snow hundreds of feet above our heads.

'We don't want to spend too much time here,' she says. As if on cue, there is a crack, and on the ridgeline the snow starts to slide.

'Shit!' Angela says, and starts to sprint away. But there's no place to go.

'It's okay!' Steve shouts over the thunder of the avalanche. 'We're too far away! We're clear!' The avalanche crashes into the soft snow a few hundred yards from the trail, and the powder absorbs the tons of snow. A blast of freezing wind and grit pummels us. I wipe the cold, wet grit from my face.

'Let's get the hell out of here,' says Angela, and we all heartily agree.

The first flakes of snow start falling as we near the Corner itself, and by the time we round the rock prow, it is snowing hard. After a quick break in the shadow of the prow, we head on.

The next section of the mountain comes to me in

dreams sometimes, and I'm no longer sure how much is memory and how much is myth of my own making. Here is what I think I remember: It is snowing, but the wind has died off, leaving the mountain as still and as quiet as a Christmas morning in the country. We are entering a maze of crevasses, the trail twists and turns like a frozen python, moving up and down over bridges of indeterminate thickness. The entrance to the crevasse field is a steep traverse along a frozen hillside. The hill slopes about forty to fifty degrees; hard, blue ice. To the right of the trail is a drop into a series of crevasses; to the left, the steep ice. The trail narrows to the width of a mountaineering boot.

'Make sure you've always got three points of contact with the ice,' Angela is saying, 'before you move. Be careful not to hang a crampon point in your gaiters when you step.'

The entrance to the crevasse field is silent, ethereal, the snow muffling even the hint of sound. The light is diffused as well, a soft, gray light that seems to glow around us. We are in the clouds. As we step onto the ice traverse, our sleds drop down the slope, sixty-pound pendulums pulling us toward the crevasses. With each step, the sled swings. Within a few steps, sweat is pouring off my body. My face is drenched. I try to set the butt of my ax, but it refuses to bite in the hard ice. Instead, I slip it into a hole left by another climber. Even the rasping of our breath is absorbed by the stillness. Landmarks vanish into the gray, until we are moving in a tunnel disconnected from time and space, placing one foot in front of the next, moving the ax, feeling the weights swing against our hips. The trail widens slightly, and I see ahead the outlines of snow bridges as the trail winds over the yawning crevasses.

'Keep the ropes tight!' shouts Steve, his voice flat and clipped.

It is like we're moving over a frozen Japanese garden, white bridges spanning sculpted streams of ice. I look down from a bridge, and see only gray, endless gray. I am as afraid as I've ever been in my life, and not just for my body.

This is where The List has brought me, I think, *to balance in the gray between heaven and hell. I am moving through the Burial Grounds.*

The trail turns, and finally climbs out of the crevasse field, away from the Burial Grounds. Everyone, I realize, is spooked.

'Whew!' says one of the other climbers.

'Gods died there,' someone else says, and I nod.

I will go through the Burial Grounds three more times, and even in the bright sunshine, the hairs on the back of my neck will stand up, and I will keep my eyes down.

Once, I will punch through into a crevasse, feel my right leg crash through a snow bridge, then swing around over . . . nothing. I will very slowly pull my leg out of the hole, hoping I can preserve the integrity of the snow bridge by sheer force of will. The bridge will hold.

We're excited when we get back to Camp 3. Tomorrow morning, we'll head back up. It will be hard, but we're moving now.

The storm hits that night, the winds ripping through Fortress Denali. With the wind comes the snow. For the next four days, it snows and it snows and it snows. At night the wind is so bad we resort to earplugs just to get a little sleep. The tent shakes and pops and snaps as the winds look for a tear, a pinhole, a way in, a way at us. The storm usually breaks in the morning for a few hours – though Steve says trying to move in the holes would be suicide. We watch one team start up Motorcycle Hill, only to retreat when a member falls waist-deep into an unmarked crevasse. A pair from Norway who've been sharing our cook tent try to move their camp to twelve thousand feet. The relentless winds hammer their tent to shreds, and they're forced to bury their remaining equipment, retreat back to Camp 3, and hole up in the cook tent, in amazingly good spirits at just being alive.

Mostly we dig. The snow is piling up in great white drifts, and we need to keep its weight off the tents. Our lives have gotten even simpler – eat, dig, wait.

I wake up one morning with a nagging headache. My throat is sore, and before I can catch myself, I have a fit of coughing.

Damn! Oh damn.

Rich and I are asleep, but like dogs, we wake up seconds before the earthquake hits.

'What is it? What is it?' says Rich, and I don't know. We're both looking around frantically, as if we can identify what fox has gotten into the hen house. Within seconds, a snowpack lifts and drops. Outside, despite the wind, we can hear the heavily loaded snow cornices let go and thunder down.

'Are we dead?' Rich asks.

'Give it a minute,' I say. 'I don't think the verdict is in yet.'

We sit up in our sleeping bags and listen as the avalanches subside, and then there is nothing left but the wind. I fall back into a fitful sleep, punctuated by deep, racking coughs.

By the third day of the storm, Fortress Denali has fallen. The snow is now level with the walls, and the entire tent platform has filled up. Five or six feet of snow. The top of the tent is a few inches below the new snowline. Part of our nightly ritual is clearing the tent vents so the air doesn't go sour – 'I know if you're snoring, the air's okay,' Rich, who's worried that we'll finally be entombed in Fortress Denali, tells me one morning. In the morning, we burrow up, out of the tent, grab the shovels, and start digging. Once we've got the tent shoveled clear, we dig a path to the bathroom, dig out the bathroom – in other words, uncover our plastic bag – dig a path to the cook tent, dig a path to the other tents. All around us, we can see members of the other teams doing exactly the same thing.

Then we lay in our tents during the storm's many lulls, reading whatever we can get our hands on and waiting for the winds to come roaring back.

At one point, Mimi, my instructor from Ouray, shows up at the tent flap at about three in the morning.

'You in there, Michael?' she shouts.

'Where else?' I say.

'Listen,' she starts. Mimi has been trapped with another party of AAI climbers at High Camp, 17,200 feet, for a week. As soon as the weather broke, they headed down. 'I'm sorry about the sled.'

It's three in the morning.

'Mimi,' I answer, 'what on earth are you talking about?'

'The sled. If I'd known how miserable it was to pull, I'd have never made you pull my stuff all over Colorado.'

'It's okay,' I say. 'Honest.'

She straightens up, then blurts, 'I hate this mountain.' She adds in a rush, 'I hate the weather. I hate being sick. I'm lucky to get off it with my life . . .' She pauses. 'I guess I shouldn't be saying this to you, huh?'

'It's okay,' I say. 'I'm beginning to feel the same way.'

The next morning, as the storm wanes, I gather up all my notes and letters and seal them in a plastic bag with a note, which reads, 'Attention! In the event of an accident, please forward the enclosed material to . . .'

When the storm finally breaks, two more AAI guides, who've been climbing a different route, show up with grim news. They discovered the frozen bodies of three climbers, just off the trail near Windy Corner. At least three other teams are coming down with cases of serious frostbite and exhaustion from fighting the storm. The mountain has shown its fangs.

'We have to move now,' Steve says. 'Our food and fuel is shrinking from being trapped. The weather's all over the place. We've got a break now, and we have to take it.'

We break camp, dig the sleds out of five feet of snow and start packing. I am feverish, with a nagging headache that won't seem to go away. I wake up feeling okay, but after three steps, I'm profoundly exhausted. I'm hardly sleeping and my appetite has slipped away. I file the symptoms away. There's nowhere to go; nothing to be done for it.

As soon as we are harnessed up, we have to break again. Dr Jim is sick – AMS – too exhausted to continue. Angela separates herself from the rope to take him down.

'It's like the worst case of flu I've ever had in my life,' Dr Jim tells me. He seems on the verge of tears 'I'm so sick.'

I pat him on the shoulder as another coughing fit rumbles up in my chest. I know what he means.

If the trip to Camp 4 was hard before, it's a living, breathing nightmare now. By halfway up Motorcycle Hill I am exhausted enough to want to just lay down in the snow, just close my eyes for a few minutes. I am burning up, dehydrated, scooping handfuls of snow into my mouth whenever I get the chance. With every step, I feel worse and worse. I imagine my body's defenses trying desperately to wage war on two fronts, fighting the infection, fighting the mountain sickness, losing on both. I know that at four-

245

teen thousand feet the body no longer has the resources to heal itself; at twenty degrees, thirty degrees below zero all the body's energies will go into making heat, shoveling whatever mean coal is left into the waiting furnace. My mind drifts, then snaps back. I have a long conversation with Ilg, who is telling me that I've forgotten that this is all a dance; that I can't dance with lead feet. *Run, Michael,* he is shouting at me. *Run up!* I wish that I had a phone, so I could call my friend Roger, Roger the windsurfer, from a hundred years ago, and tell him that I was on The Mountain, that I had let a list on a scrap of cocktail napkin lead me to some god-awful frozen place . . .

And I snap back. We are halfway up the hill to Windy Corner, and Rich, behind me on the rope, is talking. 'You're doing great,' he is saying. 'We're getting there.' My gratefulness for those words is all out of any sense of proportion.

We hear a helicopter, and above us the high altitude rescue copter is pulling the bodies of the dead climbers. Hanging from the skid of the fragile dragonfly chopper, a brightly colored package spins at the end of fifty feet of climbing rope.

'Gentlemen,' says Steve, watching the package spin in the sunshine. 'You cannot make any mistakes. None.'

I go through the Burial Grounds in a haze of pain and mind-numbing exhaustion. *I simply cannot be so tired, so shot. I am in good shape; I am strong; I have been in the field, damnit, and if I just . . . put . . . my . . . mind . . . to . . . it, I can make the pain go away.*

One leaden step after another.

It's snowing by the time we reach the cache, which, thanks to its location, is in relatively good shape. We add the weight of the food in the cache and make the last push into Camp 4. When we get there, ten hours after we started, the sun has already dropped behind a peak, and the wind has come up. It is stunningly cold. It takes forever to dig out the platform, forever to get the tents erected, forever to eat a quick supper. Steve asks me to share his tent, so he can listen to me cough. I feel so bad that I can't even bring myself to read today's note, part of the twenty-one-card package Denise has given me for the trip. It is simply too great an effort.

Morning, and welcome to Camp 4, the polyglot, totally international base at the foot of the great headwall. A Russian who's been on Everest stops by for tea; an Englishman, who remembers our tents from Camp 2, sticks his head in to see how we're making it. This is, he says, his third attempt to reach the Denali summit.

'You know,' he says, 'it gets better as you go along. The first time I came here, I was scared all the time – every morning, every hour, every minute. There are just so damn many ways to die here.'

We are above most of the world here. There is a ranger tent and a medical tent, where various climber/doctors study the deleterious effects of altitude on people. There are maybe a dozen campsites and most are occupied. There are even two 'thrones.' All the conveniences of home, plus a view.

Behind us, the headwall towers 1,300 feet over the camp. I can't not look at it – it draws my eyes, captures and holds my mind. I spend most of the day resting – I get a day off while the guys retrieve the rest of the cache.

We laugh and joke, have an early supper. Roger prays for those who were lost in the storm. '*Inshallah*,' says Tommy, who's put in time in the Middle East. As God wills it.

For me, sleep has vanished, is a memory. I am alternately cold – even in the bag, wearing long underwear and fleece pants and shirt, a silk face mask, gloves, and

247

two pairs of socks – then washed by waves of heat. My toes feel like blocks of ice. I bury my face in the wadded-up jacket that serves as my pillow, stifling the coughs in piles of fleece.

Listen, I find myself saying to my body, negotiating. *I know it's been bad ... I know we're doing our best. But I'm going to ask one more thing. Give me the headwall. Give me one more day.*

One more day.

In my head, I see the summit slipping into the mists, away from my outstretched arm. I feel the weight of the headwall, above my head.

One more day, I ask fervently, feverishly, maybe even prayerfully. *One more day.*

Around dawn, I fall into a brief, deep sleep. When I wake up less than an hour later, it is with the absolute certainty that, on some cellular level, my body has voted, and today we will climb.

The first part of the climb up the headwall is a steep, steep hike up to the icy gully that leads to the top of the great wall. Then we hook our *Jumars* – sliders that go up, not down – into the fixed ropes, ropes that were set by another team a few seasons back, for the steepest part of the climb. The idea, of course, is that the rope is protection, to catch you if you fall.

'You might not want to fall on these ropes, guys,' says Steve. 'Since we didn't put them in, we don't know whether they'll hold a fall or not. My guess is not.'

My climbing is slow, but steady, like climbing a frozen, six-hundred-foot ladder. We don't have the sleds, thank goodness, but our packs are heavily loaded with supplies. It is snowing and bitterly cold, but I feel better than I have in days.

I remember a time windsurfing before The List. I'd gone

out late one afternoon, just before sunset on a big day. For some reason, I had the beach all to myself, not a soul around. I caught the wind just right, and I sailed until my shoulders ached and my legs cramped from the pressure of holding the board on course. And just before sunset, I caught one last gust, a long, carving ride across a yacht basin that seemed to go on forever. And I thought then that single ride was the best of me, that maybe a life could be captured and marked in a single line, carved on water.

I know now that the headwall is the best of me; that with each step up, each push of the Jumar, I am carving a single, fine line. There is rock and roll playing in my head, wind screaming around my face, and a rope above me stretching into the clouds.

And finally I am at the top of the last rope. I step onto the 'balcony,' almost seventeen thousand feet high. The clouds clear, and around me, below me, as in my imagination, my dreams, the world stretches. In one direction, further up the West Buttress, is the summit itself, achingly close. I want to reach out my hand, touch it, stand there. But I am reeling. *Remember our deal,* my body echoes.

'You okay?' says Steve. 'You looked a little shaky there.'

'No problem,' I say.

The rest is dénouement. I go down, stumbling back into Camp 4 on the last of my strength.

'Are you willing to go to the medical tent now?' Steve asks.

'Sure,' I say. 'I'll walk over there.' Our conversation is all very stiff, almost formal.

At the medical tent, Dr Colin Grissom, one of the experts on diseases of altitude, is going to tell me I have AMS. That diagnosis is going to end my climb.

'You've got AMS,' the doctor says. I nod.

Walking back to the tents, Steve and I joke and talk. Finally, he states the obvious.

'You know I can't take you up again,' he says. I nod. 'You've earned your shot at the summit, fair and square. But I can't take you up.'

Down is life; up is death. So simple, so black and white. I feel dead already, inside.

'I understand,' I say, and I do.

That night, the cough gets much worse. Sometime in the middle of the night, Steve begins talking.

'You have to go down in the morning,' he says. 'I have to take you.'

I am angry – I will not kill the rest of the teams' chances at the summit. They have all earned their shot, fair and square.

'You have to go down in the morning,' Steve says, calmly but firmly, as if he is talking to a recalcitrant child. 'It's your life we're talking about here.'

'The morning,' I say, coughing. 'Something will come up.'

And something does. At dawn, another guide shouts into our campsite – 'Somebody here looking for a ride down the mountain?'

I go down.

Five days later, with food and fuel almost gone, Steve, Tom Walker, Tommy Cary, and my tentmate, Rich Davidson, reach the summit of Denali and stand on the roof of the world.

In Base Camp, I learn the full extent of the storm. Camp 1 is buried under as much as twenty feet of snow, three have died, and there are numerous injuries. At one point, two ski planes flipped landing at Base Camp – luckily, no one was injured. But food and fuel have run so low that the bush pilots do food drops.

I am tired, bone tired, but the worst of the mountain sickness lifts as soon as I come down. I feel as if I am tethered to the mountain in some undefinable way, as if the line I carved on the headwall is still connected to my soul and will never be broken. Perhaps it won't. I hear talk in the camp of 'conquering,' of 'coming back and beating the bitch,' and I am puzzled.

There is, I think, *nothing here to conquer, nothing to beat. I have come here because of a list on a napkin in a pizza joint. I am not sure what I have found here, in the cold and the snow, but the great mountain no longer makes my stomach knot with fear. The fear is gone.*

In the morning, with the sound of the bush plane in the distance, I hike one more time to the throne. I have neither bathed nor shaved in twenty-one days. I stink so badly I can smell myself. My gloves are patched with duct tape and I am still coughing badly. There are two young Japanese climbers, fresh off the plane, ahead of me in line. To my surprise, they step off the trail and bow slightly, waiting for me to pass.

One smiles.

'How was it up there?' he asks.

I smile back.

'Cold,' I say. 'Very cold.'

And then I go home.

22 The Abyss

The mountain has left me tired and at odds, as if the best parts of me are still struggling in the snow at Camp 4. I feel a bone-weary exhaustion; a sense of failure like an endless, grinding mill wheel in my head. My sleep – in a bed; in the dark – is fitful, and I snap awake at the slightest provocation, my eyes wide open, waiting for the bite of the cold, the sound of the wind.

But it is warm and quiet in Colorado; the winds I hear are all in my head.

Maybe I could have pushed harder . . . maybe I should have started the anti-altitude sickness drugs sooner . . . Maybe if I'd just wanted it more . . .

'You didn't have a choice,' Rich Davidson tells me over the telephone one Saturday morning. 'The guide wouldn't have taken you up any higher. You were sick, man.'

And I am still sick; the mountain left its mark carved in little curlicues on my lungs. I am at a clinic, staring at my chest X-rays.

'See these curls,' the doctor is saying, pointing at a series of little curves, about the size of the end of a little finger's fingernail, on the film. 'That's the residue of your high altitude pulmonary edema.'

'Will it,' I ask, 'affect my scuba diving?'

He pauses, squeezes the bridge of his nose.

'When?' he asks.

'Couple of days,' I reply. I want to finish, to see The List done. I am too tired and too depressed to care much about anything except the schedule, and am only at the doctor under duress. I am too mentally exhausted to be afraid, to be nervous. I want to get on the plane tomorrow, fly to California, and dive, dive, dive.

'The day after tomorrow?' the doctor asks.

I nod.

'Well . . .' he starts, pauses, then starts again. 'I think you're committing suicide.'

'Great,' I say. 'What kind of risks are we talking about?'

'Not acceptable,' he says. 'Those little curved scarrings can trap air, and that trapped air can lead to an embolism. You're just asking for an embolism here.'

I go home and start making phone calls, looking for a second opinion that disagrees. Finally, a diving doctor from San Francisco sums it up neatly – 'Fifty-fifty,' he says when I ask for odds. 'That's stupid.'

I hang up, then call and cancel my deep dives. It's too late to even juggle the plane tickets, so I decide to go to California anyway and at least go through the academic portion of the mixed-gas diving course.

The first thing one notices about T. Wings Stock, who's going to be my instructor, is, well, his *wings*. Awesome, multicolored wings, tattooed wings, beginning at the wristbone of each arm and climbing to his not insubstantial biceps.

'Tell me about the wings,' I say, but he just shrugs it off.

'From a guy named Lyle Tuttle in San Francisco,' he says. 'It was a long time ago.' (He's only the most famous tattoo artist in the world.)

With his huge beard and bearlike frame, T. Wings Stock looks like a remnant from the Summer of Love. It's not hard to imagine him backstage at a Dead concert, maybe working the lights.

'He always gets mistaken for one of those guys in ZZ Top,' says Ani Stock, who followed her sweetheart from the midwest to the Bay area; who waited for him to come back from Vietnam; who waited at home while he drove a long-haul truck after the war. Along the way, Wings Stock discovered scuba and no matter how he sliced it, swimming around underwater looking at wrecks struck him as a lot more fun than permanent hemorrhoids. After discussions with Ani, Wings decided that he could indeed make a living as a diving instructor.

They settled in the California community of Santa Cruz, home of the Museum of Surfing and some of the finest surf on the West Coast. Santa Cruz also anchors the top of Catalina Bay, cold, clear, and deep, home of the vast, hypnotic underwater forests of kelp. While he loves the kelp and the otters and the endless, pesky seals, Wings reserves his strongest fascination for the shipwrecks that litter the sand bottom of the Pacific off Santa Cruz, Monterey, and down toward Santa Barbara.

Here's the thing about *wreckers* – they're all just a little twisted, sort of like pieces of iron and steel exposed to years and years of depth and current. Even the name has its own spin. Wreckers was the name originally given to the landlocked pirates of the early 1800s who lured ships to their deaths on rocky shoals. Key West even has a museum dedicated to the old wreckers. The new wreckers' goal is to visit many of those very ships that scattered their bones across the bottom. Almost everybody, when they start diving, spends at least a little time on wrecks, mostly because the wrecks themselves are artificial reefs, attracting all manner of blue fishes. My first wrecks were off the east coast of Florida, and I didn't get it. I mean, all that money and time, and we were looking at a sunken tugboat in fifty feet of water. This struck me as a little like paying a hundred dollars to visit your favorite wrecked car at the junkyard.

I started changing my opinion when David Feeney, my friend and dive instructor in New York City, invited me to Cape Hatteras the previous summer to spend five days diving the deeper wrecks of 'The Graveyard of the Atlantic.'

'You're up to it, right?' David asks.

'Sure,' I reply. *Now what*, I think.

First is a routine I've already gotten used to – the frenetic assembling of specialized equipment. My dive gear consists of a face mask and a pair of flippers, plus my wetsuit from Alcatraz. I figure I can get by with a computer, a tank, and a couple of regulators.

'Any suggestions?' I asked David.

'Get something that works,' he said.

'Good idea,' I replied.

Twenty phone calls, a couple of months, and about two thousand dollars later I find myself on the *Maggie II*, bouncing through rolling seas out into the Atlantic. At the helm is Captain Art Kirchner – Cap'n Artie – one of the legendary New Jersey wreckers and part of the expedition that recovered the ship's bell from the *Andrea Doria* (though I didn't know that at the time).

My primary focus is on not throwing up as the little boat, awash in diesel fumes, goes up and down and up and down and up and down. I've also noticed, as people have started laying out equipment, that there is a substantial difference between their equipment and my equipment, not the least of which is that they each have two tanks and I only have one.

Huuummmmm.

They also have drysuits, as opposed to my wetsuit. The dreadfully expensive drysuits insulate the body with a layer of air between the suit and the skin. A wetsuit, on the other hand, insulates by trapping a thin layer of water between the skin and the neoprene of the suit. The difference between a drysuit and a wetsuit, aside from the thousand dollars or so in price, is that the deeper you get in a wet-suit, the more the neoprene compresses and the less efficient the suit becomes – when you need it the most, the worse it works.

'You knew that, right?' says David.

'Of course,' I say, vaguely remembering something from scuba class, wishing now I'd paid more attention.

Two hours of bounce, and we are over the first wreck.

'We're probably going to build up some hang time,' David says conversationally.

I shrug, not wanting to let on how nervous I actually am. A few years before, one of the big diver certifying agencies made the statement that scuba diving is every bit as safe as bowling, and they had the numbers to prove it. Statistically, that may be true, but you can bowl your entire life and never once have to stand inside the door of the bowling alley watching your watch, counting the minutes until you can step into the street without bending over double in agony, being crippled, or just plain dropping dead.

That's decompression for you.

Most everybody who's spent any time watching *Sea Hunt* on television or renting and rerenting *The Abyss* has some kind of idea about the bends. Here's the deal: nothing has changed from Denali. People are still optimized to live at sea level. But as we go down instead of up, pressure increases instead of decreases. And it increases very quickly. At thirty-three feet of saltwater, we've added the weight of an entire other atmosphere to the one already

sitting on top of us. At sixty-six feet, there are three atmospheres of pressure weighing us down – two of water and
one of air. The deeper we go, the more those atmospheres
add up. Among the things happening to us physiologically
is that excess nitrogen is being forced into all our tissues
by the pressure. On surfacing, that excess nitrogen creates
bubbles, and unless we give those bubbles a chance to dis-
sipate – *decompress* – they can cause us great pain, cripple
us, or kill us. Or maybe not. Decompression sickness is
capricious; you can do everything wrong and not get a *hit*,
a bubble that lodges somewhere in your body.

Or you can do everything right and end up in a decompression chamber with a twenty-five-thousand-dollar bill
and a lot of serious pain.

The first mention of decompression sickness in scientific
literature comes from way back, all the way in 1670, when
scientist Robert Boyle looked into the eye of a snake he
had depressurized in a chamber and saw a bubble. He had
no idea what caused the bubble or what it meant, but he
dutifully recorded the fact. The first recorded cases in man
were in the mid-1800s, when doctors discovered that
French coal miners digging in the world's first pressurized
mine became ill when they left the pressurized environment, then got better when they returned to it. The nick-
name *bends* came from the unfortunate workers on the
Brooklyn Bridge in New York City. The caissons on the
bridge foundations were pressurized with compressed air
to hold back the water, and many of the workers got sick
when they left the caissons. As their coworkers twisted in
pain, the other workers, ever New Yorkers, noted that the
sufferers appeared to be mimicking a popular fashion pose,
the Grecian Bend. After that, everyone knew about the
bends.

If you decided to live underwater, all that dissolved
nitrogen wouldn't be a problem. Coming up, though, is the

problem. The pressure drops, and our bodies try to elimi-nate the excess nitrogen. Suffice it to say that if we do not come up at a fixed, slow rate, stopping at predetermined points to let the excess nitrogen be eliminated, bubbles will form and be carried through our bloodstream to all parts of the body. Using Doppler ultrasound, you can hear the bubbles crashing through the bloodstream, transparent boulders carried along in the turbulence, waiting to do their damage.

The dive, 150 feet, is deeper than I've gone before with lousy visibility, cold water, and currents. The whole dive, my stomach is knotted with fear. A constant list of things that can go wrong – and for which I am unprepared – runs through my head. I crawl along the bottom, alternately staring at the jumbled pile of metal that used to be a ship and my computer, which is tallying my *decompression penalty*, the time to the surface. It looks like the meter of a speeding taxicab.

I know that on the way up I will have to stop at various points, determined by my computer, to let the nitrogen go away. I know that if I *violate a stop*, go to the surface too soon, I could be in trouble. What I don't know could basically fill a boxcar, but ignorance, as they say, is bliss.

Finally, I head up. But I've racked up too much bottom time, and lack the experience (or the brains) to match my decompression time with the amount of air remaining in my tanks. At the thirty-foot decompression stop, it becomes obvious to me that my air is going to run out before my time, leaving me with a Hobson's choice. I have already used up the air in my main tank and am breathing from a smaller *pony* tank I have Velcroed on my backpack.

I still have about eight minutes of decompression time left when I notice that each suck on the regulator is bring-ing me less and less air. And then there is no suck left.

There is one tremendous rush of panic, as I suck frantically on the empty bottle. *I can't breathe ... breathe ... breathe!!!* The animal rattles the cage, shaking the bars, shrieking. A more distant part of my mind notes that I am twenty feet from the surface, don't have that much decompression time left, am not at that great a risk, and that there are three people on the anchorline just below me ...

The animal abruptly stops shaking the bars of the cage.

People below me? With air?

I crawl a few feet back down the line to the closest diver, then make the universal signal for 'out of air,' a hand slashed across the throat.

I can see him laughing in his mask.

I wonder what the universal sign for 'No, really, asshole!' is.

I signal again, and he shrugs, then hands me his *octopus*, a spare regulator on a separate long hose.

I take three quick breaths, my heart rate dropping below a thousand beats a minute, the animal in my head prying his clawed hands off the bars of the cage. I smile, signal 'okay,' then settle down to wait out the few remaining minutes.

The anchorline goes limp, cut from the wreck by a diver from the boat who thought we were done. Suddenly, we are free-floating, and I am underweighted – don't have enough lead to hold me at that depth. I take a quick look at my computer – three minutes left – take three deep breaths, hand back the octopus, wave bye-bye and head for the surface.

Not an optimal beginning. But I do resolve that, no matter what is on The List, I'm not going back to the abyss until I know what I am doing.

*

Three months later, I'm finally certified as safe to dive, and Wings and I have headed for Key West and the deep, deep wrecks that lie just outside the reef there. We're joined there by Michael Menduno, editor of *aquaCORP*, the technical dive journal, and technical instructor extraordinaire, Billy Deans.

It's obvious everyone is on Key West time except Wings and I.

'You'll get used to it,' says Menduno, as we pace around Key West Divers' small dock. The heat is like a warm, wet blanket, the air thick and chewy enough to gather into balls and bounce. Out on the lagoon, the water has taken on the gray silver sheen of a piece of oxidized aluminum, the color of an old dive tank.

'Come on,' Wings says, and we retreat to our rental car with the diving computer to run simulations.

Dive planning software is a relatively new addition to the already gadget-laden sport, but for technical diving, the simulations created by the software are almost indispensable. That's because, basically, there's a wing-and-a-prayer aspect to tech diving that its participants don't particularly like to hone up to.

'You diving mix?' Dr Bill Clem, the main hyperbaric specialist at Denver's Presbyterian/St. Luke's Hyperbaric Medicine Center, asked me before I went. When I said yes, he rubbed his hands together, looking for all the world like a happy kid. 'Great! You get to be part of the experiment! We'll see which decompression tables actually work.'

Tech divers like to point out – ad infinitum, I might add – that people have been breathing weird gases underwater for just about as long as people have been diving. According to Tom Mount and Bret Gilliam, two of the pioneers of extended-range diving and the de facto historians of the sport, the first speculations on using helium to replace part of the nitrogen in air came as early as 1919. Professor and inventor extraordinaire Elihu Thompson suggested that nitrogen narcosis could be avoided if the inert gas helium was added to the mix. Unfortunately, helium at the time was twenty-five hundred dollars a cubic foot, making Thompson, who had merged with Thomas Edison's company to form General Electric, about the only person in the United States who could afford the stuff.

The Navy experimented with *heliox*, a mixture of helium and nitrogen for years, and numerous depth records were set with the mixed gases. But Jacques Cousteau's scuba pretty much changed all that. Most of the use of mixed gases were for divers wearing those funny *20,000 Leagues Under the Sea* outfits, with a long hose running up to the surface. *Scuba* – Self-Contained Underwater Breathing Apparatus – meant that the clunky suits with the tethers were passé. Throw on a couple of tanks and a mask, add some fins, and away you swim with the fishes. Compressed air became the gas of choice for scuba for a very simple reason – it's easy to compress air. Cheap, too.

The catch, of course, is narcosis. I'd already visited Narcosis World in Hal Watts's Florida sinkhole, felt the waves of nausea, the 'whirlies,' mental processes slowed to the speed of gooey fudge.

'The difference between diving deep on air and diving deep on mixed gas,' says Gary Gentile, perhaps the foremost deep-wreck diver in the world, 'is that on the mixed gas, you get to remember what you saw.'

Of course, as Bill Clem pointed out, you also get to be part of the experiment.

The gas of choice is called *trimix*, a blend that replaces as much as fifty percent of the nitrogen in the air with helium. The lesser nitrogen content makes a dive to 300 feet seem more like a dive to 150 feet, narcosis-wise.

'You will be amazed at how clear your head is at depth,'

Wings tells me. 'You'll also talk like Daffy Duck on the surface.'

Getting to dive with trimix isn't, I discovered, all that easy. The certification procedure is long, arduous, and as mentally painful as a college calculus class, with just about as much math.

Here's an example:

$$FN_2 = \frac{(END + 33) \times 0.79}{D + 33}$$

That's a formula for figuring the narcosis level of certain percentages of helium in the mixed gas.

It gets worse. There are sample questions in the textbook like: 'A mix of 16% O_2 and 40% He has 1,300 PSIG remaining in it. What will be the new mix if the tanks are topped to 3,000 PSIG with air?'

In English, the question is asking what happens if leftover trimix in a tank is pumped back up with air. The answer, by the way, is 19% oxygen, 17% helium and 64% nitrogen. Whew!

For three days Wings patiently goes over the calculations necessary to understand the mixed gas. More important, we methodically hammer away on the basics of what has been called *technical diving*, diving outside the range of conventional scuba.

'It's almost like a military operation,' he says. 'No, scratch that. There's no almost about it. A deep-wreck dive *is* like a military operation.'

We have to isolate everything that can go wrong, then decide how we would deal with that problem underwater – fill out the index cards, so to speak, for a whole range of new terrors. The biggest danger is neither from narcosis nor decompression sickness, but, surprisingly, from oxygen. The gas necessary for our survival – even in its 'normal' mix, air – is deadly below a couple of hundred feet. There's some question about oxygen toxicity; one theory holds that the higher concentrations of oxygen interfere with the enzymes the body uses for metabolism. There's no question about the effects, though. The biggie is convulsions, and convulsions underwater are a death sentence.

While we're diving deep, Wings says, our *oxygen clock* is running. Depending on the concentration of oxygen and the depths involved, we're getting dosages of oxygen. Once we reach 100 percent of our bodies' tolerance, we are on borrowed time. Like those nitrogen bubbles, we may exceed the limits and walk away unscathed. Or we may hit 101 percent . . .

'It's Russian Roulette,' Wings says. 'You pull the trigger, you may walk away. But if you keep pulling the trigger, sooner or later it's going to go bang.'

Later that evening, just for fun, I figure my oxygen clock for the deep-air dives I did preparing for these dives.

It comes to around nine hundred percent of maximum tolerance.

Click.

The dives in Key West will be on the *Wilkes-Barre*, a 600-foot-long World War II destroyer, resting in 240 feet of water – well below the 130-limit of recreational scuba diving. It is considered one of the crown jewels of technical diving, one of the most spectacular wreck dives in the world. Wings and I will be diving with Billy Deans of Key West Divers, who pioneered diving the wreck and who, along with Wings, has pushed out the limits of the abyss.

'The main thing,' says Wings, 'is that we cover every contingency and know exactly what is happening at every minute *before* we even get wet.'

We begin the planning in Santa Cruz, but we finish up in Key West. The details are these: we will be diving on a mixture of 17 percent oxygen, 50 percent helium, and the balance nitrogen, which will give us the narcosis effect of around 130 feet. As opposed to a recreational dive, where you put on a single tank and jump in, our dive on the *Wilkes-Barre* will require four tanks apiece – two oversized tanks on the back carrying the helium mix; one tank under the right arm carrying air enriched with extra oxygen (called Nitrox); and one tank under the left arm carrying pure oxygen. The Nitrox and the oxygen are for the decompression stops, the higher concentrations of oxygen helping to flush the nitrogen out of the system. The catch is that should something happen on the bottom, at 240 feet, to the main tanks, breathing from either of the decompression tanks would likely lead to fatal convulsions. In fact, it's not safe to breathe from the Nitrox tank until we're back at 100 feet; the oxygen tank is for 20 feet and less. Each tank is marked clearly and uses different styles of breathing regulators. The oxygen regulator has a surgical tubing band stretched over the mouthpiece, so the regulator can't just be stuffed into the mouth. When we get to Key West, we learn that a diver has died recently, taking a breath of pure oxygen at 200 feet. Oh yes, the 17 percent of oxygen in the mix isn't enough to supply the body on the surface, so we plan on getting to depth quickly.

We'll also be carrying two knives apiece, an inflatable bag and reel of line to allow us to decompress on our own should we get separated from the anchorline, multiple timers, extra masks, two lights apiece, and slates marked with a series of decompression alternatives, should our bottom time be shortened or extended. The gear – like the cave gear – weighs in at almost two hundred pounds.

We have run numerous computer simulations of the dive, so many that it's beginning to seem like an old friend. The intellectual challenge of dive planning is hypnotic, tempered by the knowledge that, ultimately, your life will rest on that plan.

The computer tells us that for every twenty minutes at the bottom, we'll spend over an hour decompressing. The entire dive will take eighty-seven minutes.

'So with that, we can create a run-time chart,' Wings says. 'We'll know where we're supposed to be, how much gas we're supposed to have, and how long we have to stay at that point. By the numbers – that's the way we'll do it.'

By the numbers.

The wreck first becomes visible at just over a hundred feet, run time: two minutes . . .

It floats up from the diffused green, at first just on the edges of the vision. We drift down, barely in contact with the down line, and the vastness of the wreck emerges from the green. . . . It is huge, a 600-foot capital ship, a ghost from the recent past. . . . I feel around in the back of my head, looking for the usual terror . . . *seven atmospheres, eight atmospheres, nine atmospheres . . . you're going to die here* . . . but the nagging feeling is absent, dwarfed by the wreck . . .

'Okay?' Wings signals.

I touch thumb to forefinger to agree.

We settle onto the top deck of the *Wilkes-Barre* at about 155 feet. At Wings's signal, we move down a level and disconnect our stage bottles, clipping them to a section of line – *a Jon line* – Wings has wrapped around a crusted section of railing. The lines hooked off, he taps his wrist with two fingers – time – then signals a five. Run time: five minutes – we have fifteen minutes of bottom time until we have to be back at the anchorline, ready to start back up. That translates into ten minutes of exploring time, giving me, the novice, some leeway to reattach the two additional tanks. I match Wings's movements, then signal 'okay,' and we head over the railing, into the lost world of the wreck.

I clear my head of random thoughts, take a second to visualize the rest of the dive – run time: seven minutes – then let myself drift into the world of the wreck. We swim toward the stern of the destroyer, its massive three-inch guns, now covered with a gilding of corals, point toward an enemy long gone. I feel the pressure in my ears as we drop down a deck, below two hundred feet now. I feel around for the voice in my head, and it is still silent. Wings stops swimming, and drifts down toward the deck. Then he swings his arms wide, encompassing the wreck. 'See?' he sends a message as much mental as physical. 'Do you understand now?'

And I do. We have come to one of the ends of the earth, a cathedral that will never know crowds of tourists or the swarms of recreational divers in their brightly colored matching gear. We have come to a place that will never know signs pointing to men's rooms or T-shirt sales. We have come to stand – or float – at a place where once men knew war, where now there is only the silent movement of the jacks and snappers, the razor sleekness of the barracudas, the frenetic dartings of the fluorescent tropicals. A blue tang, its fins tinged with bright yellow, darts up and tastes my glove, then jets back to the safety of the destroyer. A few feet away, a barracuda hangs motionless beneath one of the long barrels, its ancient computer racing to place Wings and I in the simple categories of the ocean – predator or prey.

I look toward the stern of the great ship, up toward its ghostly stacks. From a dozen flickering old newsreels, I imagine its awesome death, sliced apart, the sea thundering in through the rents and the tears, racing through the doors and the passageways, from deck to deck, level to level, until the ship shudders, then submits. I imagine the men that served on the *Wilkes-Barre*, wherever they are, feeling that shudder, hackles rising on their necks, as the ship died, then settled to its final resting place.

Wings taps his wrist.

Run time: nine minutes.

We drop down to 225 feet, then settle into an open hold, an elevator into the heart of the ship. I kick my fins, and Wings points to a wave of silt behind me, then shakes his finger. 'You're cave trained,' he is saying. 'You know better than to silt out an area . . .'

Run time: eleven minutes.

In the hold, I close my eyes for a moment and envision the column of water over my head, the sheer amount of weight settled onto my shoulders. An atmosphere of pressure for every 33 feet. My breathing rate picks up, the helium-thinned gas mixture flowing easily through my regulator. Too easily – I'm off my benchmark. Not dangerously so, but something to be aware of, to take into consideration. At this depth, at this pressure, there are no small mistakes. Even the smallest error, the slightest deviation, can presage a disaster. *The future's uncertain,* sang Jim Morrison so many years ago. *The end is always near.*

It's time to go.

We rise out of the hold, then swim directly toward the big guns, veering off slightly to the left to move up to the deck where the stage bottles are tethered. We crouch on the old deck, rehooking the stage bottles to our harnesses. I hook the oxygen bottle under my left arm, clumsily clipping the brass *double dogs* to my stainless steel *d-rings*. The enriched air bottle on my right side goes a little easier. I add a shot of air to my BC to offset the added weight of the bottles, then check my two times.

Run time: eighteen minutes.

I feel the pull of the wreck, the urge to stay a little longer, turn on the lights and peer into the silent inner decks, drift down the great, gaping tear in the bow. I want to stay, move through the ghostly command centers, fly through the darkened crew quarters, touch the massive engines. I run my gloved hand along the railing, along the rusting, ocean crusty metal. I want to keep going.

Run time: nineteen minutes.

Wings signals toward the surface with his thumb. I match his signal, sign 'okay,' and at run time twenty minutes we start up the line, back toward the world of air and sunshine and noise.

Sixty-seven minutes and two gas switches later, we are on the deck of the *Key West Diver*. Billy Deans, who has come up just after us is ecstatic.

'It's so damn cool,' he says.

'So what did you think?' Wings asks.

'Worth the effort,' I say, but that's not all of it. The *Wilkes-Barre*, the abyss, is the end of The List. I am reminded of Ken Kesey's legendary Merry Prankster bus, *Further*. I have ridden, I think, my own Further for all it's worth.

I know where you're going, Nancy Frederickson says as we walk along the frozen landscape of New Hampshire, but how do you plan to get back?

Eighteen minutes, versus twenty-one days on Denali. Two days on the Iditabike. Sixty seconds of free fall. Nine minutes down Mammoth Mountain. Seconds ticked off a clock that I never knew existed.

'Are you okay?' Wings asks.

'Oh yeah, fine,' I reply. I really don't know what I think. I think that some part of The Fear never really goes away – *There are so many ways to die here*, as the climber on Denali told me. The animal in your head, that screams and shrieks and cries, is always there, its hands on the bars, staring with wide, frightened eyes on a mysterious world.

And yet . . .

'We're going out to the Matterhorn in a month,' Wings is saying. 'It's a pretty cool dive, a spire rising up from the bottom. It's deep and cold, but . . .'

'Sounds good,' I hear myself saying. 'I'd like that.'

On the ride back home, Wings pulls out his Doppler ultrasound sensors and places them just beneath my collarbones. There's no *pop* of nitrogen bubbles, only the steady roar of blood seeking the heart.

23 Acceptable risks

Here is the view from the top of the mountain:

Down, a world of down.

The lift drops me off near the top of the mountain, and I step my back foot onto the snowboard and slide through the slushy snow. It is a warm July day in Colorado and I am at A-Basin, the last holdout to the summer's heat. Up high there is snow, and it is rideable, more or less. I'm wearing waterproof pants and a T-shirt, a far cry from my usual Michelin Man expedition bundling this high up. But it is summer and I am at odds.

I have never really considered what I would do after The List was completed. I'd never really thought that The List *could* be completed. But it has been.

'You know,' my mother tells me one day over the telephone, 'I never would have thought that you'd be so good at not dying.'

'It's a gift,' I reply flippantly.

But it still weighs on me, a psychic lump in my head. Pieces of experiences come to me in those gray minutes before sleep: the taste of the dirty waters of San Francisco Bay; the instant the glider takes wing, when gravity releases its grip; the searing bite of the first breath at thirty degrees below zero; the sight of mercurial air pooling in the tops of underwater caves; the illusion of the frozen castles of ice, the color of jewels in the afternoon sun. But the pieces are jumbled together, like the great ice falls on Denali, crumbled and crushed as the glaciers move inexorably toward the sea.

'We can if we so choose wander aimlessly over the continent of the arbitrary,' wrote Japanese novelist Haruki Murakami in the aptly titled *A Wild Sheep Chase*. 'Rootless as some winged seed blown about on some serendipitous spring breeze.'

I've thought a lot about the continent of the arbitrary, because that is where we will always find the edge.

I came to the risk sports looking for Indiana Jones.
Or, at least, someone like him. Some part and parcel of our mythology, cowboy or samurai, riding the edge jaggies for all they're worth, Instead, I found a group of puzzled people with a tiger by the tail, interested not so much in mythology as in touching and holding an experience as ephemeral as spider silk, ghostly as morning mist over a Montana river . . .

There is, I think now, even more to the edge than that ephemeral feeling. It has its own time, its own space. The edge has its own gravity, like a great dark star on the edge of the known universe. We approach that star only with the greatest of caution, because its gravity has the power to capture us and hold us in endless orbit, or even to pull us into its dark heart. But we continue to approach the dark star, because its gravity has the power to rip away our preconceptions, our sure knowledge of the way things are, to let us see the way things might be. The dark star has the power to give us back our feelings, sometimes in exchange for our lives.

I have never met anyone who has stood, however precariously, on the flanks of a great mountain, or who has been, however briefly, to the dark world at the edge of the abyss, and not come back changed. Changed how? More humble, perhaps; more aware of the fragility of life.

I asked one of the top triathletes in the country, an expert at brutal endurance sports, for her comments on my work-in-process – The List and the book – and one day she called me, very agitated.

'What,' she said bluntly, 'are you going to say about death? What are you going to tell them about death? Because, if you're going to be honest, you've got to tell them something.'

I started to tell her about my definition of *risk*, increased consequences of failure; of *flow*, optimal experience. But she would have no part of it.

'Bullshit,' she said. 'What we're talking about here is *dead*. I've thought about it; you've thought about it; everybody who's been out there has thought about it.'

'So what,' I ask, 'should I tell them?'

'You can get dead, but it's worth it,' she said.

'Why?'

'Because,' she said slowly, 'you get a chance to be different, to be a different person.'

'Adventure,' wrote Walt Burnett, 'is a human need.' And that it is.

'So,' asks Steve Ilg, 'what did you learn?'

I remember our conversation of so long ago, sitting in his dusty office in Santa Fe, and Ilg's great love of quotes. So I fish out a copy of an old book by Yvon Chouinard.

'Perceptions dull and we come to accept a blunting of feeling in the shadow of security,' Chouinard wrote. 'Drunk with power, I find that I am out of my senses.

I . . . long for immediacy of contact to brighten my senses again, to bring me nearly the world once more; in my security, I have forgotten how to dance . . .'

'So,' Ilg says finally. 'Did you learn how to dance?'

'The feeling I get is terribly unfocused, yet very solid,' Murakami's strange sheep detective muses in *A Wild Sheep Chase*.

His girlfriend understands immediately. 'A concentrated phenomenon based on vague motives,' she replies.

The old avalanche chute is steep, the July snow as slushy as old mashed potatoes. I maneuver the snowboard to the edge of the drop, look down at the long slope. My run is off to the left, cutting across the face. Halfway down the slope, I'll cut back to the right, then drop until the slope shallows out into an easy run down what's left of the snowy part of the mountain.

As I balance on the lip, I feel the machinery begin to wind up, the animal begin to pace nervously around the cage. I close my eyes and imagine the biochemical machine of my body dumping chemistry into my bloodstream. I feel the adrenaline begin to play tricks with time and space; the beta-endorphins stripping away the aches and pains. All around me, the parts of the external world that don't have anything to do with the next minutes of vertical drop are disappearing, shut out as a thick, quiet curtain falls around me. All in a millisecond, I feel sparks arc through my legs, the muscles tensing, resting. Through heightened senses, I feel the 164 centimeters of snowboard bound to my feet, feel the sharp heelside edge cut into the snow. I see my run, a glowing line overlaid on the gooey snow, see the point at which my weight will shift, initiating the turn. I think, as I often do, about the advice my friend Val, a professional extreme snowboarder, offered one day: 'I know if I make the first turn,' she said, 'I won't die.'

I smile, absently. The machine is fully on now, waiting for the data storm to come. *Processing*, the green light blinks. *Processing*.

We are all poised there – my mind, my body, the animal created of fear and doubt and uncertainty – waiting on the edge. The feeling, when it comes, is one of calm, of joy even, beginning at the top of my head and rolling down through my body. I feel my eyes go soft; the tension in my muscles release. In the very back of my head, where my spine connects to my brain, I hear the beginning of music, the first slashing chords of hard rock and roll.

Well, it's five A.M., the fear is gone . . .

Of its own volition, without the slightest prompt from me, the board begins its run, carving a glowing line into the first turn.

Appendix:

Stuff

One of the things that absolutely drove me crazy while I was putting together this book was the 'coyness' of some outdoor reporting. Someone would be right in the middle of explaining how some critical piece of equipment failed at exactly the wrong moment, but then they wouldn't tell you what brand of equipment it was.

Or, they'd be touting how wonderful a certain piece of equipment was, only to punk out at the last minute and not name brands. I have a closet full of stuff that failed. I have also been lucky enough to learn what works and still be here to tell you about it.

Here's another caveat – some of this stuff I got for free; some of it came at a hefty discount and some I paid pure, pure list for. In the case of guide services and instruction, it is my firm and unyielding belief that you get what you pay for. As my credit card bills will painfully attest, I paid list. On the other hand, I'm still here. Let's start with instructors and guides. This is not meant to be a complete list; it is strictly people I used myself and can vouch for. I unconditionally recommend the following people:

Wholistic Fitness

Harmony Now!
Steve Ilg
Town Plaza #240
Durango, CO 81301
(970) 259-2587 (phone and fax)

What can I say? The Way that Steve Ilg teaches is not an easy way, not a quick fix, not a seven-steps-to-blah-blah-blah. It is an honest attempt to bring together physical, mental, and spiritual, for lack of a better word, training. Before you beat yourself silly, I urge you to contact Steve and talk to him.

Climbing and Mountaineering

The American Alpine Institute
ATTN: Dunham Gooding
1212 24th Street
Bellingham, WA 98225
(206) 671-1505

AAI offers guided climbs to most of the big mountains of the world. They also offer mountaineering instruction and rock- and ice-climbing classes. AAI is the high end provider and tends to be very touchy about prerequisites. But, in my book, they are the best in the business. If you aspire to a Big Mountain, start with these guys.

Eastern Mountain Sports Climbing School
Main Street
P.O. Box 514
North Conway, NH 03860
(603) 356-5433

You can't beat these guys for ice climbing. North Conway around Chrismastime is romantic (if you ignore the outlet stores); the food is good and there are these great ice cliffs.

Clark Man
3232 Ave. San Marcos
Santa Fe, NM 87505
(505) 471-5016

If you're in Santa Fe and get tired of buying overpriced Native American jewelry, call Clark and discuss climbing lessons.

Air Sports

Hang-gliding and paragliding
Kitty Hawk Kites
ATTN: John Harris
Mile Post 13, 3933 N. Croatan Highway
Nag's Head, NC 27959
(919) 441-4124

Soaring off the dunes near where the Wright Brothers first took wing is an experience not to be missed. Kitty Hawk Kites can take you from your first tentative launches to wherever you want to go. Make a point of meeting John Harris, one of the legends in hang-gliding.

Paragliding
Fly Away Paragliding
Bill Lawrence
Golden, CO
(303) 642-0849

Small, personalized service and high-quality instruction. If Bill can teach me to fly, he can teach anyone to fly.

Whitewater

Nantahala Outdoor Center
US19W, P.O. Box 41
Bryson City, NC 28713
(704) 488-2175

If you're at all interested in whitewater, Nantahala either has or can structure a curriculum that can get you going in kayaks, canoes, or duckies. It is also nestled in one of the most beautiful spots on earth. There's some world-class mountain biking here as well. Ask the instructors about the Tsali trail.

SCUBA Diving

Technical dive training is time-consuming and expensive. It is, however, preferable to the alternative, which is becoming fish food. There are several instructors I recommend. If you're on the western side of the country, you can't do better than:

T. Wings Stock
Ocean Odyssey Dive Center
2345 S. Rodeo Gulch Road
Santa Cruz, CA 95062
(408) 475-DIVE

Wings can take you from the basics to wherever you would like to go. I can't say enough good things about Wings. He is everything an instructor should be.

John and Shelley Orlowski
AquaSpeleo
Rt. 5 Box 128E
Live Oak, FL 32060
(904) 776-1191

I would argue that John Orlowski knows as much about the caves of North Florida as any human being; Shelley gets spooked when there isn't a roof over her head.

Hal Watts
Professional Scuba Association
9487 NW 115th Avenue
Ocala, FL 34482-1007
(904) 368-7974

A gentleman's gentleman and one of the finest instructors in the world. It's worth taking a course from him just to meet him.

For more information, I urge you to contact the International Association of Nitrox & Technical Divers (IANTD) at 9628 NE 2nd Ave, Suite D, Miami Shores, FL 33138-2767, or call (305) 751-4873. This isn't the only technical diving certifying agency (Hal Watts has his own), but it is the one I chose.

Stuff

All stuff breaks down into two different types – stuff that works, and stuff that clutters up your closet. Here's a quick rundown of what worked:

Bicycles: I believe in Cannondale the way some people believe in Elvis, and, being a Memphis boy myself, this is no small declaration. They are funky, superbly made in America, reasonably priced, and they don't fail. You can get a more expensive bike, but you can't get a better one.

SCUBA Gear: My regulators, the heart of the life support system, are from a small company in Zephyrhills, FL, called Zeagle. The regulators, Tech 50s, I believe, are more expensive than most others and come in any color you want, as long as it's black. When using a single tank, I use a Zeagle buoyancy compensator (BC) as well; with double tanks, I use a set of wings from Dive Rite, a Florida company specializing in cave and technical equipment. Dive Rite also made my cave reels. I use a dry suit made by O.S.S. Systems, and it is, in fact, really warm and dry.

Mountaineering Gear: The first most important lesson in the high country is *keep warm*. I visited Malden Mills in Massachusetts, and explained my dilemma to Carol Penny. Malden makes the fabric called Polartec, a synthetic fleece, and Carol assured me that Malden could prototype some outfits that not only would keep me warm, but not make me 'look like the Sta-Puff Marshmallow Man!' The fleece outfit they made me is thin, light, and too warm at zero degrees. Ah, but when the temperature creeps lower than 30 below zero, it comes into its own. It is truly a miracle fabric. Look for it by name.

The one other company I want to overtly plug is Lowe Alpine, a bunch of homeboys here in Colorado. I have this pair of tights that was given to me by a friend from Reebok. He said they were the best tights made, and I'd wear them until they rotted off. The tights, from Lowe, are made of stretchy Polartec fleece. They are, simply said, the best winter garment I own. I wore them for eighteen days straight on Denali, used them in the Iditabike and all the training for both, wore them snowboarding, hiking, you name it. I wore them last week; I'll bet I wear them next week. They're not even expensive.

I also use Lowe packs, which fit me better than any other packs I've tried. My Lowe expedition pack helped me on the slog up Denali – it is an old friend. My sleeping bag is by Marmot, and I wouldn't trade it for a hotel room at the Holiday Inn. It's kept me warm at 30 degrees below zero and it doesn't weigh a thing. It cost me a fortune and was worth every penny. My natty, high-tech snowshoes are from Atlas, a company that got everything right.

Otherwise, I used a mixed lot of gear, usually purchased on the fly. Everything does double duty – my old REI Gore-Tex jacket gets drafted for snowboarding and climbing McKinley.